THE LAST PALESTINIAN

THE RISE AND REIGN OF MAHMOUD ABBAS

Grant Rumley and Amir Tibon

Prometheus Books

59 John Glenn Drive
Amherst, New York 14228

Inquiries should be addressed to
Prometheus Books
59 John Glenn Drive
Amherst, New York 14228
VOICE: 716–691–0133 • FAX: 716–691–0137
WWW.PROMETHEUSBOOKS.COM

21 20 19 18 17   5 4 3 2 1

Library of Congress Cataloging-in-Publication Data

Names: Rumley, Grant, 1988- author. | Tibon, Amir, 1989- author.
Title: The last Palestinian : the rise and reign of Mahmoud Abbas / Grant Rumley
    and Amir Tibon.
Description: Amherst, New York : Prometheus Books, 2017. |
    Includes bibliographical references and index.
Identifiers: LCCN 2017002122 (print) | LCCN 2017007373 (ebook) |
    ISBN 9781633882997 (hardcover) | ISBN 9781633883000 (ebook)
Subjects: LCSH: Abbas, Mahmoud, 1935- | Palestinian Arabs—Biography. |
    Munazzamat al-Tahrir al-Filastiniyah. | Arab-Israeli conflict. | Palestinian
    Arabs—Politics and government. | West Bank—Politics and government—21st
    century. | Gaza Strip—Politics and government—21st century.
Classification: LCC DS126.6.A24 R86 2017 (print) | LCC DS126.6.A24 (ebook) |
    DDC 956.05/3092 [B] —dc23
LC record available at https://lccn.loc.gov/2017002122

Printed in the United States of America

CONTENTS

FOREWORD

In the fall of 1982, on leave from the Department of State where I served as the Bureau of Intelligence and Research's chief analyst on Lebanon and the Palestinians, I wrote a short book titled *The PLO and the Politics of Survival*. The argument was pretty straightforward: the PLO—the organizational embodiment of Palestinian nationalism—confronted a set of external constraints and pressures from Israel and the Arab states and from inside the movement itself, which undermined its capacity to fashion a coherent strategy to realize its goals.

I would spend the next twenty years as a State Department negotiator watching my own arguments play out. And the challenges for the Palestinians just keep on coming. Indeed, in 2017, the Palestinian national movement is now beset by its greatest internal challenge: the movement has come to resemble a kind of modern day Noah's Ark, today split between Hamas and Fatah, where two of everything seems to be the order of the day: two statelets in Gaza and the West Bank; two sets of security services; two constitutions; and two different visions of what and where Palestine should be.

Men, Karl Marx opined writing in the late nineteenth century, make their own history, but rarely as they please. In this finely crafted and extensively researched book, Grant Rumley and Amir Tibon tell the story of Mahmoud Abbas—a man whose political life and perhaps legacy will prove Marx's point. The authors, though, go beyond Marx. Constraints notwithstanding, they argue that Abbas's career demonstrates that he never really had the leadership, let alone the "greatness gene," to make history (as he pleased or otherwise) by cutting a historic peace deal. Indeed, Abbas, they argue, passed up at least two serious opportunities to do precisely that. Many will see this as a rather harsh judgment, echoed by many Israelis and Americans who see Abbas as a weak leader clinging strongly to an unrealistic set of Palestinian demands; and, as the authors show, this view is accompanied by any number of Palestinians who see him as too willing to accommodate Israel on the peace process yet paradoxically increasingly autocratic and heavy-handed in his governing practices at home.

But anatomy is destiny, Freud wrote; and, for leaders, how they project their physical persona is critical to success. One of the strongest features of this book is the authors' focus on Abbas's personality and persona, which on balance probably worked against him. On one hand, he lacked the charisma, passion, and street cred of Yasser Arafat, which in an environment of grievance and occupation required the image of the *munadel,* or struggler. Dropping out of a Syrian military academy in his younger days in Damascus; never closely identified with the PLO's armed struggle; physically absent from the Beirut saga of invasion, siege, and exile, Abbas couldn't even pretend to project that image.

On the other hand, it was his distance from terror and violence; his quiet, courtly, and moderate demeanor; and his long track record of meeting with Israelis that made him so attractive to many Israelis and Americans. Arafat was the consummate actor and showman—always playing a role. With Abbas, you got the feeling you were dealing with a decent and emotionally attuned human being. I remember interrupting a negotiating session with Abbas and the Israelis in 1997 to say a ritual Jewish mourning prayer in honor of my mother who had passed a few months earlier and how moved Abbas said he was by an American's show of respect and honor. The authors begin the book with the story of Abbas overruling his aides and deciding to attend Shimon Peres's funeral because Peres's daughter asked him to. And his kindnesses to my own daughter, who in 2003 and 2004 was researching a book on young Israelis and Palestinians caught up in conflict, meant a lot to me. Abbas's decision to send his grandchildren to Seeds of Peace, a coexistence program for Arabs and Israelis, reflected the fact that Abbas actually believed in the possibilities of a different future for Israelis and Palestinians and not just as a talking point.

From the perspective of real peacemaking and reconciliation, there's little doubt that Abbas would indeed have been the best partner that Israel and the Americans may never have. And it is likely that this paradox—that Abbas may really have wanted to do a deal but was just not able to—may come to haunt Israeli-Palestinian peacemaking for years to come.

It is tempting to accept the argument popular in some circles that Abbas is only the latest Palestinian leader to never miss an opportunity to miss an opportunity. To be sure, it's a small set that includes only two—Arafat and Abbas. And, to be fair, the shoe of missing opportunities fits better on Arafat. The PLO leader had both the moral and historic authority and electoral legitimacy to engage with Israel, and in the Oslo process he did so in a way no other Palestinian leader could. There are many reasons final status negotiations failed at Camp David, not the least of which were unrealistic US and Israeli expectations and flawed negotiating tactics. But Arafat's transgressions there were even more serious—not for failing to sign (there was nothing that he could or would sign), but for failing to engage seriously in response to what Israel and the Americans put on the table, and then through the end of the Clinton administration choosing to ride the tiger of violence and terror from which Israeli-Palestinian relations have still not recovered.

I would argue that Abbas's options were much worse. He lacked Arafat's historic legitimacy; nor could his victory in the 2005 presidential elections compensate for the lack of it. Abbas's Israeli interlocutors—first a strong Ariel Sharon not looking for a final status deal and then a weak Ehud Olmert who lacked the capacity to deliver—made Abbas's choice on the peace process an easy one. Uniting a divided and corrupt Fatah in the wake of the passing of the historic leader was well beyond Abbas's capacity and resembled giving a student a test he could not possibly pass. And once Hamas scored big in the 2006 legislative elections and took over Gaza in the summer of 2007, Abbas became even more risk-averse. Ruling not even half of Palestine (certainly not if you factor in Israeli control of Area C in the West Bank), he would focus on hanging onto what he had, trying to prevent Hamas from taking more, coopting and undermining potential rivals, and by 2011 shifting to a Palestinian diplomatic strategy that was oriented far more toward the international arena than it was toward seriously negotiating with Israeli prime minister Benjamin Netanyahu, who, to be fair, really wasn't interested in a two-state solution that any Palestinian leader could have accepted.

We can go on and on all day about Abbas missing an opportunity by not accepting Barack Obama's March 2014 offer in the context of Secretary of State John Kerry's 2013–2014 framework negotiations, but that misses the point. If Arafat passed up the Clinton parameters in December 2000 (a much better deal than what Obama was offering), was the risk-averse Abbas going to accept a US proposal that the famously noncommittal Netanyahu hadn't?

The authors have titled their book *The Last Palestinian*. Certainly Abbas will be the last leader of a generation of Palestinians involved in the national movement from its inception who, together with Arafat, guided it through its critical years. His heavy-handedness at home has also contributed to a shrinking of the Palestinian leadership class. After Abbas there will be new leaders, albeit from a different generation and perhaps ruling as a group without one established leader. Indeed, it's difficult to envision any single Palestinian politician or security official replacing Abbas in the definitive way he replaced Arafat.

Finally, one obvious point needs to be made. Who leads the Palestinians is a necessary but hardly sufficient condition for moving forward to resolve the Israeli-Palestinian conflict. This conflict has never been about one hand clapping. Indeed, to say the least, Israelis, too, bear their fair share of responsibility for missing opportunities, adopting positions, and taking actions that make a solution more difficult. What's required, of course, are leaders on both sides who are masters of their politics, not prisoners of their constituencies or ideologies. What's needed are leaders who understand that reconciling mutual needs and requirements is essential to any chance of a breakthrough.

Right now we don't have such leaders. Still, life and politics are just too uncertain to suggest we never will. *The Last Palestinian* compels us to abandon any illusions about how difficult it may be to produce such a leader on the Palestinian side. But it should not compel us to abandon hope that under different circumstances Palestinian leaders (and Israeli leaders, too) can emerge to produce a better situation than we have today, and perhaps someday a resolution that both their peoples can support.

Aaron David Miller,
Woodrow Wilson International Center for Scholars

A NOTE ON METHODOLOGY

In addition to news articles, books, and public statements, the authors conducted approximately seventy formal interviews and dozens of informal or off-the-record conversations in the course of six months in 2016. Supplementing this research was the authors' experience covering Palestinian politics for years prior to 2016. Overall, approximately a hundred interviews and meetings with Palestinian, Israeli, American, and other sources were conducted for the writing of this book.

The authors interviewed Palestinian Authority ministers and senior officials, as well as members of the PLO's Executive Committee, Fatah's Central Committee, Fatah's Revolutionary Council, the Palestinian Legislative Council, Fatah's Advisory Committee, Hamas, the al-Aqsa Martyrs' Brigades, periphery and independent parties, and Fatah opposition groups. They also spoke to nonpolitical figures in areas ranging from refugee camps to the *muqata'a* in Ramallah. In addition, they interviewed senior officials from the Clinton, Bush, and Obama administrations, as well as Israeli officials from every government in the last two decades. Further, the authors conducted interviews with participants in every consequential Israeli-Palestinian negotiation since the 1980s.

The authors were unable to interview Mahmoud Abbas for this book. At a June 2016 meeting in Ramallah with Mr. Abbas's senior advisors—who will go unnamed out of respect for privacy—the authors asked for an interview and offered to devote a chapter of the book to its transcript. In the view of the authors, this was a chance for Mr. Abbas to address the various themes of the book and have his perspective incorporated. Mr. Abbas's advisors responded that in order to get involved, they would require editorial oversight over every chapter in the book. In their words, they wanted to make sure this was "a good book," before granting the authors access to Mr. Abbas. It was a counteroffer the authors could not accept. This is, then, an unauthorized account of Mr. Abbas's career.

Further, due to the sensitive nature of writing a book about a leader still in office, some of those interviewed on the Palestinian and Israeli sides requested anonymity. The authors respected their wishes, when possible, and have provided accurate descriptions of their positions within their respective governments.

ACKNOWLEDGMENTS

The authors are entirely grateful to their families, friends, and colleagues for their support throughout this process. In particular, they would like to thank those who read advanced copies, helped flesh out ideas, or supported the authors in their research. This includes, but is not limited to: Jonathan Schanzer, Ghaith al-Omari, Michael Koplow, Neri Zilber, Dalia Hatuqa and Charles Fromm, Gabriel Mitchell, Moran Stern, Daniel Blue, David Daoud, Gadi Baltiansky, Emanuele Ottolenghi, Clifford May, Mark Dubowitz, Hussein Ibish, Sarah Feuer, Oren Kessler, Nimrod Goren, Haneen Shibli, the al-Araj family, the Peters, the Musleh family, Avi Issacharoff, Aviram Elad, and Michal Klein. The authors are also indebted to the Foundation for Defense of Democracies and Walla! News, their respective employers during the time this book was written, for their support and flexibility.

A special thank-you goes to Mor Yahalom, who served as researcher for this project. Mor is an incredibly sharp, hardworking colleague who did a lot of the heavy lifting in preparing the research for this book. Her insight and knowledge was invaluable throughout this process.

The authors are indebted to Steven Mitchell, Hanna Etu, Sheila Stewart, and the wonderful team at Prometheus Books for their patience, guidance, and assistance throughout the process of writing this book. The authors are also indebted to Maryann Karinch at the Rudy Agency for all her support.

The authors would like to extend their sincere gratitude and love to their respective families. Mr. Rumley would like to thank his parents, Michael and Shelley, as well as his siblings, Spencer and McKenzie. Mr. Tibon would like to thank his wife, Miri, as well as his parents, Noam and Gali, and his brother, Uri. Without the support of their families and friends, the authors well know they would not have been able to complete this project.

CHAPTER 1

THE RISE OF
MAHMOUD ABBAS

On the morning of September 28, 2016, Mahmoud Abbas awoke to upsetting news. Overnight, Shimon Peres, Israel's former president and a man with whom Abbas had a long history of trying to negotiate a peace agreement, had died at the age of ninety-three. His death marked the end of an era in Israel, as Peres was the last member of the Jewish state's founding generation. For Abbas—a member of the same generation but on the Palestinian side—this was more than the passing of a neighboring leader. Abbas had long seen Peres as his natural negotiating partner.

Abbas and Peres met two decades earlier in Washington, DC, when they signed a historic agreement of mutual recognition between Israel and the Palestine Liberation Organization on the White House lawn. They had remained in close contact ever since that day, even when the conflict between their two peoples descended into its darkest hours. In 2005, Abbas became the president of the Palestinian Authority, a semiautonomous body that was born as a result of the agreement he had signed with Peres. Two years later, the Israeli negotiator became the president of his own country, a mostly symbolic post that he nevertheless used to tirelessly advocate for peace with Israel's neighbors. Just months before his death, Peres was insisting that Abbas was, in his opinion, "an outstanding man who really does want to commit to peace."[1]

As more and more world leaders announced they would attend Peres's funeral in Jerusalem, Abbas consulted with his advisors: should he also take part in the ceremony? While he had been close to

Peres, the Israeli leader was still a vastly unpopular figure on the Palestinian street. If Abbas attended the funeral, he would be exposing himself to an onslaught of criticism. This dilemma grew more difficult with each passing moment. On the one hand, the arrival of leading figures like Barack Obama and Charles, Prince of Wales, meant that the funeral could be a chance for Abbas to show his support for the peace process on a global stage. On the other hand, it was becoming clear that no Arab country was going to be represented by its leader at the event—which would make Abbas even more vulnerable to criticism from the Palestinian street if he attended.

"Why do you need this now?" a number of his advisers asked him.[2] Abbas was already unpopular at home—a recent poll showed nearly two-thirds of his people wanted him to resign—and it wasn't as if there were peace talks on the horizon. Why couldn't he just send one of his deputies? Abbas saw the logic of this approach. In his view, there was nothing bad about playing it safe. But the next morning, he surprised his staff by telling them that he was going.

One factor in his decision was a phone call he received from Peres's daughter, who told him that her father would have appreciated him coming to the funeral.[3] Abbas was touched by her plea. Furthermore, some among his staff thought that in showing up he could "disprove Israeli claims that Palestinians only believe in violence."[4] So, twenty-four hours before the funeral began, his office called the Israeli military to inform them that the Palestinian president would pay his last respects to his counterpart in Jerusalem.

On Friday the 29th, just before noon, Abbas's bulletproof motorcade arrived at the Mount Herzl cemetery on Jerusalem's western side. Soon after arriving, he bumped into Israel's prime minister, Benjamin Netanyahu, and his wife, Sara. The two leaders, who had met only once in the five years prior to the funeral, briefly shook hands and exchanged some polite niceties. Mrs. Netanyahu told Abbas that she and her husband would be happy to welcome him to their official residence in Jerusalem. Abbas smiled and simply mumbled, "long time, long time," a reference to the years that had passed since he had last visited the place.

The antipathy between the two leaders was evident when Netanyahu, during his eulogy of Peres, mentioned many of the dignitaries who had gathered at the cemetery but said nothing of Abbas. In the weeks and months prior to Peres's death, the Israeli premier had publicly accused Abbas of inciting violence and failing to condemn terrorist attacks against Israeli citizens. Netanyahu's frustration with Abbas, whom he saw as partly responsible for the deaths of innocent Israelis, wasn't going to go away simply because he had made a gesture toward the Peres family.

By the time the dust had settled, Abbas was back in a familiar position. His symbolic gesture had garnered him a chorus of condemnation from all walks of Palestinian life and did little in easing the tensions with Israel. His only comfort was the sentence in Obama's eulogy that praised him for making the trip from Ramallah. As ever, Abbas was more popular in Washington than in Ramallah, Gaza, or Jerusalem.

Mahmoud Abbas was born in 1935 to a modest family in the northern Galilee town of Safed, in what was then the British Mandate of Palestine. Together with his parents and siblings, he fled Safed during the 1948 war and settled in Damascus, Syria. He taught elementary school during the day, while finishing his studies at night, before moving to the oil-rich Qatar to work for the government. There he married his wife, Amina, raised their children, and got involved in the burgeoning arena of Palestinian politics. Before long he had made a name for himself and had joined up with other young Palestinian refugees, including a young man from Gaza named Yasser Arafat, who was the leader of a new Palestinian political organization: Fatah.

Abbas would spend the rest of his life among Fatah's leadership. His military prowess low—he admits in his own memoirs that he was flushed out of a Syrian military academy as a teenager—he viewed the "armed resistance" not as an end but a means. While Arafat and the rest of the Palestinian leadership was fighting Israel out of Beirut, Abbas was with his family in Damascus. He positioned himself as the Palestinian fundraiser and ambassador in residence: he fostered ties with the broader region and world, working especially closely with Soviet

Russia (where he completed a controversial doctoral thesis in 1982, which disputed the number of Jewish victims in the Holocaust). By the 1970s and 1980s, he was openly advocating dialogue with Israelis, and a decade later he began to openly support the concept of a "two-state solution," in which a Palestinian state would be established next to Israel in the territories of Gaza and the West Bank.

Abbas's wish became the Palestinian platform with the advent of the Oslo Accords in 1993. Through back channels in London and then Norway, Palestinian negotiators reporting to Abbas, and Israeli negotiators close to then prime minister Yitzhak Rabin's government reached a historic declaration of principles that laid out a path toward a comprehensive peace agreement. The Oslo Accords were a high point of optimism in the history of the Israeli-Palestinian conflict. After their signing, a new entity—the Palestinian Authority—was established, with Arafat as its leader. Abbas, the architect of this historic achievement, found himself back in the margins afterward. Arafat, Peres, and Rabin all received Nobel Peace Prizes. Abbas got nothing.

The next six years were a frustrating period for Abbas. He led one back-channel attempt to reach a comprehensive peace agreement with Israeli representatives, but the agreement became irrelevant following the tragic assassination of Rabin in 1995. And while the peace process was stuck, Abbas failed to navigate the treacherous waters of Palestinian politics, where his rivals portrayed him as a weak and untrustworthy negotiator who was "too soft" with Israel. In July 2000, when the Clinton administration made one final attempt to reach a peace agreement at the famous Camp David summit, Abbas was so busy protecting his own image that he contributed almost nothing to the negotiations, and in the words of one senior American official present, "was a non-entity."[5]

After the Camp David negotiations collapsed, violence erupted on the streets, leading to thousands of deaths in what came to be known as the Second *Intifada*, or uprising. During this dark hour, while Arafat was actively supporting terrorism, Abbas emerged as a rare voice of reason and moderation within the Palestinian leadership. He warned Arafat early on about the dangers of unleashing violence against Israel and regularly admonished local leaders for supporting terror attacks. What was happening, Abbas told Gazan leaders in 2002, was the "total destruction of all we have built."[6] Arafat refused to listen, however, and Abbas was again on the outside looking in.

All of that changed in 2003, when Arafat—under considerable pressure from the Bush administration—agreed to create the position of prime minister within the Palestinian Authority and name Abbas for the post. For a few months, Abbas tried to reform the Palestinian institutions, strengthen the government and put an end to the intifada. Yet despite the support he received from Washington, Abbas's tenure as prime minister ended in failure. Arafat refused to budge or cede any power to his deputy, and Abbas eventually gave up. He resigned just months into the job, with nothing but uncertainty about the future.

He had stood up to the "Old Man" however, and when Arafat died in 2004 Abbas became the immediate favorite to replace him. He was named Arafat's successor in November of that year, before winning a presidential election in January 2005. He now had a mandate to strengthen the PA's institutions and engage in peace negotiations with Israel. Yet within a year of his election he suffered a catastrophic setback when his Fatah party was crushed in the 2006 Palestinian parliamentary elections by Hamas, an Islamist party officially designated as a terror organization by the United States.

To make things even worse, in July 2007, a civil war broke out between Abbas's Fatah-dominated PA and Hamas in Gaza. Abbas would lose, his forces would be expelled or killed, and the trajectory of the Palestinian national project would forever change. From this moment on, Abbas would be a president with half a mandate. He could negotiate with Israel, but he could never deliver an agreement to all of his people. Staying in power and preventing a similar takeover in the West Bank would become the primary goal of the rest of his tenure.

Israeli prime minister Ehud Olmert was eager to reach a peace agreement with Abbas despite all of that, and in the fall of 2008 he presented to the Palestinian president a far-reaching offer that included an Israeli withdrawal from most of the West Bank and a return of thousands of Palestinian refugees into Israel. Abbas, however, never gave Olmert an answer. Olmert was himself in a weak position at the time, as a number of corruption investigations were about to bring down his government. Palestinian officials insist it wasn't a serious offer, and Americans saw it as a feeble attempt, but, regardless, it was a unique overture from an Israeli premier, one that Abbas ignored.

In 2009, Benjamin Netanyahu replaced Olmert in Israel, while Barack Obama became president of the United States. Abbas was hopeful about the Obama administration, especially after it turned out that he was among the first leaders in the world to receive a phone call from the new president. Yet with time, Abbas's excitement was replaced with disappointment as he saw the American administration devote less and less attention to the peace process. At one point, Palestinian officials even confessed that they were somewhat longing for the previous administration of George W. Bush. Faced with an uninterested White House and an Israeli prime minister whom he didn't trust, Abbas turned toward international legitimacy, launching an auspicious plan to make the world recognize Palestine as the 194th member state in the United Nations.

The "Palestine 194" campaign was Abbas's attempt at subverting the traditional peace process while placating his people. When, in November 2012, Abbas went to the UN General Assembly and upgraded the Palestinian standing, thousands celebrated in the West Bank. That's why when, in 2013, Secretary of State John Kerry offered to sponsor another round of peace negotiations with Netanyahu, Abbas was hesitant. He did not believe anything would come out of these negotiations. Many within his camp preferred making more moves at the UN rather than entering another round of unpopular talks. Yet eventually he entered the talks, only to walk away from a historic peace plan proposed by the Obama administration in March 2014, at his last-ever visit to Barack Obama's White House.

Since the civil war in 2007, Abbas—once a champion of democracy and reform—has gradually turned into an authoritarian. He's fired rivals, persecuted his antagonists, and put allies in key positions within the party. He's attacked union heads, detained journalists, and even sent his PA forces after everyday citizens for their social media posts. There was a point in his life when he viewed negotiations as the way forward for the Palestinian national project, but after coming to power he has appeared less and less interested in that. The primary focus of his reign is on consolidating as much power as he can.

Mahmoud Abbas started his presidency as a man of peace and institutions. More than a decade into his four-year term, he will end it as just another regional autocrat.

The picture on the cover of this book is of Mahmoud Abbas's first campaign stop. Two months after Yasser Arafat died, Abbas arrived in the northern West Bank town of Jenin to speak to nearly ten thousand Palestinians. It was one of the largest crowds he had ever addressed. He arrived to a mob and was carried through town on people's shoulders. In the picture, he's holding hands and waving while a poster of the Old Man, his mentor, rival, and predecessor Arafat, looks on. Weeks later, he would win the presidency by a comfortable majority. His victory would mark the golden age of Abbas's rule: a one-year period before he lost his parliament, and then Gaza, to his rivals in Hamas. This period would be the height of his political legitimacy in Palestinian politics. He would never approach it again.

Taken together, the arc of Mahmoud Abbas's career bends toward that of a missed opportunity. If Israeli officials were to describe their ideal negotiating partner, they would describe someone almost identical to Abbas, with his aversion to terror and stated willingness to compromise. But the tragedy of Abbas, and of the Israeli-Palestinian conflict in general, is in what he doesn't bring to the table. He is not a charismatic leader and thus could not convince his people to modify their version of the national narrative. Peace requires leaders who have both the courage to sign an agreement and the ability to implement it. Abbas appeared at times in his life to have the former. He was never close to having the latter.

Blame is easy to come by in the Israeli-Palestinian conflict. Surely, Abbas is not the sole reason the Palestinian people do not have their own state. But he has failed to prepare his people for the concessions necessary to live peacefully side by side with Israel. He lost half his territory in 2007 to the Islamist terror group Hamas and then also lost touch with many ordinary Palestinians, who see him and his royal court as detached from the hardships and realities of their life.

And yet, Abbas still occupies a place in the Palestinian political hierarchy few others can claim. When he speaks, he can claim to do so in the name of an entire people. He was born into the British Mandate of Palestine before the creation of the state of Israel, grew up as a refugee outside his homeland, and spent decades working next to the father of the Palestinian national movement, Yasser Arafat. Abbas has personally lived the history of his own people. He is very likely the last Palestinian leader with that kind of pedigree.

CHAPTER 2

THE NEGOTIATOR

1935–1993

O n a cool autumn day in 1994, a black Mercedes weaved its way through the quiet streets of Safed, a historic moun-taintop city in northern Israel. The luxury car passed through the center of the city before stopping at a small parking lot across from the local market. Glancing at the nearby Sea of Galilee, the passen-gers took in the scene.[1]

Sitting in the back of the car, Mahmoud Abbas looked around in disbelief. More than four decades had passed since he was last in this place, and yet it looked so familiar. The market square, the tall cypress trees, the stone-built houses, and the view of the Golan Mountains in the distance—everything was still in its place.[2] There was no doubt about it: this was the street where he was born and raised, although the house where he had spent his childhood days no longer existed. Where it once stood, there was now a Jewish religious school.[3]

Abbas walked up and down the street, passing by the ruins of an old mosque where his family used to pray. When he lived here as a child, the area was called *Harat al Jora*, which in Arabic means "the neighborhood of the pit," so called because of its location in a valley between two tree-covered hills. Now, his old street bore the name of Ze'ev Jabotinsky, an influential Zionist writer admired by the Israeli right wing. Across the market, a parallel street was named after twenty-two local children who were murdered by Palestinian terrorists in 1974.

The memory of that tragic incident was still strong twenty years later. When news that Abbas was planning a trip to Safed reached the local mayor, he issued a public warning. "People won't be happy to see him here," the mayor told the press. Undeterred, Abbas insisted he was coming anyway. Then he heard that a couple hundred angry demonstrators were waiting for his motorcade at the entrance to the city, and cancelled.[4]

Still, Abbas couldn't stay away from his hometown. A few weeks later, he chose a different tact. Now with only a few members of a security detail and no media announcement, Abbas was making his homecoming—but quietly.[5] His son, Tareq Abbas, sat with him in the car along with Ahmad Tibi, an Arab-Israeli politician and friend of the family. The visit lasted only a few minutes—there wasn't much to see. Tareq recalled years later that "the house doesn't exist anymore. When we were children, my father and grandfather told us stories that gave us an attachment to the house. But it's impossible to live there."[6]

After a short stroll, Abbas got back into the Mercedes and the small party drove to a nearby restaurant. But just as they were getting out of the city, Abbas suddenly asked to stop the car for a moment. He got out, alone, and stood by the side of the road taking in the view.[7] The last time he had looked at Safed this way was in 1948, when he was a thirteen-year-old boy fleeing the city with his family.[8] Now he was there again—this time as a grown man—accompanied by his own son and visiting with Israeli approval.

Ahmad Tibi recalled years later that Abbas, a typically stoic man, "had tears in his eyes" as he gazed over the roofs of the city. Tibi had known Abbas for decades, yet that was the only time he had seen the Palestinian politician appear so emotional. "When he got back into the car, he didn't want to talk about the past anymore," says Tibi. "From that point on, the only thing he wanted to discuss was how we can guarantee that our people have a better future."[9]

Mahmoud Abbas was born in March 1935 to a working-class family in Safed. Back then it was a "mixed town," meaning approximately six thousand Arab-Palestinian residents lived with a community of more than two thousand Jews.[10] The city, like the entire land between the

Jordan River and the Mediterranean Sea, was under British control. British soldiers regularly patrolled its streets.

Abbas's father, Mohammad, sold cheeses, olives and canned goods out of a small grocery store, which the family lived above.[11] "They weren't a rich or famous family, but they did okay," says Mustafa Abbasi, an Arab-Israeli professor and a leading historian of Safed. "There were two kinds of merchants in Safed at the time: large merchants, who traded silk, spices, and other goods with large cities in the region like Damascus, Beirut, and Amman, and local merchants, who worked mostly within the city's boundaries. Abbas's father belonged to the second group."[12]

Both the Arab and the Jewish communities in Safed had deep roots in the city that stretched back hundreds of years. The relationship was largely a peaceful one, but it had its moments of violence. One of them was in 1936, the year after Mahmoud Abbas's birth, when an Arab revolt broke out against the British rulers.[13] In Safed, Palestinian residents attacked the city's Jews, who fought back using weapons that were gathered by a Zionist militia called the Haganah ("defense" in Hebrew).

The 1936 revolt was a pivotal moment in the history of the Palestinian national movement. Yet Mahmoud Abbas, who decades later would come to lead that movement, grew up in a family that was barely involved in these dramatic events. His family chose to stay out of the revolutionary upheaval of the day.[14] Abbas himself, in a short memoir that was published decades later, described his Safed childhood in idyllic terms: "I liked school and was dedicated to studying. My childhood was enjoyable—outside of school, my days were spent with my classmates playing and exploring Safed's mountain peaks."[15]

In between studying and playing, young Mahmoud helped his father's business by doing deliveries to different parts of the city, including to Jewish business partners.[16] The family's ties with some of these Jewish merchants didn't revolve solely around business: on the last day of the Jewish holiday of Passover, Abbas's father would send his Jewish partners an offering of baked goods, sweets, and cheeses as a neighborly gesture.[17]

"The seasons of the year in Safed were well marked," Abbas recalled fondly, "winter, for instance, is cold and snowy. Spring is bright and blossoming, with the earth and mountains carpeted by multicolored layers reminiscent of a handcrafted Persian silk rug. Summer is hot, but the city enjoys an invigorating fresh breeze making it a summer attraction for tourists and vacationers. Fall, with its brisk winds, rolls in stripping the trees of their leaves and ushering them into winter with a new garment."[18]

Abbas's description, however, omits the political and religious tensions in the city at the time. By 1947, Safed was at a fever pitch. The United Nations voted to enact the famous "partition plan," which called for the creation of two national states within the historic borders of Palestine: a Jewish state on 56 percent of the land and an Arab one on 43 percent, excluding Jerusalem.[19] Safed was supposed to become part of the Jewish state, despite the fact that it had a clear Arab majority (in a census from 1944, the city's population had 9,500 Muslims and approximately 1,950 Jews).[20] The Zionist leadership accepted the partition plan, but the Arab world and the Palestinians rejected it and declared war against the newly formed state of Israel.

The British forces, as part of their redeployment all across the land, left Safed on April 16, 1948, clearing the way for an all-out confrontation between the local Arab and Jewish populations. Two weeks later, Jewish fighters captured the villages of Birya and Ein al Zeitun to the north of the city, putting themselves in a good position to conquer the city. Abbas mentions this event in later writings, stating "it never occurred to us that we would be expelled from our homes until one day the nearby village of Ein al Zeitun was taken over by the Haganah militias. After this, the western, and then only entrance to the city was closed. Safed's residents started to consider sending women and children away in fear of potential massacres."[21]

As the Jewish fighters were closing in on Safed, thousands of local Arab residents volunteered to repel the attack. According to Mustafa Abbasi, one of them was the young Mahmoud Abbas, then only thirteen years old: "His name appears in the list of people who volunteered to fight the invasion, together with the names of other men from his family. However, there was no mention of a weapon that was distributed to him, which means that he probably didn't get one."[22]

The Haganah's forces broke into the city on May seventh. It was a rainy night, and Abbas's neighborhood came under constant mortar fire.[23] Abbas's father decided to send the family's young children, including Mahmoud, out of the city. "As we were leaving the city along its eastern border, I felt an overpowering urge to turn and cast a glance backwards, as if to cement Safed's familiar details in my mind," Abbas wrote later. "I felt I might not see it again."[24]

Like thousands of Palestinian families who fled or were forced out of the Galilee, the Abbases made their way to neighboring Syria. They became part of a humanitarian crisis commonly referred to as "the Palestinian refugee problem," which has remained largely unresolved to this very day. Approximately 700,000 Palestinians lost their homes as a result of the 1948 war.[25] They settled all across the Middle East, with the largest contingencies concentrating in countries on Israel's borders, such as Lebanon, Syria, and Jordan. The Arab countries' reaction to this crisis was to insist that the Jewish state be responsible for solving it, preferably by allowing the refugees to return to their homes. It was a proposition that Israel could never accept, since a sudden influx of Palestinian refugees would vastly create a non-Jewish majority within its borders, meaning the end of Israel as a Jewish state. Many of the original refugees and their descendants, as a result, have been stuck in limbo for decades.

The refugee crisis was a focal point in the history of the Palestinians. Every year, Palestinians commemorate the event as *al-Nakba*, or "the Catastrophe." For Mahmoud Abbas, it was a defining moment in his life, as a happy childhood in the lush greenery of the Galilee was replaced with a grim struggle to survive.

"We rented a two-room house in the Akrad neighborhood of Damascus where most of the populace lived in abject poverty," Abbas wrote. "We lived with our parents in one room and in the other lived my older brother with his wife and children. All of us, with no exception, started to search for jobs. We had to have jobs to eat and to pay rent. But when it came to clothes, we often shared."[26]

Abbas began working in construction, earning "one Syrian pound" per day by working from sunrise to sundown. "I watched

sorely as other kids went to school," he recalled. "My heart broke in
sorrow and grief over what had happened to me."[27] Eventually, Abbas
saved enough money to return to his studies, and in 1953 he completed high school while simultaneously working as a teacher at an
elementary school nearby. It was this difficult period that instilled in
him the deep belief in the importance of education. "Education for
our people was the only way ahead in life," he wrote; "we had no land
to nurture, no industry to flourish and no trade to prosper. Education was therefore the only path available to us to face up to the challenges that life handed us."[28]

When large oil fields were discovered in the Persian Gulf in the
1950s, local governments needed an educated workforce to help
facilitate global trade. Young Palestinians who had studied under
the British Mandate's education system before 1948 suddenly had a
golden opportunity. Mahmoud Abbas was one of many who decided
to move to the Gulf. He took a job in Qatar, a tiny emirate that desperately needed teachers for its growing education system.[29] After
a short stint with a local oil company, he landed a senior job at the
Qatari ministry of education, which provided a good salary and
important connections in the local government.[30] His personal life
was also moving forward at this time. In 1958, Abbas married Amina,
who like him was a refugee from Safed.[31] Two years later, Amina
gave birth to their oldest son, Mazen. His friends would now know
Mahmoud Abbas as "Abu Mazen," in line with the Arab tradition of
naming the heads of households after their firstborn son. The family
acquired a comfortable and spacious house in Qatar, and other rela-
tives of Abbas—including one of his brothers—also settled in the
country.[32]

The Abbas family hadn't been politically active back in Safed,
but in his new home the young and successful Mahmoud Abbas
became increasingly involved in Palestinian politics.[33] Together with
a number of friends, he founded a local group devoted to the idea
of "launching the revolution" against Israel.[34] They had no financial
backing, organizational skills, or military background (when Abbas
tried to enroll in a Syrian military academy before his move to Qatar,
the local commander quickly dismissed him, ruling that he was unfit
for service).[35] What they did have, however, was a connection with a

similar group established by young Palestinians in the nearby oil-rich kingdom of Kuwait.[36]

Unlike Abbas and his friends in Qatar, the Kuwaiti group was organized. They called themselves *Harakat at-Tahrir al-Watani al-Filastini* ("The Palestinian National Liberation Movement"), which backward forms the acronym "Fatah." Their leader was Yasser Arafat, a short, bearded engineer who was born in Egypt and raised in Jerusalem and Gaza. Among the cadre of Fatah founders, two were close to Arafat: Khalil al-Wazir (Abu Jihad), a native of Ramle and later Gaza who was involved in planning attacks against Israel even before finishing high-school;[37] and Salah Khalaf (Abu Iyad), a native of Jaffa who was responsible for Fatah's contacts with other Palestinian groups across the Arab world.[38]

Fatah started gaining momentum in the early 1960s, with more and more Palestinians from different countries joining its ranks. "They built a network that started out in the Gulf, but spread all across the Arab world, and also into communities of Palestinian students and laborers in Europe," says Nazir Magally, a veteran journalist for the international Arab newspaper *Asharq Al-Awsat* who has covered the Palestinian leadership for decades. "Their success became a threat to Arab regimes, who wanted to use the Palestinian issue to rally up support among their own peoples."[39] For the leaders of countries like Egypt and Syria, says Magally, talking about justice for the Palestinians was "an easy way to give the people what they wanted to hear: revolutionary and nationalistic rhetoric."[40]

That's why, in 1964, Egypt helped found a Palestinian organization aligned with its own interests, called the Palestine Liberation Organization (PLO). The PLO was initially designed to be an umbrella organization for different Palestinian groups, thus giving Egyptian president Gamal Abdel Nasser "ownership" of the Palestinian effort. Arafat and his partners in Fatah had no intention of letting that happen. They viewed the PLO with suspicion, as part of an Arab ploy to actually weaken the Palestinians and stop them from starting a guerilla war against Israel.[41]

"We considered the PLO to be an Arab instrument and [its military wing] a part of the Arab armies," recalled Khaled al-Hassan, a founding member of Fatah and close associate of Arafat. "In view of our experiences with the Arabs . . . and our deep lack of trust towards them . . . we feared that the PLO would kill or divert the awakening of our people."[42] Historian Yezid Sayigh writes that al-Hassan and other Fatah officials viewed the PLO's founding as a direct challenge to "the revolutionary process among the Palestinians."[43]

"Arafat set the tone in making the Palestinian national movement a rebellious movement against the Arab regimes," recalls one of his biographers. "He talked about the war of 1948 as an event of Arab betrayal towards the Palestinians. 'There are tens of millions of Arabs, and less than a million Jews in Israel,' he would tell his crowds, 'so how can it be that the Jews won the war?' His answer to that question was simple: because the Arabs didn't really put up a fight."[44]

On January 1, 1965, Fatah carried out its first terror attack against Israel, a failed attempt to damage the Israeli National Water Carrier, near the Jewish state's border with Jordan.[45] Soon, many other attacks followed. The organization's founding leaders moved from Kuwait to Syria, a country that had a direct border with Israel, a large community of Palestinian refugees, and vast empty areas suited for military training.

Mahmoud Abbas had almost no role in any of these activities. After being turned down to defend his hometown at the age of thirteen and later dismissed within months of entering a military academy in Damascus, the aloof teacher knew armed "resistance" wasn't going to be his calling.[46] And so while Arafat and the other movement leaders organized commando missions against Israel, cycling in and out of Syrian jails (the local government arrested them out of fear of their growing popularity but had to release them for the very same reason), Abbas tried to help in more bureaucratic ways. He raised money, wrote articles and pamphlets, and helped improve Fatah's ties with oil-rich monarchies in the Gulf.[47] Fatah needed a diplomat-in-residence, and Abbas was ready-made for the job.

Then came the six-day war of June 1967. Within a week, everything changed. From June 5 to June 10, Israel fought and defeated all of its Arab neighbors. The Israeli military conquered the Gaza Strip (formerly controlled by Egypt), East Jerusalem, and the West Bank region (formerly controlled by Jordan) and brought under its control more than a million Palestinians.[48]

Amidst the sense of desperation that took over the Arab world, there was one man who saw a promising opportunity. Yasser Arafat believed that the failure of the Arab states to defeat Israel and liberate Palestine created an opening for Fatah to rise to the center of the stage. Where the powerful and glorious Arab militaries had failed, his small organization would succeed. As one scholar noted, "to many Palestinians, Fatah would become the icon of their national aspirations . . . Fatah seized the opportunity to advance an alternative approach to achieving Palestinian independence."[49]

That alternative approach was two-pronged: carry out attacks against Israelis and seize control of the PLO. Taking over the PLO was important for Fatah, since the Egyptian-founded organization had something that Fatah did not—international legitimacy. The PLO was an umbrella organization, made up of different parties and groups and speaking for Palestinians all over the Arab world, while Fatah was seen as a smaller organization focused primarily on terror attacks. If Arafat and Fatah could gain control of the PLO, they would gain broader legitimacy and a larger microphone to broadcast to the world. After an unsuccessful Israeli invasion of Jordan in March 1968 to strike a PLO camp at Karameh—in which Fatah and Jordanian fighters inflicted serious damages on the Israeli army[50]—the party had enough momentum to take over the PLO. Historian Mustafa Kabha writes that "Fatah's image as the organization responsible for redeeming Arab honor was revitalized."[51]

At the 1969 PLO conference, Fatah won enough seats to gain control of the PLO's internal parliament, the Palestinian National Council (PNC).[52] Within a year, Arafat had effectively purged the anti-Fatah leadership from the PLO, placed himself on top of the movement, and repurposed the PLO as a "state within a state" in Jordan.[53]

With a population of more than a million Palestinian refugees and a long border with Israel, Jordan was a natural choice for Arafat to set up his new base. The country's young ruler, King Hussein, was initially patient with a newfound Palestinian apparatus in his country. But by 1970, he had grown tired of his militant guests. Not only was the PLO hurting his country's image with foreign investors and tourists, they were also trying to hurt him personally. An assassination attempt put the king over the edge. In September of 1970, Hussein went on the offensive and ordered his military to drive the PLO out of Jordan at any cost.[54] Hundreds—possibly thousands—of Palestinians died in the "Black September" clashes with the Jordanian military.[55] When the dust had settled, the PLO under Arafat's leadership was forced out, defeated and humiliated.

It was during this period that Mahmoud Abbas began dedicating himself full-time to the Palestinian cause, attaching himself to the PLO's senior leadership.[56] Abbas had no military training, background, or credentials. What he did have were legal, political, and fundraising skills that would prove very valuable to Arafat as the organization suffered from the consequences of its confrontation with King Hussein.

By the early 1970s, Arafat and most of the PLO leadership settled in Lebanon, where they succeeded over the next decade in building the "state within a state" that King Hussein stopped them from creating in Jordan. Arafat himself set up his office in the capital city, Beirut, while the southern parts of Lebanon—where the PLO placed military installations, rocket launchers, and checkpoints—soon became known as "Fatah Land."[57] Mahmoud Abbas, however, did not join his colleagues in Lebanon. He abhorred the revolutionary atmosphere in Beirut and opted instead to live with his family in Damascus.[58]

Away from the center of events, Abbas began carving a new role for himself as the PLO's in-house expert on Israel.[59] For a movement focused on fighting the Jewish state, the PLO had very little knowledge about it. Abbas had known Jews as a child in Palestine under the British Mandate, but he had barely met any after fleeing in 1948. Eager to expand his understanding of his enemy, he began investing a lot of time in reading books and essays about Israel.[60] "Unlike Beirut, the atmosphere in Damascus was relatively calm which allowed me to become engrossed in reading publications and information about Israel," he wrote later. "I had dedicated a great deal of my time to becoming acquainted with Israeli society. It had been a commonplace feature across the revolutionary community and [PLO] leadership not to attend to the composition of the enemy we planned to go to war with."[61]

✦✦✦

Abbas's rationale for immersing himself in Israeli studies was any-thing but altruistic. He wasn't a peacenik, and in fact continued to raise money that was used by the PLO to carry out terror attacks. According to Abu Daoud, the PLO mastermind of the cruel mas-sacre of eleven Israeli athletes in the 1972 Olympic Games in Munich, Abbas supplied the funding for that attack without knowing what it would be used for.[62]

However, something in his approach did gradually change. By the late 1970s, Abbas was starting to suggest a different direction in the Palestinian approach to the conflict. He began talking not just about the need to study Israeli society but also to engage with it, and perhaps move toward resolving the conflict through negotiations.

There were three groups in Israel that Abbas was particularly interested in.[63] The first was Jews who had immigrated to Israel from Arab states. Israel had absorbed more than a million of them after 1948, and in the 1970s many were still speaking Arabic at home. Abbas believed this group, which was discriminated against by the Israeli founding elite, could be more open to understanding the Pal-estinian narrative. In 1977 he wrote that integrating those Jews from Arab states was a "huge success of Zionism," but that they might be the natural ones to return to Arab countries.[64] Abbas blamed the Arab countries for their mistreatment of their Jewish residents; a mis-treatment that he thought fueled their emigration to Israel.

The other Israeli demographic group that Abbas was fervently studying was the country's Arab Israeli population—Palestinians who didn't leave their homes during the 1948 war and became citizens of Israel. They were around 150,000 right after the war and grew to roughly half a million by the 1970s (there are over 1.7 million of them today).[65] At first, the Palestinian national movement treated these Palestinians as collaborators and traitors, blaming them for accepting Israel's existence, legitimizing it by participating in Israeli elections, and refraining, most of the time, from creating civil unrest.

Abbas was one of the earliest Palestinian leaders to see things differently. "He talked about us as a bridge to peace," recalls Ahmad

Tibi.[66] Journalist Nazir Magally adds that, "Unlike most Palestinian leaders at the time, who only came to Israeli Arabs with demands—'do this or do that'—Abu Mazen met Israeli-Arab politicians in Europe and spent a lot of time asking them questions, trying to understand their point of view and to learn about them."[67]

Abbas's third "constituency" in Israel, and the one he would eventually be most successful in courting, was the evolving Israeli "peace camp" that emerged in the 1970s.[68] As Israeli governments started building new settlements in the territories Israel conquered during the war—mostly in the West Bank and Gaza—a new movement was building up in the country's left wing, calling for a withdrawal from those territories in return for peace and diplomatic relations with the Arab world. The first Arab country to offer such a quid pro quo agreement to Israel was Egypt, and after a lengthy, American-brokered negotiation an agreement between the two countries was signed in 1978, leading to a full Israeli withdrawal from the Sinai Peninsula.

When it came to the West Bank and Gaza, where Israel was now ruling over more than a million Palestinians, two approaches emerged within the Israeli "peace camp." The first one called for negotiating over those territories with Jordan, since it had originally controlled the West Bank; the second approach, which was considered quite radical at the time, was to begin direct negotiations over those territories with the PLO, with an eventual aim of allowing Palestinians some form of autonomous rule. That position was only held by a small fringe group within the left, and was widely unpopular among the general public. Yet it received a boost when some PLO officials began hinting at the possibility of founding a Palestinian state, not in place of Israel but alongside it, in the West Bank and Gaza.

An important milestone was reached in 1977 when Abbas orchestrated a meeting with former Israeli general Mati Peled, who fought in the 1967 War but afterward became an advocate of negotiations.[69] Over the course of two days, the two sides constructed a mutual acceptance of principles for the establishment of a Palestinian state existing alongside, and recognizing, a "Zionist State of Israel."[70] The meeting and the document it produced had the potential to become a historic turning point, but the reactions to it both in Israel and on the Palestinian side were negative.

In his memoirs, Abbas recalls that at the time the Palestine National Council (the PLO's legislative body) "bitterly attacked" PLO officials for even meeting with Israelis:

> I discovered that none of them [PLO officials] knew what they were talking about, that their knowledge of Israel was limited to the simple fact that it was the enemy. So, I set out to work on this weakness within our ranks, to let my views on how to deal with enemies infiltrate and to suggest ways of attaining our goal. I did not scorn the gun, which was one of the means to our end, but seven years of reading and writing had enabled me to delve into issues we had not considered before; so at the PNC meeting I got up and spoke confidently to my colleagues for forty-five minutes, touching on all the ideas that I wanted them to hear in an impromptu but organized fashion. Through the expression in their eyes and the silence in the hall I realized that they were hearing such words for the first time.[71]

Abbas defended his position in the face of harsh criticism by distinguishing between various strains of Zionism—those who were willing to compromise with the Palestinians on some of the land, and those who weren't.[72] By doing that, he also exposed a similar strain within his own national movement, between those who believed it was possible to reach a compromise with Israel, and those who stuck to Fatah's original goal of destroying it.

Abbas was clearly emerging as one of the most outspoken representatives of the "compromise" group, and he was doing so at a personal risk. "People began referring to him as a traitor and a Zionist agent," says Tibi. "He never received enough credit from the Israelis for his courage during that early period."[73] One of Abbas's partners in the moderate camp, Issam Sartawi, was murdered in 1983 by an extremist Palestinian group. "Abu Mazen knew very well that the same thing could happen to him."[74]

His support for reaching a compromise with Israel, however, didn't turn Abbas into a fan of the Zionist movement. From 1980 to 1982 he would spend time at the Moscow Institute of Orientalism, writing and defending a thesis titled "The Other Side: The Secret Relationship between Nazism and the Leadership of the Zionist

Movement."[75] The controversial thesis cited Holocaust deniers, asserted a connection between Hitler and the Zionist movement, and pondered if the number of Holocaust victims was actually lower than one million.

Abbas's thesis work would garner him praise from his PLO compatriots. Years later, however, he backtracked on his own research under considerable pressure and apologized for his treatment of the Holocaust. He published an unprecedented statement for a Palestinian leader, in English and in Arabic, describing it as "the most heinous crime to have occurred against humanity in the modern era."[76]

◆◆◆

Until the 1980s, Abbas was a peripheral player in the Palestinian national movement, always separated both politically and geographically from the centers of power. When Fatah was founded in Kuwait in the 1950s, he lived in Qatar. When Arafat moved the PLO to Lebanon, Abbas chose to remain in Syria and later went to study in Moscow. Yasser Abed Rabbo, a senior Palestinian politician, describes Abbas as "a very isolated man. He's a family man. He likes to isolate himself within his family. He has a very limited number of friends. He doesn't like to be engaged too much in political activities with others."[77]

Israel's invasion of Lebanon in 1982 changed Abbas's calculus. With Israeli troops in South Lebanon and warplanes bombing the PLO's strongholds in Beirut, Arafat and the PLO were cornered. After a months-long siege, they fled the country, humiliated, in what Abbas called "the end of an era and the dawn of a new one."[78]

The experience rocked the PLO to its core. Arafat felt betrayed by the Arab world, which hadn't come to the aid of the Palestinians in face of the Israeli onslaught. Abbas shared that feeling. It was his job during the siege of Beirut to negotiate aid and support from other Arab countries.[79] Their ultimate neglect of the Palestinians spurned deep resentment. In the words of one Fatah leader at the time: "Not only Israel is the enemy, but the Arabs—Saudi Arabia, Syria, and all of them. When we get rid of the Arab rulers we will fight [Israel]."[80]

Some Fatah leaders even mused about moving the PLO's headquarters to Greece, a European country, in order to "make the Arab world look silly."[81] Abbas, who became the movement's top surrogate to Russia following his studies there, took it a step further. In a meeting in Moscow shortly before the funeral of Leonid Brezhnev in 1982, Abbas asked the Soviets if they would support a Palestinian plan to buy an unpopulated Greek island and turn it into a temporary Palestinian state. "I was amazed by his naiveté," says a PLO leader who was with Abbas in the meeting.[82] So was one senior Soviet official, who promptly burst out laughing before asking Abbas if he had ever heard of NATO, which Greece had joined thirty years prior.[83]

Despite that embarrassing event, Abbas's abilities as a negotiator, fundraiser, and in-house "expert" on Israel became very valuable to the PLO when the group relocated to Tunisia following their defeat in Lebanon in 1982. "Abbas was the first to leave for Tunisia," recalls Abed Rabbo; "he got there before all of us."[84] After operating for more than fifteen years in countries bordering Israel directly, the PLO now found itself in a difficult position, leading a struggle to liberate Palestine from over a thousand miles away. "Tunisia changed the PLO," says Nazir Magally; "in Lebanon they lived a crazy lifestyle, always driving around with guns. Tunisia turned many of them into bourgeois kind of people. They lived in nice villas overlooking the sea."[85] In the post-Lebanon PLO, Abbas believed the moderate camp within the Palestinian movement would be strengthened.

And his role within the PLO would grow more important after Arafat's two closest deputies—Khalil al-Wazir and Salah Khalaf—were assassinated in Tunis over a span of three years. Al-Wazir—the PLO's top military figure—was killed by Israeli commandos in 1988, while Khalaf was shot to death by a rival Palestinian group in 1991.[86] This made Abbas one of the last surviving "founding members" of Fatah: although he hadn't been with Arafat in Kuwait in the 1950s, he had ties to Fatah going all the way back to the pre-PLO days.

The late 1980s were a time of crisis for the PLO. In 1987, an *intifada*, or popular uprising, broke out in Gaza, East Jerusalem, and the West Bank. Thousands of young Palestinians took to the streets, rioting and protesting, while the general work force organized strikes. The PLO in Tunisia suddenly risked looking out of touch. While Palestinians confronted Israelis in front of international camera crews, the "Palestinian leadership" sat in fancy villas in Tunis, completely detached from the ground. The one Palestinian leader who managed to create good contacts with the young leaders of the intifada was al-Wazir, until Israel assassinated him in 1988.

Arafat was deeply worried about his movement's detachment from the protests, but in order to "own" the intifada, the PLO had to show the Palestinians in the West Bank, Gaza, and Jerusalem that it was indeed relevant to their struggle. Abbas writes that the PLO needed to "discuss what we can offer them," lest everyday Palestinians turn on the PLO and "throw stones at us."[87] At this point, a debate emerged within the PLO about establishing a state-in-exile. A number of senior members were against it; Abbas led the charge in favor. "Abbas believed that a government in exile would create a wider framework than could the leadership of a liberation organization," recalls historian Mustafa Kabha.[88] Arafat wasn't convinced. So, instead, the PLO pushed for an emergency summit of the Arab League in Algiers in June 1988, which subsequently produced resolutions supporting the establishment of a Palestinian state run by the PLO.[89]

The summit served the purpose of showing Arab solidarity for the Palestinians, but the most important takeaway from it was that the Arab League reaffirmed the PLO's position that the organization was the "sole, legitimate representative" of the Palestinian people. For many years, this billing had been rejected by Jordan, which was negotiating with Israel over the return of the West Bank and Jerusalem to the kingdom's control. However, in 1987, shortly before the intifada broke out, the Israeli government rejected a secret peace deal struck by King Hussein and Israel's then foreign minister, Shimon Peres. Dubbed the "London Agreement," it included an Israeli withdrawal to the 1967 lines in return for a full peace agreement with Jordan. Once the agreement was rejected by Israel's right-wing prime minister, Jordan started losing interest in regaining the West Bank, while getting used to the idea that the disputed territory would one day become the basis for a Palestinian state. Now, at the Arab League summit, this idea was receiving the support of all the other Arab states, leading Hussein to declare shortly afterward that "Jordan is not Palestine," and that "we respect the wish of the PLO, the sole, legitimate representative of the Palestinian people, to secede from us in an independent Palestinian state."[90]

It was a seismic shift in the Israeli-Palestinian conflict. Ever since 1982, the United States had promoted a peace plan based on the concept of a Palestinian confederation with Jordan. Now, Jordan was no longer willing to play along. The PLO instantly jumped on the opportunity by issuing a declaration of independence and officially endorsing various UN resolutions, including resolution 242, the cornerstone of the two-state solution. For Mahmoud Abbas, this was a seminal victorious moment. A decade after his colleagues viciously attacked him for holding peace talks with Israelis, the PLO was now officially in favor of negotiations. As he later recalled, the organization's new policy had finally "brought international legality to the PLO position."[91]

The next step, in Abbas's mind, was creating a breakthrough in the PLO's troubled relationship with Washington. The Reagan administration was now in its final weeks in the White House, and it demanded Arafat to denounce terrorism as a precondition for setting up any kind of official contacts. Abbas believed it was a worthy sacrifice to make, even if it would be received critically on the Palestinian street. In his memoirs, he described Arafat's acceptance of the American demand as a "watershed" moment that delivered "an important victory" to the Palestinians. "If America was serious about achieving a comprehensive peace settlement," Abbas wrote, "then Israel would recognize our existence, one way or another."[92]

But the honeymoon with Washington was disappointingly short. The Bush administration suspended dialogue with the PLO after Israel foiled a planned PLO raid on an Israeli beach town.[93] By 1991, as the United States went to war against Iraq for invading Kuwait, Arafat made one of the greatest political mistakes of his career: he endorsed Saddam Hussein. The decision defied not only the United States but almost the entire Arab world. "Arafat never got over the issue of the Arab world betraying the Palestinians," says Magally, "most of his deputies at the time, including Abu Mazen, were against supporting Saddam. But Arafat ignored their opinion. Arafat had a much deeper understanding of Palestinian public opinion than people like Abu

Mazen ever had. He knew that the average Palestinian, whether he's in a refugee camp or in an Israeli jail, hates America, hates the Arab regimes, and sees Saddam as a symbol of resistance. So it was clear to him that the PLO should support Saddam this time."[94]

The retaliations from the wider Arab world were harsh. Kuwait kicked out hundreds of thousands of Palestinian residents in the country after the war, causing them to relive the refugee experience from 1948.[95] Other Arab states gave the PLO clear signals that they wanted nothing to do with the organization anymore. The US government was furious at Arafat.

The PLO was once again isolated and in a state of crisis, less than a decade after its defeat in Lebanon. Abbas believed that the only way out of this deep hole was to double down on attempting to reach peace with Israel. It was the only way for the Palestinians to get back in Washington's good graces and to win back international legitimacy.

It turned out that Washington was also interested in advancing peace in the region. In the fall of 1991, an international peace conference was launched in Madrid. Israel didn't want a PLO-led delegation to attend the event, so the compromise was a joint Jordanian-Palestinian delegation that excluded the PLO. Yet despite Israel's efforts to screen out the PLO, the Tunis-based group managed to have a presence at the talks, as many of the Palestinian members of the "joint delegation" had clear ties to the group's leadership. During breaks in the conference, these members would slip out and call the headquarters in Tunisia for consultations.[96] Whether Israel, the United States, and the Arabs liked it or not, the PLO was now clearly speaking for Palestinians in the West Bank and Gaza.

The Madrid conference ended without much fanfare. Israeli premier Yitzhak Shamir left after twenty-four hours, the conference wrapped up after a few days, and Washington's focus shifted to encouraging the two sides to conduct bilateral negotiations.

The post-Madrid peace process had stalled out. Bassam Abu Sharif, one of Arafat's closest advisors, called the conference "a complete waste of time."[97] Few within the Palestinian movement saw a point in continuing negotiations. Multilateral meetings took place in capitals across Europe after the conference, but the Israeli delegation wouldn't sit in on meetings where Palestinians from abroad were present. Subsequent attempts to establish back channels to Israel's government, led by the right-wing Likud party's Yitzhak Shamir, also failed.[98]

A year after the conference, George Habash, the legendary founder of the Popular Front for the Liberation for Palestine (PFLP), led a coalition of other third parties—including the newly founded Hamas terrorist group—in opposing further negotiations with Israel. In the rejectionists' view, negotiations over Palestinian autonomy in the West Bank and Gaza would "consecrate the occupation . . . and normalize Arab-Israeli relations while ensuring Israeli supremacy."[99] At a heated PLO Central Council meeting in Tunis in October of 1992, one Palestinian leader led the charge against the rejectionists: Mahmoud Abbas.

Fortunately for Abbas, he had something to rely on: Israel had just undergone a significant political change. In the June 1992 elections, the right-wing bloc lost power, and a new prime minister had emerged from the left: Yitzhak Rabin. Abbas's pronegotiations agenda—up to then nothing more than back-channel conversations—would now be put to a real test.

CHAPTER 3

FROM OSLO TO CAMP DAVID

1993–2000

Seqtember 13, 1993, was one of the most important days in Mahmoud Abbas's life. At 10:30 that morning, he and Yasser Arafat were expected at the White House for the signing of a historic agreement between the Palestine Liberation Organization (PLO) and Israel. Three years after Arafat alienated the United States by siding with Saddam Hussein during the Gulf War, he and Abbas were about to share a stage with an American president on the White House lawn. It was a remarkable turn of events.

As Abbas and Arafat left their hotel near the Pentagon, both of them looked as they had for decades in exile: Arafat with his famous green military fatigues, clad with honorary decorations from different armies around the world, insisting on arriving to his first meeting ever with an American president dressed like a militia leader; Abbas with an ordinary gray suit and red tie, the classic appearance of a clerk-cum-diplomat, always in the background and never drawing attention to himself.

When they arrived at 1600 Pennsylvania Avenue, a White House staffer ushered them into the building. Outside, on the south lawn, hundreds of distinguished guests were taking their seats around a ceremonial stage. More than thirty foreign ministers were in attendance, in addition to dozens of the most prominent political figures in Washington.[1] All the major US networks covered the event live, while dozens of Marines provided security around the perimeter.[2]

At 11:10, the event's announcer invited former presidents Jimmy Carter and George H. W. Bush to take their seats in the front row. Two minutes later, he called upon three names: Vice President Al Gore, Israeli foreign minister Shimon Peres, and "Mr. Abbas, member of the executive council of the Palestine Liberation Organization." As the three men approached the stage, an NBC news anchor explained to the viewers that "Mahmoud Abbas, on the right, will be doing the signing for the PLO, while Shimon Peres will be signing on behalf of his country."[3]

At 11:14, President Clinton emerged out of the same corridor, with Arafat to his left and Israeli prime minister Yitzhak Rabin to his right. The ceremony was about to begin, with only seven people standing on the stage: Clinton, Rabin, Peres, Arafat, American secretary of state Warren Christopher, Russian foreign minister Andrei Kozyrev, and Abbas. Looking at them, the casual observer would not be alone in wondering who the gray-haired man standing next to Christopher was. Abbas was undoubtedly the least-recognizable person on the stage, not just to most American viewers but also to policymakers in DC and even to many Palestinians watching the event live on their television sets back in the West Bank and Gaza.

As Clinton prepared to begin his remarks, one of the anchors on the NBC news broadcast declared, "This is amazing. There are few better words to describe this sight, as common a word as it might be. It is an amazing moment."[4] Israel and the PLO—sworn enemies for more than three decades—were moments away from signing a joint agreement that would lay the foundations for future peace. Yitzhak Rabin, one of Israel's greatest war heroes and the general who commanded the conquering of the West Bank, Gaza, and East Jerusalem in the 1967 war, was standing on the same stage with Yasser Arafat, the man who was responsible for hundreds of attacks against Israelis since the 1960s. It was indeed a historic moment.

"Prime Minister Rabin, Chairman Arafat, Foreign Minister Peres, Mr. Abbas, President Carter, President Bush, distinguished guests," President Clinton began, "on behalf of the United States and Russia, co-sponsors of the Middle East peace process, welcome to this great occasion of history and hope."[5] That Abbas was personally mentioned by the president as the number two in the Palestinian delegation was mostly a matter of protocol—but on a personal level, it was a huge achievement for the Palestinian negotiator. A senior member of Clinton's Middle East team recalls that Abbas was known to administration officials "only by name" at that point.[6]

When Clinton finished his speech, it was Shimon Peres's turn. "What we are doing today is more than signing an agreement. It is a revolution," said the Israeli elder statesmen. "I want to tell the Palestinian delegation that we are sincere, that we mean business. We do not seek to shape your life or determine your destiny."[7] The crowd was on its feet as Peres closed with words of hope: "Let's say together, in the language of our Bible: 'Peace, peace to him that is far off and to him that is near, said the Lord, and I will heal him.'"

The next one to speak was Abbas. As was his custom in almost every public appearance, Abbas chose to speak in Arabic, despite his proficiency in English. "We have come to this point because we believe that peaceful cooperation and coexistence are the only means for reaching understanding and for realizing the hopes of the Palestinians and Israelis," Abbas declared. "The agreement we will sign reflects the decision we made in the Palestine Liberation Organization to turn a new page in our relationship with Israel."[8] Clinton, standing behind him, beamed when the English translation of that sentence was read aloud.

The news broadcasts alternated between Abbas and a group of young Palestinians in the West Bank city of Jericho, who were watching the event with great excitement. Abbas was likely just as excited, but he kept his stoic tone steady throughout the speech. When he was done, he and Peres each sat down to sign the mutual recognition agreement. Officially called the "Declaration of Principles on Interim Self-Governing Arrangements," the agreement set out the creation of a Palestinian governing authority that would assume responsibilities for millions of Palestinians while final-status negotiations took place.[9]

In signing the declaration of principles, Shimon Peres and Mahmoud Abbas became the highest ranking Israeli and Palestinian to ever reach such an agreement. But it was incomplete without their bosses' approval, and Clinton knew it. He wrapped his long arms around the backs of Yitzhak Rabin and Yasser Arafat and almost physically pulled them together for a handshake, as if against their will. It was an image that would come to embody the entirety of the peace process.

"The enthusiasm was electrifying," one senior Palestinian official wrote in his memoirs.[10] Mahmoud Abbas shared that feeling, but as one of the architects of the agreement, he was also aware of the challenges waiting down the road. "We know quite well," he warned in his speech, "this is merely the beginning of a journey that is surrounded by numerous dangers and difficulties."[11]

◆◆◆

Fourteen months earlier, a new government was sworn into office in Israel. In July of 1992, for the first time in more than a decade, the left-leaning Labor Party formed a coalition without the participation of any right-wing parties.

The new prime minister was Rabin, the iconic former general, and while his ruling coalition had only a slim majority in the Knesset (Israel's parliament), it was bolstered by the informal support of Israel's Arab parties, who had declared they would assist Rabin if he tried to pursue peace with the Palestinians. "Abu Mazen encouraged us to take this position," recalls Ahmad Tibi. "After Rabin won, Abu Mazen told us it was important to signal to Rabin that if he tries to make peace, he can count on our support."[12] It was a watershed moment in Israeli politics. The Arab-Israeli parties had not traditionally interfered in the coalition bargaining. Now, with Abbas's encouragement, the Arab-Israeli parties were entering the fray. Their support would be critical to Rabin later.

Rabin's rise was, in part, due to the failure of the previous government to deal with the Palestinian uprising, the intifada. Chaos and violence reigned in the streets, and the Israeli people trusted Rabin, with his storied military background, to restore calm back to the country. It also didn't hurt Rabin that he was viewed as more amenable to the United States, which the previous Israeli premier, Yitzhak Shamir, had fought often with over settlement construction. Both of these crises fueled Rabin's rise to power, but they also related back to a central question: more than two decades after the 1967 war, what was Israel going to do with the West Bank, Gaza, and East Jerusalem?

By 1992, these territories were home to approximately two

million Palestinians.[13] These Palestinians were not granted Israeli citizenship yet were subject to Israeli laws. Now, Israel was unable to quell their mass-scale uprising. Rabin's new coalition brought with it the possibility of a different Israeli policy on the Palestinian question, and some in the PLO immediately realized that potential. "We knew that Likud would not take one single step towards a [peace] settlement," wrote Abbas.[14] When the right-wing party was defeated that year, Abbas could barely hide his glee. "So much for the Likud," he wrote.

But the first months of Rabin's rule were disappointing for those hoping to see a breakthrough in the peace process. While Rabin wasn't an enthusiastic supporter of settlements, he also wasn't ready to accept the two-state solution or hold direct negotiations with the PLO. Some in the Israeli government still hoped that Jordan would reverse its position and reaccept responsibility for the West Bank. Others believed Israel could solve its problems by negotiating directly with a new, local leadership in the West Bank and Gaza rather than dealing with the Tunis-based "Arafat gang." And indeed, the only official negotiations taking place at the time involved a delegation of politicians and academics from the West Bank and East Jerusalem who were meeting with midlevel Israeli bureaucrats for fruitless discussions in Washington.[15] When President Bush lost his reelection bid in November 1992, this channel became wholly irrelevant.

But that didn't mean all channels were closed. In December 1992, negotiations finally started moving—not in Washington, but in London. Yair Hirschfeld, a left-wing Israeli academic who had been involved for years in unofficial "track two" talks with Palestinian activists and academics, arrived at an economic conference in the British capital knowing that Ahmed Qurie, a senior PLO official close to Abbas, would also be in town. With the help of the same Palestinian academics who were involved in the Washington channel and frustrated by its stagnation, Hirschfeld sent a message to Qurie that he would be happy to meet him secretly while in London. Hirschfeld's purpose was clear: he was close to Israel's new deputy foreign minister, Yossi Beilin, and he knew Qurie was close to Abbas; together they could, perhaps, open their own back channel for negotiations.

Years of trying to advance peace had left Hirschfeld disillusioned and disappointed. He believed a peaceful, negotiated agreement between Israel and the Palestinians was in Israel's best interests, but he had grown frustrated with both his own governments and the PLO. To one Palestinian friend, he complained about his inability to reach out to Arafat and the PLO leadership: "When we talk to Egypt or Syria, there is a very clear structure of power. We know who we need to talk to. With the Palestinians, it's like trying to communicate with a number of boats in the middle of the sea, [with] each one going in a different direction."[16] His Palestinian associate replied that if Hirschfeld really wanted to make progress with the PLO he had to go through one person: Mahmoud Abbas. Now, with both him and Abbas's associate visiting London at the same time, was a rare opportunity to make it happen.

Back in Tunis, meanwhile, Qurie—the son of a wealthy family from Jerusalem who was one of the PLO's financial experts—briefed Abbas about Hirschfeld's offer. Abbas was responsible for all the PLO's connections with Israelis and had met many Israeli peace activists over the years, but few of them had such solid connections to the Israeli government. Hirschfeld was a member of the ruling Labor Party and enjoyed direct access to the deputy foreign minister. The potential for a breakthrough with him seemed real. Abbas and Arafat authorized Qurie to hold the meeting and waited patiently to hear the results.

For Qurie, known also as "Abu Alaa," this would be the first meeting in his life with an Israeli. "I was very reluctant to sit together in a room with any Israeli," he wrote in his memoirs. "At that time, we thought of Israelis with enmity and hostility. They hated us and we hated them."[17] On December 4, 1992, he met Hirschfeld for breakfast at a hotel in London, and to his surprise, it was a pleasant experience. Over the next forty-eight hours they held two more meetings. Hirschfeld told Qurie that, while he was acting on his own, he had good contacts in the Israeli government, and that there was now a real opening for peace.

When Qurie returned to Tunis, he immediately briefed Arafat and Abbas. Abbas writes in his 1995 semi-autobiography, *Through Secret Channels*, that after going over Qurie's written report of the meeting, he became convinced that the Israeli professor "could not have acted on his own initiative, he must have received authorization from his bosses, Peres and Beilin."[18] Hirschfeld, he believed, was "sent to sound us out," which meant that there was now a "faction in the Israeli government" that wanted to engage directly with the PLO.

Hirschfeld suggested that he and Qurie hold more meetings in the future—not in London, but in Oslo, Norway, where the government was interested in supporting unofficial dialogues between Israel and the Palestinians. Abbas and Arafat gave their blessing to the idea but told Qurie that these meetings had to remain a complete secret—unknown even to the Palestinian academics from the West Bank who had introduced him to Hirschfeld to begin with. These academics, members of the Palestinian delegation to the Washington talks, would continue to hold "dead-end" talks with the Israeli delegation over there, unaware of the progress being made by Qurie and Hirschfeld on the other side of the ocean.

Qurie arrived in Oslo with Hassan Asfour, a top official in Abbas's committee for contacts with Israeli society. Hirschfeld was joined by Ron Pundak, another Israeli intellectual and peace activist considered close to Yossi Beilin. More meetings followed, and by the spring of 1993 the talks began to yield results. Both sides had largely agreed on a framework agreement that would include a declaration of mutual recognition. That document would become the foundation for the "Oslo Accords," the unofficial name of the agreement signed by Abbas and Peres a year later at the White House.

As the negotiations advanced, the leadership on both sides got more involved. On the Palestinian side, the most important person throughout the talks was Abbas. Ahmed Qurie mentions in his account of the talks at least ten occasions in which he briefed Abbas about the negotiations. Yair Hirschfeld responds, "We knew that Abu Mazen was the one who oversaw the talks. Abu Mazen ran the diplomatic department and he made the decisions."[19] He adds that, "In Oslo, like in every negotiation, we played some games. The Palestinians' game was to announce once in a while that they need to take a break and 'call Tunis.' And we knew that the person they called was always Abu Mazen. Not Arafat." On the Israeli side, the updates went to Beilin, and later directly to Shimon Peres.

By the summer of 1993, the Oslo talks finally yielded a historic mutual recognition agreement between Israel and the PLO. The agreement would lead to the creation of a new body in the West Bank and Gaza, one that would allow the Palestinians to govern themselves. The idea was to create such an interim governing body so that it would gradually take control over the Palestinian cities and villages before a Palestinian state was negotiated. Israel would continue to have overarching say over security matters in the West Bank, Gaza, and its settlements in both territories, but for the first time in decades the Palestinians would have a level of control over some territory.

This new governing body would be run by the PLO, which Israel would recognize as representing the Palestinian people. The PLO would recognize Israel's right to exist in peace.[20] Arafat and the organization's leadership would be allowed to move into Gaza and the West Bank, where they would now be responsible for managing the daily life of Palestinians.

Both sides saw victory in the agreement. For the Israelis, the Oslo Accords provided a way out of the intifada taking place in the West Bank and Gaza. It also delayed a final, comprehensive agreement for five years, during which many in Israel hoped a new, organic Palestinian leadership might emerge. For the exiled PLO of Arafat and Abbas, the agreement provided legitimacy. They were able to show Palestinians that the PLO not only represented them but could also squeeze concessions out of Israel on their behalf.

Yet from the start, questions riddled the agreement. Who would officially sign it? Where would the signing take place? The Israelis had briefed the Americans earlier that year about the secret talks, and both sides agreed that some level of American involvement was necessary for creating international legitimacy—but how much? Eventually, both sides agreed to have the signing in Washington, yet that only presented further dilemmas.

The Clinton administration's top experts on the region believed that having Yasser Arafat attend the signing would be a bridge too far. Arafat, after all, was responsible for the murder of hundreds of Israelis and a number of American citizens. But if Arafat could not participate in the signing ceremony, then neither could Rabin. Clinton's advisors urged him to hold the ceremony without either of the two leaders, instead just having Shimon Peres and Mahmoud Abbas sign the agreement. Clinton, however, strongly objected: he believed the signing of the accord was a historic moment that would be incomplete if the leaders of the signing parties were absent.[21]

This was somewhat of a loss for Abbas. Without Arafat in attendance, it would have been his moment of triumph, and his alone. For a man who had for so long wallowed in the lower echelons of the Palestinian leadership to suddenly be the top representative at the White House would have been a massive boost. Instead, he was again overshadowed by Arafat. Insult was added to injury a few months later when Arafat, Rabin, and Peres all received the Nobel Peace Prize. Abbas, whose role in paving the way for the agreement was just as important as theirs, was left out. "I'm the equivalent of Peres on the Palestinian side," he reportedly complained to the Norwegian ambassador to Israel.[22]

Despite his fifteen minutes of fame at the signing ceremony, the Oslo negotiations and their aftermath had left Abbas feeling unappreciated. The long-time negotiator had been meeting with Israelis for years in order to reach an agreement, and here he was overshadowed by his boss, Arafat, and at the same time, threatened by Qurie's rise to stardom as the negotiator who actually participated in the secret talks in Oslo. While others were winning Nobel Prizes, Abbas was largely forgotten. Soon, however, he would have an opportunity to truly make his mark on peacemaking. He would bring the Palestinians closer to a comprehensive peace agreement with Israel than they'd ever been.

The optimism of September 1993 quickly succumbed to the realities of the region. Suspicion and mistrust grew between the Israeli government and the newly formed Palestinian Authority. Tensions were clearly visible the following spring when the two sides met in Cairo to sign an agreement detailing Israel's withdrawal from Gaza City and the West Bank city of Jericho. At one point in the signing ceremony, which was broadcast live in Israel and across the Arab world, Arafat refused to sign the geographical annex to the agreement for several minutes, despite the fact that all sides had already previewed and accepted it. The episode was a shocking embarrassment for Rabin, Peres, and Egyptian president Hosni Mubarak, who were all on the stage waiting for the ceremony to proceed. At one point, Mubarak was overheard cursing at Arafat to sign the maps already.[23]

The agreement was already off to a rocky start when mere months after the Oslo ceremony, in February 1994, a Jewish extremist from the West Bank settlement of Kiryat Arba broke into the Ibrahimi mosque in Hebron, murdered 29 Palestinians and wounded 125 more before being beaten to death.[24] Baruch Goldstein's rampage in the Cave of the Patriarchs compound, sacred to both Jews and Muslims, was a massacre with far-sweeping implications. When hundreds of Palestinians took to the streets to protest the attack, the Israeli military placed the city under a closure. It was a stark reminder to every Palestinian in the West Bank that despite the pretty pictures from the previous September they were still living under an Israeli occupation. Meanwhile, large demonstrations against the Oslo Accords took place all across Israel, led by the religious and right-wing opposition. In an attempt to calm his opponents, Rabin quietly authorized the construction of nearly a thousand new settlement units in the West Bank.[25] If both sides had had a rosy view of the Oslo Accords, the first year of the agreement had tarnished that visage.

To make matters worse, shortly after the Declaration of Principles was signed at the White House, the ultraorthodox Shas party left Rabin's coalition, dealing the Israeli premier a serious political blow.[26] Rabin now had to rely on the Arab parties in order to maintain a majority in the Knesset. On the one hand, Abbas looked incredibly prescient at that moment: it was he who had pleaded with Arab-Israeli lawmakers to support Rabin in case he lost support from Jewish parties. But, on the other hand, Rabin was now vulnerable. His opponents within Israel began casting his Oslo moves as illegitimate since they were "based on the support of the Arabs."[27] As one Rabin biographer wrote, "Opponents of the agreement would seize on this to discredit the approval process, advancing the unsavory argument that Jewish votes alone should count when broad national issues are at stake."[28] Rabin strongly rejected this thesis, but he was painfully aware of its effectiveness on public opinion.

Despite all of that, negotiations between the two governments continued. The Palestinian Authority increasingly gained responsibility for areas in the West Bank and Gaza, and Israeli military and intelligence services were beginning to work together with their new Palestinian counterparts against a common enemy: the Islamist terror group Hamas. In the months after the signing of the Oslo Accords, Hamas—which violently objected to the peace process—unleashed a murderous wave of terror attacks, killing dozens of Israeli citizens in buses, cafes, and busy street corners. Israeli officials were furious at Arafat for what they perceived as his indifference and at times even support for these attacks, but they found partners within the new Palestinian security forces who realized what a danger Hamas was to the stability of the agreements.

Hamas emerged from the First Intifada as an offspring of the Egyptian Muslim Brotherhood. Officially founded in Gaza in 1987, the Islamist terror group rejected any type of peace with Israel. Its founding charter, released a year later, would urge Palestinians to launch a *jihad* against Israel.[29] In the 1990s, the group would conduct terror attacks specifically designed to thwart any progress made in Fatah's peace negotiations with Israel.

Despite Hamas's terror attacks, the peace process soldiered on. In September 1995, Israel and the PA signed the Oslo II agreement, which increased the PA's autonomy in the West Bank and Gaza by dividing the territories into three areas: A, B, and C. Area A would be under the PA's control, Area B would be under Israel's military responsibility but the PA's civil administration, and Area C would be under full Israeli control. The agreement also allowed for the safe passage of Palestinians between the West Bank and Gaza.[30] It was a historic redeployment of Israeli forces in the territories, and one that has endured for more than two decades.

Throughout this period, Mahmoud Abbas was involved in the negotiations, but he had lost some of his influence in Arafat's orbit. Unlike most of the PLO leadership, he didn't immediately move back to the West Bank and Gaza following the creation of the Palestinian Authority, choosing instead to remain for some time in exile.

"He thought Arafat was not doing the right thing," recalls Yasser Abed Rabbo, a member of the PLO's highest decision-making body, the Executive Committee. "He disagreed with how he was running the PA. [He thought] it was a one-man show. . . . So, he stayed in Tunis."[31]

Despite being a leader within Fatah, Abbas rejected the way Arafat was filling the PA with Fatah cadres, choosing to appoint political allies to key positions instead of creating a professional leadership rank. It was another instance of Abbas rejecting Arafat's style of politics. When Arafat had run Fatah and the PLO in Lebanon, Abbas had stayed in Damascus. Now, with Arafat inserting Fatah into the PA from his new offices in Gaza, Abbas wanted to stay in Tunisia. He wouldn't return to Gaza and the West Bank until September of 1995.[32] He retained his position as chief negotiator within the PLO, but he wasn't given any formal title within the new Palestinian Authority.

This made him an excellent choice to manage a secret back channel with the Israelis. Just weeks after the Oslo signing ceremony, in October of 1993, Yossi Beilin met with Arafat to discuss further steps in the peace process. Beilin, a former journalist and long-time protégé of Shimon Peres, brought a message of his own—unapproved by his superiors—to the meeting with the Palestinian leader. "We have to start working on a final-status agreement," he pleaded, "now is the time. We can't wait."[33] For Beilin, the calculation was clear. "The idea was that we need to capitalize quickly on Oslo," explains a former Israeli official who was close to Beilin at the time, "because the agreement's opponents on both sides were so shocked by how quickly everything was happening. We had to start working on a final-status deal before they could get out of their shock and regroup."[34]

Arafat seemed to agree. He told Beilin to start working on it with Abbas. Despite the fact that both Beilin and Abbas were deeply involved in the Oslo process, the only time they had ever met was a brief handshake during the White House ceremony. Now, these two men were set to work on finalizing a comprehensive agreement between Israel and the Palestinians. This time, unlike in Oslo, Abbas wanted complete control over the back channel. He didn't want a deputy, like Ahmed Qurie, involved. Instead, he instructed Beilin to meet with two academics based in London: Hussein Agha and Ahmed Khalidi.[35] The two of them—dubbed by the Israeli side as "the Londoners"—were close to Abbas and unknown to Israelis: together they were the perfect negotiators for a secret channel.

The Londoners soon began holding meetings with Hirschfeld and Pundak, the former Oslo negotiators who were chosen by Beilin to be his representatives in the talks.

The back channel that emerged, known later as the "Beilin-Abu Mazen talks," was a classic example of what diplomats refer to as "track-two negotiations," where the negotiators are not strictly official representatives of their respective parties. Typically they are academics, activists, or prominent members of society with close ties to government officials. The key advantage to a track-two negotiation is that the negotiators are not bound to a constituency or government pressures; they are largely independent. For Beilin and Abbas, the benefit was two-fold: their delegates could negotiate freely on their behalf, and—if things went wrong and the channel's existence became known to the public—both parties could deny their involvement. If that were to happen, they could both claim that the talks were nothing more than an academic exchange of ideas between four distinguished intellectuals who just happened to be friendly with people in official positions.

Abbas's relationship with Agha and Khalidi went back decades. The two academics had grown up together in Beirut and joined the Palestinian national movement at a young age. For Khalidi, it was a natural avenue: he hailed from an aristocratic Palestinian family based in Jerusalem. His family fled to Lebanon, where his father, Walid Khalidi, became one of the leading Palestinian intellectuals of the twentieth century. In a 1978 article for *Foreign Affairs*, titled "Thinking the Unthinkable: A Sovereign Palestinian State," Walid Khalidi laid out one of the first academic arguments for the two-state solution.[36] The family's home in Beirut was a center for Palestinian activism and intellectual discourse, a fact that had a strong influence on Walid's children, including Ahmed. One Israeli who had negotiated with Ahmed Khalidi recalls hearing from him a childhood memory about a "short man with a beard coming to their home to speak with his father about the Palestinian revolution."[37] That man was Yasser Arafat.

If the Khalidis were the hub of Palestinian intellectualism, the Aghas were something entirely different. To begin with, they weren't even Palestinian. Hussein Agha was born to a Lebanese Shi'a family with roots in the Iranian aristocracy.[38] Agha's father was a successful businessman with ties all across the Middle East. The younger Agha's decision to join the Palestinian national movement was influenced by his friendship with Khalidi. In the heyday of the PLO, it was not unusual for non-Palestinians to join the movement, and in some cases even carry out attacks against Israel.

Agha and Khalidi, however, did not become part of the "armed struggle." Like Abbas, they were intellectuals and instead embarked on an academic career, earning advanced degrees from the most prestigious universities in the United Kingdom and publishing articles in the world's most esteemed newspapers. They were also among the earliest within Palestinian politics to engage with Israeli academics. This made them natural allies of Abbas, who shared their worldview and fields of interest.

Their meetings with Hirschfeld and Pundak began in the summer in 1994. Nimrod Novik, a former senior adviser to Peres, joined in on some of the discussions. Like Hirschfeld and Pundak, he was impressed by Agha and Khalidi. "We were very optimistic about this channel," he recalls. "We thought these guys were professionals and that we could really cut a deal with them."[39]

And, indeed, by mid-1995 the two sides had smoothed out the edges of an agreement. Secluded from the day-to-day headaches of politics, violence, and crisis, Beilin and Abbas's negotiators reached multiple understandings.[40]

The two sides agreed that Israel would withdraw from the Gaza Strip and from approximately 90 percent of the West Bank, making way for the creation of a Palestinian state in those areas.[41] The remaining 10 percent of the West Bank—where most of the large "settlement blocs" close to the 1967 border are located—were supposed to be annexed by Israel, which was going to compensate the Palestinians by giving them an equivalent amount of land to the south of the West Bank.[42]

Jerusalem, under the proposed agreement, was to be "an open and undivided city" with a reformed higher municipal council and two sub-municipalities that would administer their respective boroughs. The western part of the city, home to most of the Jewish population, would be recognized as the Israeli capital "Yerushalayim," while the eastern part, home to most of the Palestinian population, would be recognized as the Palestinian capital "al-Quds."[43] On Palestinian refugees, Israel would acknowledge the "moral and material suffering caused to the Palestinian people" and support the establishment of an international commission to facilitate the final settlement of Palestinian refugees within either the Palestinian state or neighboring Arab countries. Israel, however, would allow a limited number of refugees into its territory on a humanitarian basis, as well as commit funds to improve Palestinian refugees' situation abroad.[44] Finally, the agreement allowed Israel to keep a limited presence of military forces within the West Bank and Gaza for twelve years following the creation of a Palestinian state.[45]

The detailed agreement was finalized in October 1995.[46] It was twelve pages long and included additional understandings on water distribution, diplomatic cooperation, and cultural relations programs. Abbas arrived in Tel Aviv and the parties toasted the agreement. The atmosphere was joyous: after almost a century of conflict between Jews and Arabs in historic Palestine, representatives of both sides had, for the first time, constructed a comprehensive peace agreement that would end hostilities. It was a major achievement for Abbas, Beilin, and the rest of the negotiators involved.

"Abu Mazen was perhaps at his best as a negotiator during our work on that agreement," says Novik. "He very quickly authorized his negotiators to present his red lines and didn't change anything fundamentally afterwards. It was clear to us that he realized Israel isn't going to be flooded by refugees and there was no point in opening that for discussion."[47]

A former Palestinian official explains that Abbas's flexibility during the talks was partly a result of his decision to remain separated from Arafat and the rest of the movement after the establishment of the Palestinian Authority. This detachment from Arafat "gave Abu Mazen a degree of freedom, and he could come up with ideas and explore things."[48] The same former official adds that he thought "Arafat understood the value of having someone within his inner circle that could explore but also had a degree of deniability."[49] Eventually, however, Abbas returned to the Palestinian Territories in 1995. Palestinian, Israeli, and even some international officials had coaxed him back in the hopes that he might dilute Arafat's growing autocratic tendencies.[50]

Now, with a peace agreement in its final stages, Abbas had a massive challenge on his hands: convincing Arafat to accept it. The Palestinian leader had green-lit the negotiations back in 1993, but that didn't mean he agreed with what was being discussed by October 1995. The Beilin-Abu Mazen agreement included compromises on some of the PLO's oldest and most important issues, like refugees and settlements. It was far from certain that Arafat would agree to it. Similarly, Beilin was going to have to do the same with Peres and Rabin on the Israeli side. It was a massive hurdle for both these negotiators, and it was also why, while toasting the agreement, the two men did not pull out pens to sign it.[51]

Yasser Abed Rabbo, who still considers the Beilin-Abu Mazen agreement "the most balanced proposal for peace," says that Abbas "never gave it to Arafat as a document."[52] He discussed it with him in general terms but decided to wait for answers from Rabin and Peres before asking Arafat to officially adopt it. Beilin, for his part, had contacted Rabin's office and asked for time with the prime minister to present the agreement to him. He and the other Israeli negotiators were optimistic, mainly because the Palestinians had compromised on Rabin's top priority: security. With an Israeli military presence in the Jordan Valley for more than a decade, they believed Rabin would be willing to seriously consider the text.[53]

Beilin, however, never managed to present the agreement to Rabin. On November 4—a week after the "Beilin-Abu Mazen" agreement was finalized—a right-wing Jewish extremist murdered Rabin at the end of a pro-peace rally in Tel Aviv. Rabin's death, which came after months of rabid incitement against him by opponents of Oslo, put everything on hold. The "Beilin-Abu Mazen" agreement was now the last thing on anyone's mind.

Shimon Peres took over as prime minister and was immediately faced with a dilemma: call elections right away or wait until the fall of 1996, when the elections were originally scheduled to take place. Peres, who himself had a troubled past and rivalry with Rabin, decided to wait until the following May. According to those close to him, he "didn't want to win on Yitzhak's blood."[54] Peres wanted to win the election on his own merit.

Arafat, meanwhile, was deeply disturbed by Rabin's assassination.

"I lost my partner," he famously told reporters.[55] His first-ever visit to Israel came days after Rabin's funeral, when he quietly visited Rabin's house in Tel Aviv to pay his respects to the grieving family. "We lost a great man who made the peace of the brave with us," Arafat reportedly told Rabin's widow, Leah.[56] Abbas, too, was saddened by the tragedy, according to a former senior American official: "They [the Palestinian negotiating team] were all shaken by it."[57]

But they didn't have long to wallow in grief. 1996 was to be a pivotal election year. Both Israelis and Palestinians would have to answer to their respective publics on the progress made in peace talks. The democratic contest was decidedly easier on the Palestinian side, where Arafat was clearly headed for an easy victory. Mahmoud Abbas, for his part, was appointed the gatekeeper for the first elections in the history of the Palestinian Authority. As head of the newly formed Central Elections Commission (CEC), Abbas was in charge of organizing, supervising, and verifying the results of the election.[58] It was his first job in the Palestinian Authority. The biggest challenge, Abbas told reporters, was that "the ballot boxes which were designed to international standards filled up at 11 o'clock, four hours after the polls opened."[59]

Arafat and Fatah coasted comfortably in the elections, which were held for both the presidency and the parliament. Arafat defeated his competitor for presidency, the female activist and charity worker Samiha Khalil, by garnering nearly 90 percent of the vote.[60] Fatah secured a majority in the Palestinian Authority's parliament, the Palestine Legislative Council, by winning sixty-five of the council's eight-eight seats.[61] The very existence of those elections was an achievement for the Palestinians and a sign of actual progress reached thanks to the Oslo Accords. Five years earlier, Arafat was an international pariah and the leader of an organization struggling to remain relevant; now, he was the first democratically elected leader in Palestinian history.

As for the Beilin-Abu Mazen agreement, both sides knew it would have to wait. Peres believed that unveiling it before the May 1996 Israeli elections would be a dangerous gamble that could play into the hands of the right wing. Already perceived by many Israelis as too weak on security, the last thing he needed was to run on a platform based on a secret peace agreement under which Israel would give up a majority of the West Bank to Arafat. Instead, what occupied Peres's mind was the need to show Israelis that he was tough on terror, just like Rabin had been.

In January of 1996 an opportunity emerged for Peres to do just that when the Shin Bet—Israel's internal intelligence agency—discovered the hiding place of a top Hamas terrorist: Yahya Ayash. Hamas's chief bomb maker was known internally by the nickname *al-Muhandis* ("the engineer"). He was the mastermind behind many of Hamas's cruelest terror attacks in the post-Oslo years.

Eager to get rid of Ayash, Peres authorized the Shin Bet to carry out an assassination attempt. Israeli intelligence had found a way to get a two-ounce radio-controlled bomb into Ayash's phone, and when he spoke they triggered the detonation. On the morning of the assassination, Ayash's father called his roommate to ask to speak with his son. "I left the room," recalled his roommate. "Five minutes later I returned because I thought he had finished his conversation. I saw Yahya lying on the ground covered in blood. He had no head."[62]

Israel braced for a harsh response from Hamas. So, too, did the PA's security forces, which by then were working on a regular basis with their Israeli counterparts in Gaza and the West Bank. Yet both sides were caught off guard by the magnitude of Hamas's retaliation. Over the next two months, more than sixty Israelis were killed in suicide bombings in Jerusalem and Tel Aviv.[63] Any public support Peres had won in taking out Ayash was now lost amid the panic in the streets. The terror wave hurt his standing and pushed many Israelis to support Benjamin Netanyahu, the young leader of the Likud.

Then, in March 1996, two months before the elections, another "bomb" exploded—this time a political one, aimed directly at Peres's campaign. The Israeli newspaper *Ha'aretz* published the entirety of the Beilin-Abu Mazen agreement on its front page. Presented as a secret peace deal that was struck on Peres's behalf, *Ha'aretz* alleged the agreement would be implemented after the elections. The journalist who revealed the story was the paper's veteran security affairs reporter, Ze'ev Schiff. Perhaps coincidentally, a decade later, Schiff would publish a book together with Agha and Khalidi, the two Palestinian negotiators in the Beilin-Abu Mazen talks. To this day, the

Israelis who took part in the secret channel blame their Palestinian counterparts for the leak (an accusation that Abbas's associates have denied).[64]

"It was leaked by their side," says Yossi Beilin. "I don't know why. Maybe as some sort of a gesture to a friend, or maybe they didn't realize what would be the consequences. Ze'ev Schiff called me and he said—I'm sorry, I have this document, and as a journalist, I have to publish it."[65]

The leak was political gold for the Netanyahu campaign, who seized on it immediately. Ads soon littered the country claiming that "Peres will divide Jerusalem."[66] For religious and conservative-leaning Israelis, it was the ultimate rallying cry. Peres tried to distance himself from the agreement, but the similarities between this secret channel and the one that preceded Oslo—mainly, Beilin and Abbas's involvement—made that almost impossible. The damage proved to be beyond repair.

Abbas was also among the leaks' casualties, as he was blasted by other Palestinian officials for compromising on issues like the "right of return" and Jerusalem. Under pressure to save his own skin, Abbas denied any involvement with the negotiations. "As soon as it came out, he rejected that he made the agreement," says Abed Rabbo, despite the fact that "he himself negotiated it with Beilin."[67] Some Israeli officials understood Abbas's behavior in this case: admitting he was involved could have ended his political career. Others were less forgiving, insisting his rebuttal of the Beilin-Abu Mazen agreement was the first in a long history of rejectionism.

On May 29, Peres lost to Netanyahu by a slim margin of roughly thirty thousand votes.[68] Netanyahu's rise to power left the fate of the Oslo Accords on uncertain ground. But while many in the Palestinian Authority and the international community had sensed doom, others—among them Mahmoud Abbas—believed that it was worthwhile to at least give the new leader a chance. Netanyahu was a hawk and a strong supporter of settlements, true, but so was a previous Likud prime minister, Menachem Begin, who surprised the entire world by signing Israel's historic peace deal with Egypt in 1979. Abbas, as the PLO's leading expert on Israeli politics, understood this better than most. Perhaps Netanyahu would be the second "Likudnik" prime minister to prove his critics wrong by pursuing peace with Israel's neighbors?

Within forty-eight hours of Netanyahu's victory, Abbas was in Tel Aviv to meet with Yair Hirschfeld and Yossi Beilin. He told his Israeli friends that he now wanted to establish some contacts within Netanyahu's camp. Dore Gold, a close associate and advisor to Netanyahu, had already called Abbas and expressed his interest in opening a channel of communication with him. Gold, it turned out, had previously met Abbas's friend Hussein Agha at academic events. In between Agha and Gold, Abbas saw a ready-made back channel that could serve him and Netanyahu to exchange ideas and positions. With Hirschfeld's help, Abbas arranged funding from the Swedish government in order to fly Agha to Jerusalem.[69] Netanyahu, meanwhile, assured the Palestinians that he would respect Israel's commitments under the Oslo process.

It didn't take long, however, for Abbas to lose faith in Netanyahu. Through the back-channel talks, Gold had asked Abbas to convince Arafat to shut down two Palestinian offices that were operating in East Jerusalem. For Netanyahu, this was a personally important issue: he had campaigned on keeping Jerusalem undivided, and he could not be seen as accepting any hint of official Palestinian presence within the city. Abbas told Arafat that in return for shutting down those offices, Israel would permit Palestinian workers into Israel, launch peace talks, and settle the open question of a redeployment from the Palestinian city of Hebron. Arafat was sold. But soon after closing the offices, Netanyahu threw Abbas a curveball. "What Gold meant by moving on these issues was not to act immediately on them," explained President Clinton's envoy, Dennis Ross, "but rather to be open to discussing them."[70] Soon after, Israel demolished a Palestinian building in East Jerusalem and announced new settlement units in the West Bank.

Abbas was mortified. His image on the street as someone who was "too soft towards Israel," in the words of one senior Palestinian official, was now solidified.[71] Abbas felt "burned" by his back channel with Gold.[72] Weakened, he stepped back from negotiations and focused instead on establishing ties with Israelis outside of Netanyahu's camp. Every couple of weeks he met with left-leaning Israeli politicians in the opposition at the house of Egypt's ambassador to Israel, Mohammed Bassiouni.[73] Together, Abbas and the Israeli participants—many of whom were involved beforehand in the Oslo process—discussed ways to advance the peace process with the help of the international community. "Sometimes, after we finished our discussions, as we were leaving the place, a small motorcade with darkened windows would drive into the ambassador's residence," recalls one Israeli participant in the discussions. "Inside it was the US ambassador, Martin Indyk, who came to receive an update from Bassiouni about the ideas we'd discussed."[74]

Abbas also developed a close relationship during this period with Israel's top military official, IDF chief of staff Amnon Lipkin-Shahak. The senior general had been involved in negotiations with the Palestinians under Rabin's government and was known to have a rocky relationship with Netanyahu. During the course of negotiations, Abbas and Lipkin-Shahak became personal friends. "Amnon was respected by all the Palestinians," says Ross, "but the one person who I felt had an emotional connection to him was Abu Mazen."[75] Abbas's friendship with Lipkin-Shahak would become part of a recurring theme: he usually fostered stronger relationships with the Israeli security establishment than with Israel's elected politicians.

Even more interesting than his connection to Lipkin-Shahak was Abbas's attempt during the same period to establish a relationship with another Israeli war hero, one whom Palestinians loathed more than anyone else: Ariel Sharon. In Palestinian circles, Sharon had the reputation of something between a demon and a monster. As defense minister in 1982, it was Sharon who orchestrated the Israeli invasion of Lebanon and subsequent siege of Beirut. On top of his military exploits, Sharon had been a fervent supporter of settlements since the 1970s. Now, however, he was a minister in Netanyahu's cabinet, and Abbas, despite Sharon's terrible image on the Palestinian street, believed it would be smart to meet him and hear his views about the conflict.

A meeting between the two of them was organized in June

1997 at Sharon's ranch in southern Israel. They spent a long Friday afternoon together, discussing different ways to advance the peace process. When the details of the meeting were leaked, an Israeli commentator wrote that it was "one of the most important developments that has happened in the process of reconciliation between the two nations."[76] Hyperbole or not, Abbas's willingness to see past popular opinion in order to make progress was a sign that his belief in peace was still strong.

Abbas's good intentions, though, were far from enough. Netanyahu's three years in office (1996–1999) were largely a stagnant period for the peace process. Where there was progress, it was minimal. In January 1997, the two sides agreed to redeploy Israeli troops in Hebron, and in October of 1998 they signed the Wye River Memorandum, in which the PA promised to clamp down on terror in exchange for minor Israeli redeployment in the West Bank.

Unlike some of his peers, Abbas had no personal animosity toward Netanyahu. In conversations with American officials, he confessed that he liked the Israeli premier.[77] The problem with the young Likud leader, Abbas felt, was that he would "always be limited by his base."[78] Many of Clinton's top advisers shared this assessment of Netanyahu, but they also had their fair share of complaints about Arafat. "The time for calculated ambiguity has passed," Secretary of State Warren Christopher told Arafat after the Oslo signing, "our success now depends on you being straightforward in your condemnation of and action against terror."[79] But years of Arafat's skittishness had infuriated Clinton officials. His "unwillingness to take responsibility for stopping the violent acts of his own people would come to be recognizable as vintage Arafat," wrote Indyk. "It would do more than anything else to undermine the trust so necessary to the success of his new partnership with Israel."[80]

If the Americans saw Arafat as duplicitous, their opinion of Abbas was the complete opposite. During the up and down negotiations in Netanyahu's term, Abbas endeared himself to the Clinton administration. According to Ross, Abbas was "the one guy on their side who, if he tells you something, you're more likely to be able to count on it." The president himself, adds Ross, considered Abbas and Ahmed Qurie as the two most serious and trustworthy officials on the Palestinian side.[81] "We saw him as the architect of Oslo and of the PLO's moderation and pragmatism," recalls Indyk. "He was somebody we could talk to and work with."[82]

Abbas's good reputation in Washington and Jerusalem, however, ran the risk of becoming a problem for him in the West Bank and Gaza. "Arafat wouldn't trust Abu Mazen to be alone with any Israelis," recalls Abed Rabbo. "He was afraid of the concession approach of Abu Mazen."[83] The problem was also clear to some of Clinton's advisors. "Abu Mazen is every Israeli's favorite Palestinian," Ross once warned the Israelis. "The surest way to kill him is to communicate that."[84] One senior Palestinian official offers a less polite view on Abbas's negotiations tactics: "His approach to the Israelis was very simplistic, and in my mind, also very idiotic."[85]

After the signing of the Wye River Memorandum in October 1998, Israel agreed to release several hundred Palestinian prisoners. But rather than releasing the prisoners Arafat demanded—most of them convicted terrorists—Netanyahu at first released an entirely different batch, mostly made up of unknown petty criminals.[86] Palestinians thought Arafat had been duped. "The Palestinian Authority," wrote Qurie, was "in a weak position in the eyes of Palestinian public opinion."[87] Arafat needed a fall guy, and Abbas was ready-made to take the heat. Anonymous sources accused Abbas of "neglecting the prisoner negotiations" and being too soft with the Israelis. Palestinians protested in front of Abbas's home in Gaza. Some threw stones.[88] Abbas was in shock. "It was a very hard experience for him," says Munib al-Masri, a Palestinian businessman who was close to Arafat and has known Abbas for decades. "It showed him what a price he could pay for his support of peace."[89]

This was Abbas's first taste of Palestinian politics at the ground level. No longer was he in a Tunisian villa coordinating back channels with Israelis. Palestinian politics are a contact sport, and someone had brought the battle to his house. His first suspect was Mohammad Dahlan, a rising political star within Fatah.[90] Young and ambitious, the Gaza-born Dahlan first emerged on the national scene during the First Intifada, when Israel expelled him to Jordan for fomenting unrest on the streets of Gaza.[91] His actions caught Arafat's attention, and when the Palestinian Authority was formed after Oslo, Dahlan became responsible for setting up and commanding the PA's security forces in Gaza. He quickly developed a reputation as a ruthless opponent of Hamas. His forces routinely tortured and interrogated members of the Islamist group.

Abbas knew what everyone else in Gaza knew: no one could protest against a Palestinian leader in Gaza without the approval, implicit or otherwise, of Dahlan. This crisis would be the spark of a furious rivalry between Abbas and Dahlan, one that would last for decades and come to represent a wider generational battle within Fatah between the "old guard" of Tunis and a younger, Gaza and West Bank-born group of politicians.

Two months after Wye, Clinton arrived for a historic visit in Gaza. He was there to open Gaza's international airport and to oversee a change in the PLO's charter. For decades, the PLO's charter had called for Israel's destruction. Now, at Clinton's behest, Arafat would convene the PLO's parliament, the Palestinian National Council, to remove those calls. At the Shawaa Center in Gaza City, Clinton— flanked by Arafat and the speaker of the PLO's parliament, Salim Za'anoun—entered the hall to a standing ovation.[92] Za'anoun spoke, and then Arafat, before Clinton gave what one of his advisors called "the best speech ever given on peace."[93]

"By turning this page on the past, you are taking the lead in writing a new story for the future," Clinton told the parliamentarians, "and you have issued a challenge to the government and the leaders of Israel to walk down that path with you."[94] Palestinians were moved. Another Clinton official recalls seeing tears streaming down the faces of the delegates as they annulled their founding document.[95] A page, seemingly, had been turned.[96]

Abbas beamed in the front row. Clinton's trip was a result of the Wye River negotiations, in which Abbas and his deputy, Ahmed Qurie, had played a vital role. For a sitting US president to visit the Gaza Strip as the guest of the PLO was an incredible change from just a few years ago. "We ourselves regarded the visit as a major milestone on the road to establishing the independent state," wrote Qurie. "Millions of Palestinians were thrilled by the scene. . . . The two presidents, the American and the Palestinian, stood together, shoulder to shoulder. Until recently they had represented two opposing poles of world politics. Now, in the interests of peace, understanding was the order of the day on both sides."[97]

In early 1999, the political tremors caused by these developments had reached Israel, as Netanyahu's government collapsed after a small right-wing party accused him of offering too many concessions in the peace process and quit the coalition.

Israel went to new elections, and Ehud Barak, a former general and the leader of the Labor Party, emerged as Netanyahu's main challenger. Abbas was in Washington on election night and invited Dennis Ross to watch the election results with him at his hotel. As Ross arrived, the Palestinian negotiator jokingly told him, "Either we toast the outcome or we jump out the window together."[98] The Clinton administration actively worked to help Barak in the hopes of defeating Netanyahu and reigniting the peace process.[99] When the results came in and it was clear Barak had won by a landslide, Abbas was elated. "These are our natural partners," he told Ross, referring to the Israeli Labor Party. "We can now make peace."[100]

A few weeks after Barak's election victory, one of his wealthy supporters hosted a meeting between the new prime minister and Abbas at a luxurious villa outside of Tel Aviv. "Barak was very impressed with [Abbas]," recalls Gilad Sher, Barak's former chief of staff. "He thought Abu Mazen was the one who could bring Arafat to a historic decision."[101]

Abbas had no official position within the Palestinian Authority at the time. "It was his preference," says one of his former aides. "He was responsible for the negotiations with Israel, and that was the mandate of the PLO, not the Palestinian Authority."[102] On paper, Abbas was Secretary General of the PLO, effectively the number two in the entire organization. In this role he was also the head of the negotiations affairs department with Israel. The downside of it was that, unlike those who held official positions within the Palestinian Authority, Abbas could not secure a political "base" of support for himself. It's not clear, however, if Abbas even cared about any of that. "He's not a people person," recalls a former staffer. "Abu Mazen is not in touch with the people."[103]

Outside the political arena, after the PA was established it was widely reported that Abbas's three sons established a business empire worth millions of dollars. His oldest son, Mazen, settled in the Gulf region, where the family had some business and political connections going back to Abbas's time in Qatar. "Mazen took care of the family's holdings in the Gulf, but he also made new connections of his own, and was quite successful," says Israeli journalist Dani Rubinstein, who covered the Palestinian leadership for decades.[104] Abbas's two younger sons, Yasser and Tareq, focused on the West Bank and Gaza, where they invested in tobacco, telecommunications, and various contracting firms.[105]

Were Abbas's sons benefitting from their proximity to the Palestinian Authority's leadership? That question has been repeatedly raised over the years, but as of this writing it has never been resolved. Arafat himself had hid over a billion US dollars from public funds by the time of his death, and many other Palestinian officials found ways to use the Palestinian Authority's budget for their own benefit.[106] In Israel, this was viewed as a fact of life. "Our entire approach was to kind of ignore signs of corruption within the PA," says one senior Israeli official. "The logic was—since we're not giving them real features of sovereignty and statehood, at least for the time being, we have to let them secure their power in their own way—which was, by corruption, by throwing money in every possible direction to keep everyone happy."[107]

The dangers of this issue, however, received little attention beyond Israeli circles. Instead, the world's focus was on peace negotiations. The target date for the completion of final-status negotiations according to the Oslo Accords, May 4, 1999, had passed without any significant progress. With a new government in Israel and a year left in the Clinton administration's final term, all sides felt a sense of urgency. Barak, who had campaigned on this issue, was eager to put Israel on a new path, which he discussed with Abbas at their meeting after the election.

Barak was one of the most ambitious prime ministers in Israel's history. He stayed in power for only eighteen months but managed within that short time to pull Israel out of Lebanon after eighteen years of bloodshed and hold serious negotiations with both the

Syrians and the Palestinians. The Syrian track was his first priority. Yet, when those negotiations failed in early 2000, Barak decided to focus all of his attention on reaching a historic deal with Arafat. "Barak wasn't the kind of leader who wants to be prime minister for the sake of being prime minister," says one of his aides at the time. "His motivation was different: to get big things done."[108]

Barak's approach to peacemaking was not only different from Netanyahu's but also from Peres's and Rabin's. While those former Israeli leaders were all committed to the gradual Oslo process, the new prime minister thought it was a waste of time to negotiate small Israeli withdrawals from the West Bank and Gaza over long stretches of time. Instead, Barak wanted to jump headfirst into negotiating a comprehensive peace agreement. This strategy led him to ignore previous commitments to gradual withdrawals made by Netanyahu, something that angered the Palestinians and ended the early sense of optimism in Ramallah.

Barak felt the gradual withdrawals were just political maneuvering. He wanted the two sides to sit down and hash out all the details of a comprehensive agreement in one big summit. In that regard, Barak was particularly interested in the Beilin-Abu Mazen formula from 1995, and he invited Yossi Beilin, now his minister of justice, to present the agreement to him in person. He liked certain elements of the deal, but he believed that giving 90 percent of the West Bank to the Palestinians was too much. "He thought he could get them to accept a state on 48 percent of that territory," Beilin recalls.[109]

What Barak wanted most, by late 1999, was to have a secret channel, ideally with Abbas's involvement. In the fall of that year, his close adviser Gilad Sher flew to London to meet with Abbas's negotiators Agha and Khalidi. "Abu Mazen gave his approval, and we met at a hotel suite for a discussion that lasted for hours," recalls Sher, a former colonel in the Israeli military.[110] Like Yair Hirschfeld and Ron Pundak before him, Sher was highly impressed by Agha and Khalidi. "It was a pre-negotiation meeting. We mapped the gaps between the two sides, and the actual negotiating was supposed to start at our next meeting. I left London with a sense that we made good progress and that there was room for optimism. These were two very serious people."[111]

A week after the London meeting, a leading Israeli commentator published an article assessing the state of the peace process since Barak's election. The article's conclusion was that since everything looked stuck on the surface, there must be some type of secret channel. The article contained no details, but, according to Sher, it caused panic on the Palestinian side. Abbas soon backed away from the secret channel: "He blamed us for leaking it to the press and decided to freeze everything."[112]

Sher thought Abbas overreacted. But Abbas was still haunted by the price he paid for the Beilin-Abu Mazen agreement in 1995. According to Ahmed Tibi, "The Israelis never understood how much political risk Abu Mazen was taking upon himself by doing these secret negotiations time after time, while they continued to build in the settlements."[113] Another leak from yet another secret channel would only reinforce his image on the Palestinian street as someone who was too soft with the Israelis. Thus, after one meeting, the London back channel died.[114]

Barak, however, still wanted a back channel, and so did Arafat. A few months later, the Swedish government intervened and offered to host secret negotiations between the two sides. Abbas, who had good ties with the Swedish foreign minister, knew about the invitation and discussed it with Arafat a number of times. Abbas had no doubt that when the negotiations happened he would be the one representing the Palestinians. Yet, to his shock, Arafat chose to send Ahmed Qurie instead to Stockholm. Abbas was appalled. He was the chief negotiator for the Palestinians, and here was his deputy going to Sweden for secret talks with Sher and Shlomo Ben-Ami, a senior member of Barak's cabinet. "It was a classic Arafat move," says a former senior Israeli official. "[He was] playing Abu Ala'a [Ahmed Qurie] and Abu Mazen against each other."[115] In order to mitigate threats from potential challengers, Arafat often played his various deputies and protégés against each other. For Arafat, it solidified his rule by creating tiers of leadership—Abbas and Qurie were the clear second-tier leaders—but it also divided the movement at crucial junctures. Palestinian negotiators, therefore, were forced to keep one eye on Israel and another on their position in Arafat's court.

Eventually, the Americans were also brought into the picture.

According to Dennis Ross, Qurie actually told him that he wanted to invite Abbas's proxies, Agha and Khalidi, to join the channel at some point in order to involve Abbas.[116] The talks were promising. "Somewhat to my surprise," recalled Qurie, the Israeli side's ideas "did not wholly contradict mine." A rough framework was outlined, with both sides feeling they were on the same page. "We were in agreement that progress could be made only by tackling problems head on," said Qurie.[117]

But for Abbas, the fact that Qurie had been sent to the secret negotiations instead of him was a giant insult. During the secret negotiations in Oslo in 1993, it made sense for Qurie to meet with the Israelis abroad while Abbas stayed in Tunis laying the political foundation with Arafat. Oslo was, after all, initially a thought experiment. This time, however, the Israeli side was represented by two senior government officials, and the goal wasn't mutual recognition but a historic peace treaty that would create a Palestinian state. Abbas had been working his entire adult life toward that moment, and now Arafat had kicked him aside in favor of his deputy.

The channel went ahead without him. "It was super-secretive," recalls Sher. "I think only ten people, from all sides, knew about its existence."[118] But then, in the middle of one of the negotiation sessions, Sher's mobile phone rang. It was an Israeli number on the screen, and it belonged to Raviv Drucker, an Israeli journalist. Drucker asked Sher where in the world he was at the moment, and if it was true that he was leading a secret negotiation channel with Ahmed Qurie. When Sher informed the other negotiators of the phone call, "the channel was essentially over."[119] Qurie "shut down" afterward and refused to participate in any meaningful discussion. Like Abbas before him, he was afraid of his concessions getting leaked to the public.[120]

For the second time in a row, a secret back channel had collapsed because of leaks to the Israeli press. This time, however, Israeli, American, and even some Palestinian officials believed that Abbas had sabotaged the talks himself. "I could not help wondering if [the leak] had been made for trivial personal reasons by someone on our side who wished to wreck the effectiveness of this channel," Qurie recalled, "jealous that the Palestinian leadership as a whole had confided in me the responsibility for its success."[121] The event came to be known as "the Swedish betrayal."[122]

Abbas and Qurie had enjoyed a good relationship for years. The achievement in Oslo created tensions, but at the end of the day it was large enough for both of them to take credit: Abbas as the manager of the negotiations and Qurie as the man who actually sat in the room with the Israelis. Everything changed after the failed Swedish channel. Abbas now looked at Qurie as a rival and a challenger who was trying to usurp his mandate. The Americans feared Abbas would completely detach himself from negotiations. His lifelong proclivity for withdrawing himself when things didn't go his way was well-known in DC. The administration dispatched Ross to Ramallah for damage control. After a tough conversation, Ross came to the conclusion that Abbas had "the posture of someone who did not want anything to happen soon."[123]

Abbas felt cornered. He was furious with Arafat for choosing his deputy and furious with Qurie for betraying him. At the same time, he was increasingly wary of his young rival Mohammad Dahlan, who, thanks to his control of the Palestinian security apparatus and his personal charm, had grown to be one of the Americans' favorite officials on the Palestinian side. Abbas felt he was under attack from every direction.

But then something changed. The American administration announced that in July 2000 a peace summit would be held at Camp David, the presidential retreat where Israel's peace accord with Egypt had been signed two decades prior. Arafat needed Abbas and Qurie's cooperation during the summit, and he encouraged them to make peace with one another. The alarming rise of Dahlan also served as a wake-up call to the two veteran negotiators: while they were busy bickering with one another, Dahlan and his main political ally, Arafat's financial adviser Muhammad Rashid, were positioning themselves as the new favorites of the American administration. According to one former senior Israeli official, Abbas and Qurie finally made amends during a joint trip to Saudi Arabia: "They talked it over, and realized that Dahlan and Rashid were a bigger threat to both of them, than they were to each other. They couldn't let these young guys take over, and working together was their only way to stop it."[124]

In the background, a larger question was looming. Arafat was getting up in years and a new cadre of leaders was emerging. Infighting had driven the Palestinian leadership into different political camps. Qurie wrote longingly of his "desire to be free of the constant challenges and criticisms of my many Palestinians rivals."[125] In the lead-up to Camp David, a decisive division had emerged: it was the "two Abus"—Abu Mazen and Abu Ala—against "the Muhammads"—Dahlan and Rashid. At the peace summit in July, this rift would prove destructive.

Of all the failed attempts to reach an Israeli-Palestinian peace accord, none was more consequential than the Camp David summit of July 2000. For two weeks, the Clinton administration—including the president himself—invested unprecedented efforts in trying to bridge the gaps between the two sides, only to walk away empty-handed. Instead of producing a historic peace deal, the summit led to a deadly, multiyear period of violence that cost thousands of lives.

The summit's failure has been discussed at lengths by various participants, with different conclusions. President Clinton put most of the blame for the failure on Arafat, accusing him of avoiding any constructive engagement. "[Arafat] could only get to step five," Clinton said a year after the talks, "and he needed to get to step ten."[126] Martin Indyk thought Arafat simply wanted to "live to fight another day" and that the summit "revealed Arafat's true capabilities rather than his true intentions."[127] The Americans also placed some blame on Barak, but it was clear the United States placed most of it on the Palestinians.

On the Israeli side, the failure of Camp David was a death blow to the country's left-leaning "peace camp." Ehud Barak lost power six months after the summit. Most of the Israeli participants at Camp David shared the American analysis, claiming that Arafat was to blame. "He did not negotiate in good faith; indeed, he did not negotiate at all. He just kept saying 'no' to every offer, never making any counterproposals of his own," the Israeli prime minister charged.[128] He even added that Arafat believed Israel "has no right to exist, and he seeks its demise."

The Palestinian point of view on Camp David has been different. "The Americans never listened to Palestinian advice," wrote Akram Haniyeh, a member of the Palestinian team. Saying no to the United States, according to Haniyeh, was "politically, nationally, and historically correct and necessary to put the peace process on the right track."[129] Similarly, Abbas's confidante Hussein Agha wrote that, structurally, Arafat would never have been able to accept an offer at Camp David. Together with Rob Malley, a member of the American team, he argued that "Camp David seemed to Arafat to encapsulate his worst nightmares."[130] The Palestinian delegation severely misunderstood the US-Israeli relationship, Agha and Malley wrote, and in failing to put forward their own counterproposals, "the Palestinians deprived the Americans of the instrument they felt they needed to further press the Israelis."

Abbas felt the summit was doomed for failure from the start. "We agreed with Secretary Albright that [we] would have two weeks to prepare," Abbas told the PLO's Central Council, an advisory committee, in September 2000. "We were later surprised by a telephone call from President Clinton inviting us to a summit that was to be held within a week."[131] As Abbas recalled:

> We were faced with two choices: to go knowing very well that the
> summit will fail and that the Americans may blame us for its failure
> or to refuse to attend and be accused of sabotaging the peace
> process. So we took the first choice.[132]

While analysts on all sides certainly disagreed on the specifics of Camp David, there was near consensus on one issue: Mahmoud Abbas's unhelpful conduct at the summit. Abbas was an "obstructionist" in the words of one Palestinian negotiator,[133] a "non-entity" in the words of a former American official,[134] a "man who wasn't there" as one Israeli puts it.[135]

Abbas arrived to Camp David with a grudge. He may have made up with Qurie, but that didn't mean he trusted him or Arafat. He was also disturbed at how close his young rival Dahlan was to the Americans. Making things even worse for Abbas was the fact that he seemed to have no partners on the Israeli team at Camp David. Beilin and

Peres, though members of Barak's cabinet, were not invited to the summit.

"Barak felt it was more important for him to bring centrist figures to Camp David, so that if an agreement is signed, it will have more public legitimacy," recalls Gadi Baltiansky, Barak's spokesperson during that period. "I asked him before the summit if he wanted to perhaps bring Yossi Beilin with him, since Yossi was such an experienced negotiator and also had a close relationship with Abu Mazen. His reaction was that he doesn't want Yossi there, and that Abu Mazen is going to be a negative factor in the summit anyway, so it doesn't matter what kind of influence Yossi would have on him."[136]

Barak's assessment regarding Abbas was based on what his intelligence officials were telling him. Prior to the summit, Israeli intelligence had concluded that Abbas was increasingly ostracized from Arafat. Coincidentally, some of these same intelligence chiefs also had a close relationship with Dahlan, as a result of his position as the head of Palestinian security forces in Gaza, and perhaps their opinion on Abbas was influenced by conversations with his young rival. "Dahlan had some close friends on the Israeli delegation in Camp David, mainly the intelligence guys," recalls Baltiansky. "Abbas had no Israeli counterpart. All the people from the Oslo process, who respected and appreciated him, weren't there."[137]

The Americans also isolated Abbas, according to negotiators at the summit. In the lead-up to the summit, they invited Dahlan for a meeting at the White House with national security adviser Sandy Berger. According to Indyk, "This convinced Abu Mazen that the United States was supporting Dahlan for succession to Arafat and thereby conspiring to rob him of his birthright as the number two official in the PLO."[138] Abbas's fears were reinforced when the American negotiators engaged primarily with Dahlan in the opening days of the summit.

As the talks began, a poisonous dynamic quickly emerged on the Palestinian side. While "the Muhammads"—Dahlan and Rashid—seemed eager to find compromises and reach an agreement, "the Abus"—Abbas and Qurie—took hardline positions. "The negotiations were taken hostage by the race to succeed Arafat," says one of the Israeli participants.[139] "The younger guys like Dahlan, Muhammad

Rashid and Hassan Asfour were pushing for a deal," recalls one of the Palestinian negotiators present, "but the older guys felt it will either compromise the Palestinian position, or, if they agree to it, would give the younger crowd more credit."[140]

Abbas was anything but discreet in blaming other members of the negotiating team. In response to a reporter asking him about Clinton's offers, Abbas replied, "Unfortunately, these . . . Israelis, Americans, and few Palestinians are deluding themselves. . . . Unfortunately, few of our brothers—Palestinians and non-Palestinians—found these [American] offers tempting."[141] The "non-Palestinian" comment was a clear reference to Dahlan's ally Muhammad Rashid, who was Kurdish.

Abbas and Ahmed Qurie quickly emerged as the two least-flexible members of the Palestinian delegation. It was a shocking revelation for American and Israeli negotiators. Here were the two Palestinians considered the strongest proponents of the Oslo peace process, suddenly unwilling to negotiate or compromise. The officials Clinton once referred to as "the good guys" were suddenly obstinate.[142] Midway through the talks, Clinton lost his patience, famously raising his voice to Qurie and scolding him in front of the other negotiators for his intransigence.[143] After that dressing-down, Qurie shut down completely and lost any interest in what was happening at the summit.

Abbas wasn't any more cooperative. In the middle of the summit, he suddenly declared he was leaving Camp David and going back to the Palestinian territories in order to attend a family wedding. The abrupt departure disturbed the Americans. "For me, it was really unsettling to see Abu Mazen [like that]," Ross recalls. "I remember saying to Clinton at one point, every deal that's been done, it came down to Abu Mazen and Abu Ala'a convincing Arafat that it was okay to do it. With Arafat, every deal—even one he's already decided he wants to do—required him to have some people around him who could rationalize it and say that it's okay."[144] Abbas and Qurie, the two oldest and most experienced members of the Palestinian leadership, were the ones who usually played that role. But at Camp David, when Arafat was presented with the most important decisions he had ever faced—ending the conflict, signing a final peace agreement with Israel, and giving up the right of return—they were playing the opposite role.

"In Camp David, Abu Mazen, along with other members of the old guard, feared that progress would politically benefit their young guard rivals and as such took hardline positions on substance," recalls a member of the Palestinian negotiating team.[145] This hardline position trickled up to Arafat from his top two negotiators: "Before Camp David, Abbas and Abu Ala'a were not on speaking terms. Perceiving a common threat from their young guard rivals, and fearing that progress might politically benefit the latter, they adopted hardline positions and argued against compromise."

This, of course, didn't absolve Arafat from his responsibility as a leader and the final decision maker. While his delegation was torn between the more pragmatic group, led by Dahlan, and the less flexible one, led by Abbas and Qurie, Arafat "didn't take sides," according to the former senior Palestinian official: "It was typical Arafat. He let them fight it out while he remained above the fray. I think this was one of the most striking moments of Camp David. There was such internal rivalry within the team, I'm not sure the team was capable of reaching any decision or agreement. The fact that Arafat wouldn't throw his weight behind either of the camps shows he was willing to let that rivalry be the prevailing theme."[146]

Barak's negotiating style wasn't exactly helpful, either. He refused during the summit's first days to negotiate directly with Arafat, despite the fact that the very reasoning behind convening such a summit was to allow the two leaders to engage each other in a neutral environment. Instead, Barak left most of the negotiations to his deputies, creating a sense of confusion and mistrust on the Palestinian side.[147] "We felt as if we were in a prison," Abbas told a local paper in the West Bank. "This was a trap. From beginning to end, and we survived it."[148]

The Palestinian team believed they could get more and more out of Barak if they held out at the summit, and the Israeli leader reinforced their line of thinking. Barak arrived at Camp David believing he could get Arafat to agree to a state on roughly half of the West Bank. By the end of the summit, he had offered approximately 90 percent of the territory.[149] He also changed his position on Jerusalem, moving from a solid "no" on any division of the city, to a detailed proposal splitting it into two respective capitals.[150]

The irony of all this is that before the summit Gilad Sher and Shlomo Ben-Ami both asked Barak to use the Beilin-Abu Mazen document as the basis for the Israel's "red lines" in the negotiations, but Barak rejected the idea. In Barak's calculus, Beilin-Abu Mazen contained too many far-reaching Israeli concessions. Yet by the end of the summit Barak had offered Arafat more than what Beilin had agreed to with Abbas in 1995 on multiple issues. Though short of putting forth a comprehensive agreement ("We had only made proposals on borders and Jerusalem [at Camp David]," Dennis Ross later remarked[151]), Arafat still walked away from Barak's proposals, which also turned out to be temporary. Barak again offered the Palestinians more just months later at the January 2001 Taba Summit, which also ended without an agreement.[152]

Eventually, on July 25, 2000, the Camp David summit ended without an agreement. Two months later, the Second Intifada broke out in East Jerusalem, Gaza, and the West Bank. Arafat harnessed the anger on the street to unleash a fiery wave of terror. Both Fatah and Hamas escalated the chaos into violence and terror aimed at Israelis, to which Israel reacted with brutal force, shooting more than a million bullets in the occupied territories over a period of three weeks.[153] The peace process was now officially dead, despite last-minute attempts by the Clinton administration to revive it. Both Clinton and Barak's days in office were numbered.

This descent into violence and terror was ostensibly the end of the road for Abbas. He had spent the past two decades convincing the Palestinian leadership to negotiate with Israel, but now, after rounds and rounds of peace talks with no progress, Arafat had reverted back to terror. Abbas was angry and bitter. His Israeli and American counterparts blasted him for his conduct at Camp David, while his Palestinian colleagues cheered the death of his beloved negotiations program.

It would have been easy for him to resign and live out his life in relative seclusion. Instead, Abbas chose to stay in the public arena, and in so doing was setting himself up for the greatest battle of his life, one that would shape the future of the Palestinian national movement.

CHAPTER 4

YEARS OF TERROR

2000–2003

Mahmoud Abbas entered Yasser Arafat's office in the Palestinian presidential complex, commonly referred to as the *muqata'a* (Arabic for "compound"), in the center of Ramallah. It was October of 2000, and violence was raging in the streets. Dozens of people had already died in clashes between Palestinians and the Israeli military. Hundreds were wounded. This was no longer just a burst of outrage—it was coordinated, and it was turning into another intifada.

When Abbas arrived at the muqata'a, Arafat was busy taking phone calls from world leaders. France invited Arafat and Barak to attend a peace conference in Paris, the United States was willing to renew its efforts as a mediator, and Egypt was also working behind the scenes to calm the situation. Abbas was involved in all these efforts, but it wasn't the main thing he had come to discuss with Arafat. Inside the Palestinian leader's office, where a large photo of Jerusalem hung on the wall, Abbas delivered a stark warning to Arafat: if you don't instruct all of the Palestinian Authority's security forces to stop the violence, the Palestinian people will suffer terrible consequences.[1]

Arafat, in fact, was doing the exact opposite: he was actively encouraging his security forces to participate in the violence. At one meeting with his top security officials, he reportedly asked: "Why do the Jews not have more deaths? You know what to do."[2] Qaddura Fares, a former PA cabinet member, explains that "Abu Ammar [Arafat] led Palestinians according to our reality. So, when there was a need to struggle and fight, he did."[3] Abbas found this direction extremely disturbing. "We are losing control over the street," he warned Arafat, according to a source with knowledge of the conversation. "This thing will turn against us."[4]

Arafat acknowledged his deputy, but refused to commit to ending the violence. Over the next weeks, things only got worse. On October 12, two Israeli soldiers accidentally entered Ramallah after taking the wrong turn at a checkpoint. They were arrested by PA police officers, taken to a local station, and then brutally lynched to death by hundreds of angry Palestinians, including members of the PA security forces.[5] Horrific pictures from the event were broadcast for hours on Israeli television. Israel retaliated that evening by bombing, for the first time since the creation of the Palestinian Authority, office buildings used by its security agencies. The two sides were now practically at war, just three months after the failed peace summit in Camp David.

If his role during the summit was that of an intransigent hardliner, Abbas's conduct during the first weeks of the Second Intifada was almost the opposite. "Abu Mazen was one of the first to warn against [violence]," says one of his former advisers. "This might not have been terribly popular, but it did distinguish him from others."[6]

In opposing the violence and calling for moderation, Abbas was resisting not only his boss but the sentiment of the street. "He was the only one to stand up to Arafat and tell him about the dangers posed by the intifada," says Avi Dichter, who was the head of the Israeli Shin Bet at the time. "He realized very early where this was going, and why it had to be stopped. Arafat refused to listen to him."[7]

Ahmad Tibi, a close associate of Abbas's, explains that his opposition to violence was a mixture of morals and politics: "He believed it was morally wrong to use violence, and also that it was against the Palestinian people's interests. He never thought violence would lead to the end of the occupation."[8] What Abbas wanted, says Tibi, was a "non-violent intifada" consisting of civil protests that would draw the world's public opinion to the suffering of the Palestinians. "He thought violence would have the opposite effect."

Ahmed Qurie, Abbas's former deputy, wrote in his memoirs that "At this time, there were also internal differences within the Palestinian leadership. In private discussions, there were sharp disagreements between us."[9] Arafat had unleashed the violent elements within his own party and coordinated with Hamas and Palestinian Islamic Jihad, another terror group. There was little Abbas and the negotiators in the leadership could do to stop it. "Some Fatah leaders in the field," wrote Qurie, attempted to "construct their own organizational bases inside Fatah." The party was fracturing, and older leaders like Abbas and Qurie were ceding influence to a younger, more hostile generation.

In December of 2000, President Clinton, weeks away from leaving the White House, presented both sides with a last-minute peace proposal, known as "The Clinton Parameters," which included a Palestinian state on 94 to 96 percent of the West Bank and all of Gaza, Palestinian sovereignty over the Aqsa Compound (known also as the Temple Mount), a split Jerusalem based on ethnic lines, and a gradual Israeli withdrawal from the West Bank and Gaza.[10]

"I knew the plan was tough for both parties," Clinton wrote in his autobiography, "but it was time—past time—to put up or shut up. [. . .] It was a hard deal, but if they wanted peace, I thought it fair to both sides."[11] Barak, who had lost his majority in the Knesset and was forced into early elections, accepted the parameters. Arafat rejected them. "The deal was so good I couldn't believe anyone would be foolish enough to let it go," recalled Clinton, who thought Arafat's rejection was an "error of historic proportions." Clinton believed that unlike Arafat, who said no, "Abu Ala and Abu Mazen also would have agreed but didn't want to be at odds with Arafat."[12]

By rejecting this offer, Arafat essentially put the last nail in the coffin of the peace process, while simultaneously green-lighting the escalation of the intifada. "[Arafat] saw that repeating the First Intifada in new forms would bring the necessary popular, international, and Arab pressure upon Israel," recalled Fatah leader Nabil Sha'ath. Arafat's wife, Suha, famously recounted her husband urging her to leave before the violence rose: "He said, 'you have to leave Palestine, because I want to carry out an intifada. [. . .] He ordered me to leave him because he had already decided to carry out an intifada after the Oslo Accords and after the failure of Camp David."[13]

Arafat took most of Fatah on this turn toward terror. Mahmoud Abbas was part of a small group of officials who refused to follow him. For much of Abbas's life, he had been politically isolated. Yet at no point was he more politically removed from the bastions of Palestinian power than during the Second Intifada. Abbas was the most prominent Palestinian leader to completely reject Arafat's turn to violence, and that left him on the outs with the terror aspects of his own party. "During that period," recalls Fatah parliamentarian Nasser Juma'a, "there wasn't one Palestinian who declared his or her objection to the intifada."[14]

"He was very unhappy with Arafat," recalls Martin Indyk, then the US ambassador to Israel. "He didn't at all agree with what was going on. He thought it was tremendously destructive. He was very clear about this, and also very frustrated, because he didn't have the influence to stop it. He did the right thing, and he paid a political price for it, but he wasn't strong enough to stop Arafat."[15] Munib al-Masri, a close associate of Arafat, adds that, "Abu Mazen didn't hide his opinion. He went to Fatah gatherings and said very clearly: this is wrong and it won't help us end the occupation."[16]

Jerusalem expressed a similar sentiment regarding Abbas's conduct during this period. "I think he risked his life," says one former senior Israeli official. "He walked around and told the young Fatah activists who were organizing to carry out terror attacks 'this is a mistake, you are ruining the Palestinian dream.' This episode convinced me and many others in Israel that despite all his other shortcomings, his opposition to violence and terrorism was sincere."[17]

Some Palestinian officials, however, are skeptical about Abbas's efforts and impact. No one doubts that he was opposed to the violent nature of the intifada, but there is a debate on how effective that opposition was. "Abbas was against the Second Intifada, but he did nothing," argues Juma'a. "He did not express his views in an influential way. Had he been clearer and more influential—and even stronger—he may have found many who share this opinion."[18] "I'm not sure this was the biggest disagreement between [Arafat and Abbas] at the time," says Qaddura Fares, the former cabinet member. Fares adds that the friction in the relationship between the two leaders was perhaps just because "Abu Ammar was ignoring Abu Mazen at the time."[19]

Failing to influence the direction of the Palestinian uprising, Abbas found himself in a familiar position of exile. Just as he had done in the past when he disagreed with Arafat, he physically removed himself. He traveled frequently to places like Tunisia and the Gulf.[20] His eldest son, Mazen, was running a successful business out of Qatar, which for decades was somewhat of a second home to the Abbas family. Mazen Abbas was personally close to Hamad Bin Jassim, the Qatari foreign minister, and also enjoyed a cordial relationship with Eli Avidar, an Israeli diplomat stationed in the rich emirate. The two would play tennis together from time to time. "During those matches, Abbas Jr. often spoke of his despair at the failure of the Camp David summit and his anger at Arafat's attempts to remove his father from the circle of senior leadership after he had severely criticized the *rais*'s [president] conduct at Camp David," Avidar wrote in his memoirs.[21]

While the Abbas family began spending more and more time in Doha, terror kept raging in the West Bank and Gaza. Frustrated with Barak's failure to tamp down the violence, the Israeli public rewarded Ariel Sharon with a landslide victory in the February 2001 special elections. Any prospect of peace negotiations was now gone: Arafat was fully committed to terrorism; Sharon was fully committed to crushing it. In addition, the personal enmity between them, going back to their 1982 standoff in Lebanon, was beyond repair.

With the derailment of the peace process, Abbas's political standing was at a historical low point, despite the fact that his early warnings about the dangers of the intifada were undoubtedly coming true. "Arafat was very skillful at cutting down any critics; he was a master at that game" says Martin Indyk. "Ridiculing, spreading rumors, bashing—whatever he needed to do in order to discredit those who dared speak up against him."[22] Abbas wasn't doing himself any favors, either. "When Arafat was besieged in the muqata'a, Abbas invited some cadres within Fatah to meet and write a document critical of Arafat," recalls Yasser Abed Rabbo. "Even if you agree with him on the principles, the time was the worst. Arafat accused him of treason: 'I am under siege, and you are joining my enemies in criticizing my leadership style?!'"[23] Even after all these years of politicking within the Palestinian national movement, Abbas did not understand the finer points of dealing with Arafat.

The tongue-lashings from Arafat didn't stop Abbas from

campaigning against the intifada. "What have we achieved?" he demanded at a closed-door meeting of local leaders in Gaza in 2002. "What positive or negative aims have we accomplished?" In the heat of a popular uprising, here was the number two official in the Palestinian national movement criticizing everything his colleagues had supported since September 2000. The thousands of lives lost, the international condemnation, the destruction of Palestinian institutions—it all weighed heavily on Abbas. "What happened over these two years," Abbas bemoaned at that event, "has been the total destruction of all we have built and all that had been built before that."[24]

Underlying the intifada's gruesome terror attacks was an escalating battle between the two largest Palestinian political parties, Fatah and Hamas. Some analysts have argued that a large part of Arafat's decision to launch the uprising was to take a swipe at a surging Hamas's "resistance" appeal.[25] Hamas, an offshoot of the Muslim Brotherhood, saw the uprising as an opportunity to replace Fatah as the leaders of the Palestinian national movement. In Abbas's view, this bloody competition between his party and Hamas was devastatingly destructive to the national cause.

The events of 2002, the bloodiest year of the intifada, certainly strengthened his case. In late March, following the murder of thirty Israeli and foreign citizens by a suicide bombing in the Israeli city of Netanya, Israel carried out a wide military operation throughout the West Bank, seizing back complete control over the Palestinian cities that had been handed over to the Palestinian Authority under the Oslo Accords. The Israel Defense Forces (IDF) also surrounded the muqata'a, putting Arafat under siege within his own compound, parts of which were destroyed in the fighting. Two years earlier, Israelis and Palestinians were negotiating over an Israeli withdrawal from approximately 90 percent of the West Bank; now, Israel was undoing the withdrawals it had already committed in the mid-1990s, and Arafat, instead of being invited to another signing ceremony on the White House lawn, was eating pita bread in the dark while Israeli tanks and snipers surrounded his office.[26]

Abbas's warning that the Palestinians could lose everything as a result of the intifada had come true. And yet, even then, Arafat still refused to listen to him.

✦✦✦

President George W. Bush entered the White House in January 2001, just four months after the beginning of the intifada and a month before Sharon's election victory. It didn't take long for him to develop a negative opinion of Yasser Arafat. The outgoing president, Bill Clinton, famously told Colin Powell, Bush's secretary of state, regarding Arafat, "Don't you ever trust that son of a bitch. He lied to me and he'll lie to you."[27] Bush appeared to take that message to heart. Despite expressing support for Palestinian statehood at his first UN General Assembly speech that fall, Bush was not eager to launch a full-bodied peace initiative. Instead, the new administration was looking to avoid the fruitless peace process in which Clinton had invested so much. Bush's senior advisors viewed Arafat more as a menace and less as a partner for peace.

"I would divide it into three periods," says Elliott Abrams, Bush's top Middle East expert. "The first is pre-9/11. There's a general distaste for Arafat and a desire not to engage with him. But on the other hand, he is 'Mr. Palestine,' and Powell, among others, is saying we have to deal with him, that he is what he is."[28] But then 9/11 happened, and the White House's calculation shifted dramatically. All of a sudden, the Bush administration was engaged in a war on terror, and Arafat's support for terror in the Second Intifada put him in full view of the administration.

The question for the administration in this second period of Bush-Arafat relations was basically what to do with Arafat and his connection to terror. According to Abrams, "That question [was] not answered until the *Karine A* affair in January 2002."[29] Less than six months after the events of 9/11, Israel seized a cargo ship laden with weapons bound for the Palestinian Authority in Gaza. According to the Israeli military, the freighter carried over fifty tons of war equipment.[30] Arafat denied the freighter was bound for his PA, but the Bush administration wasn't buying it. "The administration basically concluded that [Arafat] really is a terrorist," recalls Abrams, "Bush [was] for a Palestinian state, but Arafat cannot lead that state."[31]

Palestinian officials, too, could see the writing on the wall after

9/11 and the *Karine A* affair. "It was obvious immediately after the 9/11 events that the intifada was extremely harmful to Palestinian interests," says Juma'a. "The whole formula on the international level changed. Suddenly countries of the world were being classified as either pro-terror or anti-terror. [. . .] That's when we started to lose the international compassion and sympathy for our cause."[32]

These political developments, dramatic as they were, became somewhat meaningless for Abbas in June of 2002, when his oldest son, Mazen, died of a heart attack at the age of forty-two.[33] Besides running the family's business interests in Qatar, Mazen was also one of his father's most trusted political advisers. "He was very close to Mazen and very proud of him," recalls Ahmad Tibi, a longtime friend of the family. "His death was a terrible blow to the entire family. He was still young and had a bright future ahead of him."[34] Mazen's body was flown to Ramallah, where hundreds attended a state funeral, including Arafat. "We went to the mourning house, and Arafat left the muqata'a to join," recalls Fares. The Palestinian newspapers were filled with condolence advertisements for an entire week.[35]

While Abbas was grieving the death of his beloved son, the developments on the ground in the West Bank and Gaza continued to make him look prophetic. In his conversation with Arafat in October of 2000, Abbas had said that if Fatah and the PA encouraged terrorism, they would eventually lose control and strengthen their own internal rivals. In October of 2002, a group of Hamas terrorists assassinated a senior commander of the PA's police force in Gaza in broad daylight. When the heads of the security agencies in Gaza asked Arafat to order a painful retribution against Hamas for the assassination, Arafat refused to do so, disappointing his own security chiefs and causing the entire PA establishment to appear weak and crumbling. "When they didn't even try to take care of that problem in Gaza, it became clear to many Palestinians how weak they had become in just two years," says Avi Dichter.[36] Two years prior, Arafat had refused Abbas's demand to use his security forces to stop the violence against Israel. Now, he was too weak to use them to stop violence against his own institutions.

With Israeli tanks rolling into Ramallah, the sense among Palestinians was that the intifada was failing them. Aaron David Miller, a longtime State Department advisor on Arab-Israeli issues, recalls visiting Arafat with Bush administration envoy General Anthony Zinni: "[We] saw Arafat when he was being besieged by the Israelis and the muqata'a was a scene out of a bunker: all the windows were blocked and Arafat was there in candlelight with his pistol on the table. Zinni described Saeb [Erekat, a top negotiator] and [Yasser] Abed Rabbo looking like a bunch of drowned rats."[37]

A possible peek into Abbas's mindset during that period, after two and a half years of a bloody and ultimately failed uprising, can be found in an article coauthored by his close confidant Hussein Agha in the *New York Review of Books*: "[Abbas] looks around him and sees Palestinian land thoroughly reoccupied by Israel, the Palestinian Authority destroyed, widespread economic distress, and political mayhem. Practically anyone can acquire a gun and claim to make policy by showing it off. This is not resistance; it is anarchy. [. . .] In the court of international official opinion, the Palestinians have lost the moral high ground so patiently acquired for years."[38]

Agha and his writing partner, former Clinton adviser Rob Malley, wrote in 2003 that, in Abbas's eyes, "the last two and a half years [. . .] have been disastrous for the Palestinians, and Arafat, who, better than anyone else, could have brought the disaster to an end, chose instead not to exercise his full authority. There was nothing new about Arafat's behavior; Abu Mazen was familiar with it as much as he was familiar with the man himself. Only this time, the result was an unmitigated catastrophe because it violated so many of Abu Mazen's cardinal rules: do not confront Israel with violence but deal with it through negotiations; maintain bridges with the Israeli public; do not dissipate the Palestinians' international legitimacy."[39]

Abbas emerges in these years as the anti-Arafat. He gains the respect of a small group of peers while also making himself known in Israel and Washington as a man of principle. It's a testimony to his character that he was averse to terror, yet it's a barometer of his political acumen that he was unable to stop or even slow down the bloody onslaught. Confronting Arafat and the Fatah militant class would have been a tall order, but in secluding himself abroad or avoiding the spotlight he showed his tendency to retreat in times of confrontation. It would become a theme in Abbas's political life.

Arafat's gamble on terrorism and violence had unleashed a disaster upon his own people. Abbas failed in his attempt to stop it. But in defeat he had also etched out a position for himself as leader of the disunited opposition. It was a position that would lead to a power struggle between the founder of the Palestinian national movement and his stubborn deputy. Soon, Abbas would get another chance at righting what had gone so terribly wrong, in his view, during the intifada.

CHAPTER 5

OUR MAN IN RAMALLAH

2003

O n a sunny afternoon in May 2003, a convoy of bulletproof vehicles arrived at the official residence of Israel's prime minister in Jerusalem. Inside the convoy, surrounded by a security detail, sat Mahmoud Abbas. Two months earlier, in a surprising political development, he had been appointed as the Palestinian Authority's first-ever prime minister. Now, he was about to meet his Israeli counterpart.[1]

Abbas and Ariel Sharon held the same title—prime minister—but could not have been in more different domestic positions. Under Israeli law, the Jewish state's official leader is the country's president, but, in practice, the Israeli prime minister is the chief executive, and Sharon was an especially powerful one at that point, having recently won reelection by a landslide. Abbas, on the other hand, was lost in bureaucratic no-man's land. Few truly understood the limited powers allotted to him as prime minister other than that his position was subservient to Arafat, who was officially still the leader of both the Palestinian Authority, Fatah, and the PLO. This left Abbas in a constant struggle with Arafat, who had no intention of sharing power with him.

And yet, as Abbas's motorcade was speeding through the drive from Ramallah to Jerusalem, it was Sharon who seemed unusually nervous ahead of the meeting. "By that point, he had already met everyone and visited everywhere," recalls Dov Weisglass, Sharon's chief of staff, "but this meeting was very important to him. We decided to hold it at the residence, not the office, in order to create a good atmosphere between them. Sharon inspected the room before

89

Abu Mazen arrived and had all kinds of suggestions about the food and the sitting arrangements. He really wanted the meeting to be a success. This was an opportunity we could not afford to lose."[2]

It wasn't that Sharon had turned into a man of peace—at least, not yet. In private conversations with his closest confidantes he was cautiously speaking in more pragmatic terms, mentioning the need to separate from the Palestinians as part of a two-state solution. "The Palestinian state is hardly my life's dream," he told a cabinet meeting, "but looking ahead, it is not right for Israel to rule over three and a half million Palestinians."[3] Still, his intentions weren't always clear. What he saw in Abbas, much more than a possible peace partner, was a potential ally against his decades-long nemesis, Arafat. He knew that Abbas and Arafat had clashed over the intifada in 2000, and that a combination of internal and international pressure had forced Abbas's appointment as prime minister. If by empowering Abbas he could weaken Arafat, then Sharon was intrigued.

Prior to the meeting, Israel's security establishment had urged Sharon to make a gesture of goodwill toward Abbas by withdrawing the IDF from several of the Palestinian cities that it had invaded in a major anti-terror operation in March 2002. Sharon quickly accepted the proposal and asked his aides to prepare a plan that he could present at the meeting. When Abbas arrived, he and Sharon exchanged niceties and talked about their general visions for peace, and then Sharon presented the withdrawal plan. "Abu-Mazen listened carefully, and then he surprised all of us by saying 'I think it's still too early for this plan,'" recalls Weisglass. "He explained that he wants us out of the cities, and the sooner the better, but only after the Palestinian Authority's security forces will be ready to assert control. Because otherwise, our redeployment will create chaos."[4]

Sharon was impressed, according to Weisglass, who was his private attorney for more than two decades before joining him in the prime minister's office. "The meeting lasted a few hours and all of it was very pleasant, but this dialogue really changed Sharon's perception," Weisglass recalls. When Abbas left for Ramallah, Sharon told his advisers, "I was sure that half an hour after I made that offer, he would convene a press conference and declare that he threw the Jews out of the cities."[5] In the press release eventually approved by both sides, there was a clear reference to an Israeli redeployment, but without a timeline.[6] Abbas, in Sharon's eyes, chose the long-term benefits of a gradual Israeli withdrawal over the short-term political gains of an immediate one. "He's a responsible man," the Israeli premier said of Abbas. Coming from Sharon, it was quite a compliment.[7]

A year earlier, Sharon arrived at the White House for a visit with President Bush. The intifada was still raging on the ground, with Israeli soldiers patrolling the centers of Palestinian cities in the West Bank and terrorists blowing up Israeli buses.[8] The Bush administration, meanwhile, was speeding up its preparations for the Iraq war. Bush tried to assemble a large coalition—just a week earlier he had hosted the Saudi crown prince at his ranch in Texas.[9] From Bush's interactions with both Western and Arab leaders, it was clear to White House officials that some sort of action on the peace process was preferable in order to create broad international support for the administration's wider Middle East policy.[10] The challenge for Bush was how to make progress without giving any legitimacy to Arafat, a Palestinian leader he viewed as beyond the pale because of his support of terrorism.

Elliott Abrams, Bush's senior adviser on the Middle East, explained the president's dilemma: "You have a problem. You have just said in the fall of 2001 that you are for a Palestinian state. But the *Karine A* [affair] confirmed that Arafat is a terrorist. He believes in the use of terrorist violence. He is even connected to Iran."[11] Abrams and many in the White House wondered where that left their peace process vision: "How do you square the circle?"

Bush conveyed this by doubling down on Palestinian statehood while simultaneously demanding that Arafat be sidelined in order for it to happen. Bush started hinting at this plan in a joint press conference with Sharon right after their 2002 meeting. "I have been disappointed in Chairman Arafat," Bush stated. "I think he's let the Palestinian people down. I think he's had an opportunity to lead to peace and he hasn't done so."[12]

Bush doubled down yet again a month later, declaring in a televised speech that "peace requires a new and different Palestinian leadership."[13] He didn't mention Arafat by name, but he called on the Palestinian people "to elect new leaders, leaders not compromised by terror." His message was clear: "If Palestinians embrace democracy, confront corruption and firmly reject terror, they can count on American support for the creation of a provisional state of Palestine. With intensive effort by all of us, agreement could be reached within three years from now. And I and my country will actively lead toward that goal."

As Abrams notes in his memoir, "Bush was offering Palestinians both more and less. Previously, his support for Palestinian statehood had seemed more like a one-liner than a key policy objective, and here it was being given substance and a timetable, and turned into a direct pledge. But previously, that support had seemed unqualified, and here the offer was being made conditional."[14] The speech was the first in a series of speeches and policy memos that would become the administration's new peace plan: the Road Map for Peace.

The plan consisted of three phases. The first called for a cessation of all acts of terror and for the Palestinian Authority to begin institution building and preparations for elections. The second phase called for a transition phase of Palestinian statehood "with provisional borders and attributes of sovereignty" until an international conference would be convened to provide economic and material support to the Palestinians.[15] The third and final phase would be reached once "Palestinian reform is consolidated and its institutions stabilized" and would entail another international conference to get both parties to sign a final, comprehensive agreement by 2005.

Inside this plan was one important detail: as part of building state institutions, the Palestinian Authority would appoint a prime minister who would serve under Arafat, but, at the same time, ideally weaken his complete hold on power. The United States wouldn't pursue outright regime change, but it would try to diffuse the myriad levers of power Arafat held over the Palestinian body politic. "The administration's position was: we're not supporting a dysfunctional Palestinian state. Why does the world need another failed state? It doesn't," recalls Aaron David Miller. "Therefore, regime change, pursued in an incremental manner, seemed to be the way to go."[16]

Both Abrams and Weisglass insist that in between Sharon's visit in May and Bush's speech in June, there was no American-Israeli dialogue on who should become Arafat's prime minister. "Abu Mazen's name wasn't mentioned in the White House meeting, nor in any other conversation that I was aware of," says Weisglass.[17] Abrams explains that the conversation was more about diffusing Arafat's power to another person and less about who that person should be. The Road Map, according to Abrams, "wasn't formulated with Abbas in mind. It was not tailored to this man."[18]

Abbas, in fact, seemed like an odd choice for the job. His tense relationship with Arafat had turned him from a liability in Arafat's eyes to the downright leader of the anti-intifada opposition. How could the Palestinian president's first prime minister be his biggest critic? The two would be destined to clash.

Yet there were some Palestinians who saw merit in elevating Abbas precisely for his criticism of Arafat. As the most prominent opponent of the intifada, Abbas was undoubtedly in line with Washington's demands for nonviolence. In addition, by 2003 Arafat was starting to face a quiet but stern revolt within the PLO's top ranks, many of whom were starting to realize how much damage Arafat's choices had brought upon the movement. The appointment of a prime minister presented a window of opportunity for those critics to promote one of their own.

"Abu Mazen was convinced, and the other Palestinian leaders here were convinced that Arafat was an obstacle," recalls Radi Jarai, a member of Fatah's internal advisory body.[19] Yasser Abed Rabbo echoes that sentiment: "At that time, we all had problems with Arafat. We felt that Abbas was with us because he was critical of Arafat's policies, and we were all very critical of Arafat's policy of using suicide attacks. We told Arafat he was gambling with this. We told him he would turn the whole world against us. We told him this was not the way."[20] Arafat's rampant support for terrorism was hurting the Palestinian Authority, just as Abbas warned it would.

"This is one of the things that defines his career," says one of Abbas's former advisors. "He would stake out advanced positions that were not popular, but as time progressed they would become the mainstream thinking and he would find himself a representative of that phase."[21] Indeed, his opposition to Arafat's terrible miscalculation was politically costly at first, but now, with more and more people realizing how right he was, it turned into an asset. Combined with his seniority and diplomatic experience, Abbas suddenly emerged as the leading candidate for prime minister.

In March of 2003, Arafat reluctantly gave him the job.[22] On paper, the two were supposed to confer over forming a new cabinet and finalizing the separation of powers between them. In actuality, however, they feuded from the very start. "The whole world wanted to see a change in the Palestinian government, and there was a lot of pressure on Arafat, so he agreed to appoint Abu Mazen as prime minister," recalls Ashraf al-Ajrami, a former Palestinian Authority minister. "But he also made sure that Abu Mazen wouldn't succeed."[23]

Within weeks, high-level negotiations between members of the PLO's Executive Committee and Fatah's highest decision-making body, the Central Committee, had broken down in Ramallah. Ostensibly, this was a debate over control within the Palestinian Authority— yet when the PA was the *de facto* property of the PLO and Fatah, the debate escalated to the upper echelons of the Palestinian body politic. The stalemate was so bitter that Egypt's intelligence chief, Omar Suleiman, had to fly to Ramallah to try and break the deadlock.[24] "The moment he was appointed," Abbas's former advisor recalls, "Arafat began undermining him."[25]

By the end of April, both sides compromised. Arafat realized a protracted fight with a new prime minister would only hurt his image abroad, while Abbas began to realize his power would be diminished if he didn't reach a truce with Arafat. In a crowded hall in Ramallah, over seventy Palestinian parliamentarians met to vote on the new Palestinian Authority government. After Arafat, without great enthusiasm, urged members to approve Abbas's appointment and the new government, Abbas stood up to speak. "There will be no other decision-making authority except for the Palestinian Authority," he declared. "On this land and for this people, there is only one authority, one law, and one democratic and national decision that applies to us all."[26] His words could have just as easily been directed at the man sitting to his right.

◆◆◆

In March of 2003, the Bush administration officially unveiled the Road Map. By June of that year, Bush was in the Jordanian city of Aqaba for a summit to celebrate the initiative. On the shores of the Red Sea, the president took the stage together with Sharon, Abbas, and the local host, King Abdullah II. Arafat, of course, wasn't invited. A decade earlier, he had overshadowed Abbas during the signing ceremony of the Oslo Accords in Washington; now, he was under Israeli siege in the muqata'a while the world watched the rise of his deputy.

The participating parties agreed that Abbas's speech at the summit would come right after Sharon's. This presented a challenge for the Israeli prime minister, who didn't want to sound too conciliatory in his own speech if Abbas was going to take a tougher position right after him. Sharon, who had obtained a copy of Abbas's speech, read it carefully and then called Weisglass into his room. Pointing at one specific paragraph in the speech, he told his chief of staff, "Come on, he isn't going to say this."[27] In that paragraph was a strong and unequivocal denunciation of terrorism, without any distinctions or exceptions. Sharon couldn't believe that a Palestinian leader— even someone like Abbas—would say such words in public.

Yet when Abbas took the stage in Aqaba, he did not skip a single word from his written remarks. "Let me be very clear," he declared. "There will be no military solution for this conflict, so we repeat our renunciation of terrorism against the Israelis wherever they might be." This sentence effectively meant that even violence against Israeli settlers in the West Bank and Gaza—which some Palestinians claim is legitimate under the fourth Geneva Convention—was unacceptable to Abbas. "Such methods are inconsistent with our religious and moral traditions and are a dangerous obstacle to the achievement of an independent sovereign state we seek," he said. "These methods also conflict with the kinds of state we wish to build based on human rights and the rule of law."[28]

Watching the event in Ramallah, Arafat was livid—not only because of the warm reception bestowed upon Abbas by the leader of the free world as well as the Israeli and Jordanian leaders, but also because the new prime minister didn't even find it worthwhile to mention him in his speech.

"He showed it to me before he gave the speech," recalls Abed

Rabbo, "and I was shocked that there was no mention of Arafat. He didn't even ask to release him [from the muqata'a]! He didn't ask to lift the siege! I told him, if this going to be your speech, you should start it with: 'I'm here representing my president, Yasser Arafat. And, in the name of Arafat, so on and so on.' I told him you should ask in a very clear way for the removal of the siege. If you don't do that, you will be killed by the Palestinians!"[29]

Instead, Abbas started his speech by thanking the Jordanians for supporting the summit, before saying, "I also would like to thank the Israeli Prime Minister, Sharon, for joining us here in Jordan. And many thanks especially to President Bush who took the longest journey for peace of all of us."[30] When Abbas returned to Ramallah, Arafat flew into a rage. "You traitor," he snarled at his prime minister. "You didn't mention me? You didn't mention my name? You didn't mention that man sitting in a prison who cannot get out to see the sun?"[31]

Even members of his own party, Fatah, criticized and made excuses for Abbas. "You have to understand that Abbas has been deceived by the Israelis," declared Fatah Central Committee member Sakhr Habash. "He was obligated to [deliver] the text demanded of him, while the Israeli Prime Minister, Ariel Sharon, did the opposite."[32]

Hamas was less kind. "Abu Mazen tells us certain things and makes promises behind closed doors, and later we're surprised and shocked [when we hear] that he speaks to the entire world and promises Bush and Sharon [that he will] restrain the intifada," declared a spokesman for the Islamist group. "We noticed that Abu Mazen uses double language, one that he uses behind closed doors and another [when he speaks] to Sharon and Bush, and we understood that he has thrust a knife deep into the Palestinian dialogue."[33]

In truth, the tensions between Abbas and Arafat were not the result of the speech alone. "The undisguised difference they had on the subject of violence was a clear point of tension," says Hussein Ibish, a former senior fellow at the American Task Force on Palestine. "Abbas was never a good fit. It was never a good fit between them. As long as Abu Mazen was just a business guy, it was okay. But once he was in the national leadership the two could not coexist well."[34]

Arafat waged a two-front war against Abbas. Privately, he began consolidating his grip on the epicenters of power in Palestinian politics: the security agencies and Fatah. Under the Road Map and the newly established Palestinian Basic Law—a pseudo-constitution to guide the Palestinian Authority—control of some of the security agencies was to fall to Abbas as the prime minister of the PA, rather than to the president, Arafat. This was part of the plan to demilitarize the violent uprising by shifting the security chiefs to the nonviolent Abbas. "But Arafat would not play ball," recalls an Abbas advisor. "It was clear to the security chiefs that they might pay a courtesy call to Abbas, but they would get their marching orders from Arafat."[35]

Inside Fatah, Arafat began deploying his loyalists to deride Abbas publicly. From television to radio to public speeches, the upper echelons of Fatah blasted Abbas at every occasion. "Arafat mobilized all the members of the Central Committee to go out and trash Abu Mazen. They were the attack dogs for Arafat, [he] mobilized a lot of his people to go after Abu Mazen," remembers an Abbas aide. "In Ramallah atmospherics, the muqata'a was much more buzzing than it had been for a while. Arafat began having daily Fatah meetings to prove he was the one in charge."[36]

Arafat wasn't mincing his words, either. In an outburst during one July meeting with the UN's envoy for peace, Terje Larsen, Arafat called Abbas a traitor. "Abu Mazen is betraying the interests of the Palestinian people," Arafat declared. "He is behaving like a tyro who doesn't know what he's doing. How does he dare to stand next to an Israeli flag and next to Sharon and to act friendly with a man whose history is known to all the world?"[37]

Despite Arafat's constant barbs, Abbas still managed to achieve some progress on the two most important fronts—fighting corruption and ending the violence. He pushed forward internal reforms within the Palestinian Authority with the aid of his finance minister, Salam Fayyad, an esteemed economist who took the job after a successful career at the World Bank and the International Monetary Fund. Fayyad had wrested control of some of Arafat's funds, and with Abbas as prime minister the two worked hard to reorient the PA's financial mechanisms toward helping build state institutions and serve the general public, instead of enriching Arafat and his cronies.[38]

On the security front, Abbas succeeded in convincing the various Palestinian factions to accept a temporary ceasefire (*hudna*) with Israel in June 2003.[39] The agreement was seen by the Palestinians as proving their compliance with the first phase of the Road Map—stopping all acts of terror. July, the following month, was indeed the least violent month since the beginning of the intifada.[40] Abbas had delivered to Israel, but Sharon reneged on his promise to release a large amount of Palestinian prisoners (many of them convicted terrorists). A prisoner release was, perhaps, the one thing that would have saved Abbas's image on the Palestinian street. Yet Sharon at first refused all together, and then, repeating Abbas's traumatic experience from the Wye River negotiations, released "criminal" prisoners instead of "national" ones. Sharon had also promised to take down fifteen illegal outposts built by the settlers throughout the West Bank, yet some of those outposts were rebuilt just hours after their evacuation.[41] It also didn't help that at one Israeli cabinet meeting, Sharon referred to Abbas as "a chick that's not grown feathers," meaning a new leader who still hadn't proven himself.[42] The remark was leaked to the press and only further weakened Abbas's political standing.

David Landau, Sharon's biographer, accuses the Israeli prime minister of shortsightedness in his treatment of Abbas—weakening him instead of doing everything within his power to help the rise of a moderate Palestinian leader.[43] Dov Weisglass, Sharon's chief of staff, rejects the accusation: "No one wanted to help Abu Mazen more than the Israeli government. We were happy when he succeeded and sad when he failed. But we also had our own constraints."[44]

Sharon went through a political evolution in 2003. By the end of that year, he would break his decades-long bond with the settlement movement and unveil a groundbreaking plan to evacuate seventeen settlements from the Gaza Strip, losing his status as the leader of the Israeli right wing and becoming instead a hero of the center-left. But in July all of that was still months away and unknown to anyone but a handful of the premier's closest aides. When Abbas could have used more gestures from him, Sharon was still consumed in his own political battles, mainly with Netanyahu, now his finance minister and main challenger within Likud. Sharon's references to a Palestinian state were already bad enough in the eyes of many of his party's members. More concessions toward Abbas would have created political hardships for Sharon. And, unlike Abbas, he had the choice of avoiding them, for now.

On August 19, a little more than a month after the beginning of the ceasefire, all of that became irrelevant when a Hamas suicide bomber hit a crowded bus in Jerusalem, killing twenty-three Israelis, many of them young children.[45] The ceasefire was now officially over, and with it, Abbas's hopes of creating a long-lasting change in Palestinian politics. For months, Abbas had demanded Arafat give him more control over the PA's security and intelligence agencies, in order to rehabilitate them and turn them into effective forces in the fight against terrorism. Arafat refused. Now, with violence flaring, Abbas realized he was fighting with his hands tied behind his back.[46] On September 6, he angrily tendered resignation.[47]

On his way out, Abbas blasted not only Arafat, but also Israel and the United States, which he accused of lying to his government and not giving it enough support. "The US (and the international community) did not exert sufficient influence on Israel to implement its commitments in the road map to push the peace process forward, or to end its military escalation," read a statement from his office.[48] The "fundamental problem," it added, was "Israel's unwillingness to implement its road map commitments and to undertake any constructive measures."

Had he gotten in over his head? His peers certainly thought so. "I think Abu Mazen came to the prime minister job with a lot of naiveté," says Nizar Farsakh, a former member of the PLO's negotiations department. "He totally underestimated the power politics. There were powerhouses there already that were not just going to roll over."[49] One of Abbas's advisers explained at the time that "he has simply had enough of all of them. He [felt] very badly let down, betrayed even."[50]

"He was basically abandoned," recalls Ghaith al-Omari, a former advisor to Abbas and a member of the Camp David delegation. "One day our office is packed with everyone wanting to see the prime minister. The next day: no one. He walks in and it's a ghost town. This was not lost on Abu Mazen, he was keenly aware that he was abandoned by those so-called allies."[51]

There was no precedent for the role of a former first-time prime minister of the Palestinian Authority. What should he do? Teach at a university? Write a column? Abbas was a man without a purpose. He was persona non grata in Arafat's court, the Israelis and Americans had little reason to call him, and his own people were largely indifferent to his plight. "Many thought this was the end of his career," says al-Omari. "He had dared to defy Arafat and he lost. It was bad to be seen with him at that point."[52]

When he resigned in September of 2003, there was no guarantee he would ever hold a position of power in the Palestinian Authority again. Sure, he was still the number two in the Palestine Liberation Organization, but Arafat had defanged him in all but title. Abbas had no idea in that September if he'd ever get a meaningful word in the national debate again. Arafat was still on top, he showed little signs of slowing down, and Abbas's competitors within Fatah were rejoicing in his defeat. Times were undoubtedly bleak.

Underlying all of Abbas's efforts in his short tenure as prime minister was a fundamental disconnect with Palestinian politics. Arafat and the PLO had built the base, developed that support, and mobilized it within the Palestinian Authority. Abbas's politics, which were always a closer fit with Soviet-style palace politics, were an especially poor fit in an Arafat administration that required clout with the street to make any moves. One diplomat told the *New York Times* shortly after Abbas's appointment in 2003 that "so many big people will rally around the prime minister [Abbas] that he will quickly establish a power base."[53]

How wrong they were. And to make matters worse, Abbas's on-again, off-again rival Ahmed Qurie (Abu Ala'a) had replaced him as prime minister, and was having more "success" than his predecessor. Qurie chose the path of least resistance with Arafat, choosing to be a good and faithful servant rather than a thorn in the Old Man's side. Abbas didn't realize it at the time, but the contrast between the two would actually play to his advantage in the court of Palestinian politics. "Because Abbas didn't compromise or crawl back to Arafat, [that] created a sense of respect for him," says al-Omari.[54]

That sense of respect was also apparent by the reactions to his resignation in Washington and Jerusalem. Abrams says that Abbas left "a good taste in our mouths in Washington. We thought this guy was a good guy, and Arafat proved it by working so hard to sideline him. And then [Abbas] proved it by quitting. On the one hand, he failed the political test, but on the other he passed the good governance test."[55]

For Sharon, meanwhile, Abbas's failure reinforced the notion that it was impossible to reach a peace agreement with the Palestinians, at least as long as Arafat was around. "We tried to marginalize Arafat by empowering Abu Mazen, and eventually Abu Mazen was the one being marginalized," concluded Weisglass.[56] For the Israelis, it was time to try a different formula.

It took Sharon three more months to reveal this formula, but when he did, in December 2003, he shook the very foundations of Israeli and Palestinian politics alike. "If in a few months the Palestinians still continue to disregard their part in implementing the road map, then Israel will initiate the unilateral step of disengagement from the Palestinians," Sharon declared in a groundbreaking speech at the Herzliya Conference that year. "The disengagement plan will include the redeployment of IDF forces along new security lines and a change in the deployment of settlements, which will reduce as much as possible the number of Israelis located in the heart of the Palestinian population."[57]

Sharon's announcement surprised just about anyone who had followed the man's career. He was, after all, a longtime supporter of settlements and one of Israel's greatest hawks. Now, he was promising to take down settlements without asking the Palestinians for anything in return.

One person who was perhaps less surprised, however, was Mahmoud Abbas. In his memoirs, Abbas mentions a strange conversation he once had with a senior member of the Israeli communist party. The Israeli politician recalled seeing Sharon in the Knesset hallway, shortly after the 1982 invasion of Lebanon, and refusing to shake Sharon's hand. Sharon, in Abbas's telling, responded to the insult by saying, "One day you will realize that it is I who will establish the Palestinian state."[58] It's hard to know if the story is accurate, but roughly a decade after Abbas included it in his book, Sharon was about to take a massive step toward making it look prophetic.

CHAPTER 6
PRESIDENT ABBAS
2004–2005

When Israeli tanks besieged Yasser Arafat's headquarters in Ramallah in 2002, the Palestinian leader famously declared, "Oh God, grant me a martyr's death."[1] Two and a half years later, his wish came true, in part. In November of 2004, the "Old Man" died in Paris after suffering a brain hemorrhage.[2]

Arafat's death left Fatah in disarray. The Palestinian leader was unconscious for days, yet when he finally passed away the party he had led for decades seemed to be unprepared for this historic moment. In the middle of the night, members of the party's highest body, the Central Committee, and the PLO's highest body, the Executive Committee, huddled in their offices in Ramallah and discussed what, exactly, should happen next. There was a funeral to arrange, a burial ceremony in Ramallah to take care of, and other pressing matters to address. But the most urgent question facing the elders of the Palestinian national movement was who, out of all of them, would succeed Yasser Arafat as the leader.

A passionate debate ensued, and many of those in attendance wanted more time to deliberate. Yasser Abed Rabbo, a veteran of the PLO and close ally of Arafat, was having none of it. As a ranking member of the Executive Committee, Abed Rabbo was not going to allow chaos to reign. When a number of senior officials asked to delay a decision by three days, the veteran politician replied, "You have three hours."[3]

In the bowels of the PLO's headquarters, while the foremost members of Palestinian politics argued over who should succeed the

Old Man, Mahmoud Abbas sat in the corner, silent. Technically, the PLO's bylaws dictated that power should go to him, since he was the organization's secretary general. Still, some Palestinian officials were not convinced that he was up to the task.

Eventually, it was the members of smaller factions within the PLO, like Abed Rabbo (a political independent), that steered the decision in Abbas's direction. "They [Fatah] quarreled with us, so we said if they don't do it we'll do it for them," remembers Abed Rabbo. "We told them the Executive Committee's choice was Abu Mazen. They had to approve it. We said 'our candidate is Abu Mazen, and if you want someone else, go meet in the next room and get us another name.' But we could not wait three days. We had to tell people today there was a leader."[4]

Early in the morning on November 11, 2004, as ordinary Palestinians woke up to the dramatic news of Arafat's death, Fatah finally came to a decision on his successor: "Abu Mazen it is."[5]

◆◆◆

The next morning, Mahmoud Abbas stepped down onto the tarmac at Cairo's international airport, accompanied by a small delegation of senior Palestinian officials.

Yasser Arafat awaited them there. After passing away in Paris, the Old Man's body was flown to the Egyptian capital, where President Hosni Mubarak was awarding Arafat the honor of a state military funeral. At least sixteen heads of state were in attendance; dozens of other countries sent delegations.[6] The delegation from the Palestinian Authority was officially led by Abbas. When Mubarak—back then the strongest leader in the Arab world—arrived at the mourning tent where foreign dignitaries were gathering, Abbas was among the first dignitaries he went to greet.

The funeral procession moved through the streets of Cairo as a horse-drawn carriage pulled Arafat's coffin to the famous Almaza Air Base. Abbas walked at the front of the procession next to Tunisian leader Zine el Abidine Ben Ali, a fitting ode to Tunisia's place as a "home away from home" for the Palestinian leadership in the 1980s. Next to Ben Ali walked Mubarak. Abbas may have seemed like a timid and uncertain leader next to the two long-standing strongmen, but despite his improbable rise his rule would outlast them both.

On Egypt's official state television, the announcer described the scene. "Hosni Mubarak is flanked by his brothers, [by] leaders of the Arab countries leading this procession for their brother, Yasser Arafat," he explained, adding some revisionist history. "Yasser Arafat, who often put his hands in their hands on the path to working for the Arab interests, on the path to liberating every inch of the Arab land, and on the path to achieving the highest interests of the Arab world."[7]

The somber funeral service in Cairo was the exact opposite of what happened later that day in Ramallah, where "Abu Ammar" (Arafat's nom de guerre) was finally laid to rest. Tens of thousands rushed to the helicopter that carried Arafat's coffin, making it dangerous for the pilots to land. One senior Palestinian official yelled at the crowd to give Arafat "the honor he deserves," but to no avail.[8] Members of Fatah fainted on the scene, security forces discharged their rifles upward, and mourners began chanting, "With our blood, with our souls, we are yours!"[9] Chaos and confusion swept over the event. The fact that the funeral took place during the month of Ramadan, during which Muslims refrain from eating and drinking for most of the day, made things even more chaotic.[10]

"People didn't seem to believe that their leader was dead," recalls Al Quds University president Sari Nusseibeh. "Maybe they expected him to pull off another of his daredevil stunts, like the time he crash-landed in the Sahara and walked away with barely a scratch. Perhaps they thought the Old Man could trick death itself."[11]

Eventually, after hours of confusion, the crowds dispersed. Rawhi Fattouh, the speaker of the Palestinian Authority's parliament, was named interim president of the PA. Elections were set for sixty days, and Mahmoud Abbas was now chairman of the PLO. The era of Yasser Arafat was over.

The hours after Arafat's death saw a dramatic turn of events for Mahmoud Abbas. Just a year earlier he had resigned from the premiership and was in political exile. He had retained his position as the PLO's number two, technically, yet many believed his political career was effectively over. Still, by merit of his position as number two in the PLO and a founder of the Fatah party, he was in a different tier of leaders.

As the reality of Arafat's death sank in, the only thing the panicked Fatah and PLO leaders could agree on was that protocol should be followed, and protocol meant Abbas would be the guy. In a few short hours, Abbas had suddenly become the leader of the Palestinian national movement. As his negotiating proxy Hussein Agha wrote a few months later, "A multitude of divergent interests has coalesced around him."[12]

Just two decades earlier in Tunisia, there were maybe six or seven Fatah leaders in front of Abbas in seniority in the group.[13] Now he was the leader of the Palestinian national project. Fatah's hierarchy was coalescing around him, the PLO was under his effective control, and he would soon campaign for president of the Palestinian Authority. How, exactly, did he end up in this position?

"Abbas maintained a degree of integrity. He looked like he was his own man," recalls his former aide, Ghaith al-Omari. "It didn't hurt that the world didn't fail to notice this. The Americans who remained in contact with him saw he was not willing to compromise on these [governance] issues. So when the moment came, Abu Mazen had just accumulated enough respect to succeed Arafat."[14]

It also didn't hurt that on the international scene Abbas's short stint as prime minister made him a personal favorite of world leaders, including President Bush and British prime minister Tony Blair. His willingness to confront Arafat, both on terrorism and internal reform, impressed them even if it didn't lead to actual results.

"We [thought] this is wonderful," recalls Elliott Abrams, the Bush administration's senior director for the Middle East and North Africa at the National Security Council at the time. "We're very happy, and the same was true of the European Union. There [was] no friction in this relationship. We wanted reform of the security services, and he says 'Yeah, sure.' We wanted an end to corruption, and he says 'Yeah, sure.'"[15]

Abbas's appointment was seen in Washington as the culmination of a multiyear process of weakening Arafat. "I call on the Palestinian people to elect new leaders," Bush said in a speech in June 2002, "leaders not compromised by terror."[16] To Bush administration officials, that was Abbas. "[He was] appointed prime minister and we welcomed it because it's seen as sort of a vindication of the Road Map: that, in essence, we were looking for an alternative leadership untainted by terror," recalls Robert Danin, a member of the National Security Council at the time. "The President says Palestinians deserve a new leadership untainted by terror, and that's Abbas."[17]

In Jerusalem, Abbas's appointment was also received warmly, although perhaps with tempered expectations. Sharon remembered very well how things ended up the last time Abbas took a leadership position, and he wasn't sure how it would work out this time. He decided that Israel would continue with its unilateral disengagement plan, without relying on Abbas in any way. Still, said a former senior Sharon adviser, Abbas was obviously preferable to Arafat, whose death "was not a very sad event, from our point of view."[18]

The Americans were happy. The Israelis were content. Fatah and the PLO were satisfied with Abbas's ascendance. Now, all he had to do was actually win an election.

In 1994, Nader Said was a pollster at the Arab World Research and Development center in the West Bank. He and his team wanted to gauge the thoughts of everyday Palestinians on the newly returned leaders of the Palestine Liberation Organization. So, Said first put out a poll asking Palestinians if they supported Yasser Arafat as president, and, to no one's surprise, a vast majority did. Said then followed up with a poll asking Palestinians to choose who should be president, Arafat or Sheikh Ahmed Yassin, a leader of the terror group Hamas. Arafat still won a majority. The next day, Said received a handwritten note from Arafat, containing only three words:

> *Eh da, Said!*
> "What's this, Said!"[19]

It was less of a question than a statement, and it was in Arafat's typical Egyptian dialect. The "Old Man" never shook his linguistic upbringing. The next month Said put another poll in the field. This one asked Palestinians who they thought should be Arafat's vice president. The post didn't exist, and there was scarce talk of creating it, but the pollsters wanted a sense of who Palestinians saw as Arafat's number two. The day after the poll was released, Said received another handwritten note from Arafat:

Eh da, Said!!!!!!!!!!

"Ten exclamation points!" recalled Said laughingly. "So, he was okay with us polling about presidential candidates, but not a vice president."[20] Arafat's paranoia loomed large, and the logic was simple: naming a number two in the public eye would give the public another natural leader if and when Arafat stumbled. Arafat rejected even the mere discussion of such a possibility.

And yet, when he did sneak a look at the poll results, Arafat could easily see that there was one man he had absolutely no reason to worry about: his longtime adviser and negotiator, Mahmoud Abbas.

Among those vice presidential figures listed in the poll, Mahmoud Abbas garnered a measly 1.5 percent of the vote. "At the time, nobody knew Abbas at all," recalls Said. "Abbas was always in the background. He was never a populist. He was not a people's person. He didn't care—not in a bad way—but it's just not his style. Unlike Arafat, who was always out there, always saying the right things, the sloganeering. Abbas is not into that. He doesn't give a damn about that."[21]

December 28, 2004, was Mahmoud Abbas's first-ever day on the campaign trail. The sixty-nine-year-old Fatah nominee for president had never campaigned for a job in his life, and he was suddenly running for the highest office in the West Bank and Gaza. His advisors knew that, in order to win, the soft-spoken peace negotiator needed to appeal to all of Fatah, not just the bureaucratic elite. That meant Abbas had to go to the beating heart of the Second Intifada, to win over Fatah's militant base: the refugee camp of Jenin, in the northern West Bank. Jenin, home to over thirty thousand people, had been an epicenter of the violent clashes with Israel ever since the beginning of the uprising. In order to win an election, Abbas first needed to win his party, and to do that he had to go into unfamiliar territory. "2005 was a continuation of the Second Intifada," recalls his campaign manager, Mohammad Shtayyeh, and Abbas was about to go into the belly of the beast to "call for the demilitarization of the intifada."[22]

But he faced an uphill battle. The aging Fatah leader had never mobilized big crowds or captivated packed halls. "Abu Mazen is an elite person, he has a selective audience," says Shtayyeh. "The biggest group he ever spoke to was maybe the PNC [the parliament of the PLO]. He never went to rallies or demonstrations. That was a big challenge."[23]

Tensions were high in Jenin at the time. Fatah's armed wing, the Aqsa Martyrs' Brigade, had filled a soccer stadium with machine-gun clad supporters, and they were not exactly receptive to Abbas's nonviolent approach. Abbas entered the stadium cautiously, safe inside his motorcade. When he finally did emerge, it was for the all-important embrace with Zakaria Zubeidi, the most prominent terror chief in Jenin and a media darling who gave exclusive interviews to journalists from hidden bunkers.[24] There was perhaps no other figure in Palestinian politics who was more different than Abbas, both in resume and temperament. Yet Abbas needed to win Jenin, and to win Jenin he needed Zubeidi.

Zubeidi was a tough sell. He had initially supported Marwan Barghouthi, a former colleague within Fatah's terror wing who launched his own presidential bid from an Israeli prison, where he was serving five life sentences. But when Barghouthi, despite his vast popularity on the Palestinian street, dropped out of the race, Zubeidi decided to fall in line with the Fatah elite. He greeted Abbas warmly in Jenin and hoisted him on top of a mob of supporters. With a scarf draped around his neck reading "Abu Mazen for President," Zubeidi marched Abbas through town while Abbas waved to supporters.

"Zubeidi was carrying him on his shoulders, and Abu Mazen was saying, 'I am against the militarization of the intifada,'" recalls Abbas's campaign manager. But then Zubeidi was confronted by a journalist asking how he could support the nonviolent Abbas for president. "I was worried he would drop him!" remembers Shtayyeh. "But Zakaria, luckily, said something that was nice. [He said] 'I am under the political leadership; I am under the legitimacy of Abu Mazen. Whatever he says, I will live with it.'"[25] Abbas returned from Jenin victorious: despite his opposition to the armed struggle, those who participated in it were lining up behind him.

Ashraf al-Ajrami, who served as a cabinet member under Abbas, explains that "he was never a man who had strong support on the street. People knew his name ever since the Tunis days, but he wasn't one of the big shots. My generation, the generation of the First Intifada, looked up to Arafat, Abu Jihad, and Abu Iyad—they were the three giants of the Palestinian movement. Nobody looked up to Abu Mazen. People who were more involved in politics knew that he was an important player, but if you mentioned his name to the kids fighting with Israeli soldiers on the streets, they wouldn't have any opinion of him."[26]

"He promised to continue the public sector reforms that he began in 2003 and were blocked by Arafat," recalls al-Ajrami. "When that promise was combined with his seniority within Fatah and his international standing, it was enough for people to be convinced. People were eager for a change after Arafat's rule. There was a sense that the armed struggle was over anyway, so now [was] a good time to focus on things like proper government, the economy, and the education system, things that Arafat never really cared about."[27]

There were at least seven candidates for president of the Palestinian Authority during the two-month campaign, but the only serious threat to Mahmoud Abbas came from Mustafa Barghouthi, a physician and long-time political independent. Barghouthi, a distant relative of the terror leader Marwan, had run for the PA's parliament in 1996 but narrowly missed getting a seat. In the heat of the Second Intifada, Barghouthi and several prominent Palestinian academics had formed a new third party called *Al-Mubadara*, or the Palestinian National Initiative (PNI). The party's platform was simple: it opposed the Israeli occupation and pledged full support to Palestinian refugees abroad. Now, that party was his platform for staging a presidential run.

"[Fatah] was taken by surprise on the first day of the campaign because we had filled the country with posters and activists and volunteers," recalls Barghouthi of the 2005 presidential campaign. "We forced them to campaign. The more we moved in the campaign the more they thought there was real competition. . . . They became more and more irritated the closer we got to the election date."[28]

Barghouthi may have been forcing Fatah and Abbas to campaign, but he never became a real threat. While Barghouthi was campaigning in Jerusalem and across the West Bank, Abbas was limiting his public appearances and allowing Fatah to mobilize on his behalf. Fatah was the best-organized political vehicle in the West Bank; if the party endorsed a candidate that candidate had the support of party cadres in every village and town. Meanwhile, Barghouthi was harassed in Hebron by rival parties and was even briefly detained by the Israelis for campaigning in Jerusalem.[29] Did Abbas face such Israeli restrictions? "No, of course not. There were no restrictions. But he didn't go to Jerusalem anyhow."[30]

"There is much evidence proving that the elections are not fair and that the local media and the Arab media are biased in favor of Abu Mazen," complained Abdul Sattar Qassem, another independent candidate for president.[31] Abbas's rivals were crying foul not only at physical intimidation, but in the media. "Only yesterday Abu Mazen was an isolated and insular individual, yet today, after Arafat's passing away, he has turned into a media hero supported by those who [previously] fought against him. All the Arab and world media are rushing to help him win the Palestinian elections."

But Abbas and Fatah ran a smart campaign. They honed their approach. They conducted city-specific polls and made sure their people in each city were addressing the most relevant issues among Palestinians. Whereas Barghouthi's slogan was "Put our issue in trusted hands," Abbas's was "Peace and reduction of poverty."[32] His campaign advisor remarked that Abbas used to repeat a verse from the Qur'an in every stump speech and interview: "The one who fed them and the one who secured them from fear."[33] The 106th Sura seemed a natural slogan for the lifelong negotiator and reformer.

The elections on January 9, 2005, were largely seen as free and fair. An observer mission led by former president Jimmy Carter concluded the elections were a "clear expression of the democratic will of the Palestinian people."[34] However, the monitors noted that last-minute rule changes that allowed Palestinians to vote simply by presenting identification without having registered prior were "prob-lematic," and they concluded that "some people took advantage of the rule change to cast more than one ballot."

The election monitors also backed up some of Abdul Sattar Qassem's allegations of media bias toward Abbas, noting, "Publicly owned broadcast media demonstrated heavy bias toward the Fatah candidate."[35] In Jericho and Ramallah, observers recorded "busloads of [Palestinian Authority] security personnel" and likely Abbas voters being hauled in to vote under the new rules change. Finally, the Jimmy Carter–led observer mission concluded there were "scattered incidents of intimidation and harassment by some Fatah activists of some voters, [and] supporters of other candidates."

Clearly, Fatah was not going to allow any other party to try to succeed the founder of the national movement, Yasser Arafat. "Fatah decided he was the candidate and everybody rallied behind him," remarks Shtayyeh. Was there ever a thought that Abbas might lose the election?

"No."[36]

The first exit polls proved that Abbas's confidence was justified, as they showed him winning 66 percent of the vote to Barghouthi's 19 percent.[37] Abbas was ready to exhale. "Victory is beautiful," he told reporters, "but it will be more beautiful to fulfill the pledges."[38] Abbas insisted his priority as president would be to meet with Israeli prime minister Ariel Sharon as soon as possible, and soon after he declared victory he received a congratulatory call from President Bush in Washington. Bush then did what he had never done for Arafat: he invited Abbas to Washington.[39]

In the end, Abbas received 501,448 votes to Barghouthi's 156,227.[40] Barghouthi did not contest the results, but he did com-plain about the last-minute rule change. "I'm not saying we won the election," recalled Barghouthi more than ten years later in his office in Ramallah. "But I think we got much higher than just 20 percent."[41]

In retrospect, the presidential election of 2005 should have been a warning sign for the Fatah party. Almost ten years earlier, its can-didate had won a presidential contest by a margin of 88 percent to 11 percent.[42] Though its candidate then was the indomitable Yasser Arafat, the drop-off in support could have been seen in some Fatah circles as a sign of a possible downward trend. But Fatah had never been a movement of self-inspection, and any soul-searching that perhaps would have saved the group from the biggest defeat of its existence the following year was wanting. It would be another year before Abbas and his allies would realize how badly they misjudged the Palestinian public. For now, they were celebrating.

One week after winning the presidential election, Mahmoud Abbas gave his inaugural address to the Palestinian Authority's parliament, the Legislative Council. It was the most important speech of his career to that point. "I dedicate this victory in the name of our whole people to the soul and memory of our eternal leader, the symbol of our cause, Yasser Arafat," declared Abbas. "It was he who planted the first seed of this democratic process, it was he who held its banner high, and it was he who consolidated its traditions. Our respect and gratitude go to your noble soul, Abu Ammar, on this day of Palestinian democracy."[43]

Abbas then got down to brass tacks. His goals as president were simple: end the Second Intifada, reform the Palestinian Authority, and push to renew the peace process. In order to do so, the longtime negotiator would have to reorient the Palestinian national project. He viewed his election as a referendum of popular support for his mission:

> The people have voted for the rule of law, order, and pluralism, the peaceful transfer of authority, and equality for all. The people have chosen [a] just peace, ending the occupation, and coexistence based on equality and international legitimacy.[44]

His inaugural address also reiterated his negotiating stance:

> The greatest challenge before us and the fundamental task facing us is national liberation. The task of ending the occupation, establishing the Palestinian state on the 1967 borders, with Jerusalem as its capital, and reaching a just and agreed solution to the refugee

problem on the basis of international legitimacy, first and foremost
[UN General Assembly] Resolution 194 [of 1949] and the Beirut
Arab Summit Resolution [of 2002].[45]

"To achieve these national goals," Abbas continued, "we will
remain committed to the PLO's strategic choice: the choice of
achieving just peace and our national goals through negotiations.
The path to these goals is what we and the world have agreed upon
in the road map. We have repeatedly stated that we are committed to
our responsibilities in the road map. We will implement our obligations as a matter of Palestinian national interest. In return, Israel has
to implement its obligations."[46]

Israel and the United States were more than happy with the
change of leadership. Condoleezza Rice writes that the United States
"welcomed Abbas's election by offering to donate $200 million annu-
ally to the Palestinians," as well as having President Bush encourage
"the wealthy Persian Gulf states to dramatically increase their aid."[47]
A week after Abbas's inaugural address, Israeli premier Ariel Sharon
decided to nix a massive military operation in Gaza to quell the terror
of the intifada. According to one government official, Israel wanted
"to give him [Abbas] a chance to operate."[48]

Three weeks after his inaugural address, Abbas was in Egypt
for a summit with Sharon, Hosni Mubarak, and King Abdullah of
Jordan. In accordance with the Bush administration's Road Map,
Abbas announced the Palestinians would "cease all acts of violence
against the Israelis."[49] Abbas pledged himself to "restoring the peace
process," while acknowledging that "we differ on several issues. And
this may include settlements, the release of prisoners, the wall [which
is] closing institutions in Jerusalem. We will not be able to solve all of
these issues today, but our positions towards these issues are clear and
firm." In short, the Palestinian leader would no longer be leading
the violent uprising against Israel. Rather, he'd prefer negotiations.

In the short term, Abbas had to corral the violent elements of
the intifada, both within his party and across the Palestinian political
spectrum. The first step was pushing the Arafat loyalists out of government. Abbas needed to reorient the Palestinian Authority from
a position of fighting Israel to one of governance and state-building.

And to do that he needed to purge the militant elements within Fatah.

"The whole world is watching, and we have a lot to do," Abbas told parliamentary members a month after assuming office.[50] Then he fired seventeen of the twenty-four cabinet members of the Arafat era and replaced them with allies. The message was clear: get on board with the new strategy or get out.

Many Palestinian militants chose the latter. Abbas immediately tried to clean house upon moving into the PA's headquarters, the muqata'a, at one point literally. When Abbas forced out six militants who had sought refuge in the muqata'a since 2002, they retaliated by shooting at the compound before attacking a local restaurant.[51] At a March gathering in Ramallah of thousands of Fatah activists, gunmen from Fatah's own military wing, the Aqsa Martyrs' Brigade, burst into the hall and dispersed the meeting by firing their rifles into the air.[52]

Abbas may have been president, but the chaos of the post-intifada era still loomed large. Factions still dominated camps across the West Bank, the PA security forces were diminished, and the governing bodies were depleted or nonexistent. Strongmen still lingered in cantons across the Palestinian territories. Even Zakaria Zubeidi, who had hoisted Abbas on his shoulders in Jenin during the presidential campaign, was unwilling to bow completely. When one of Abbas's security chiefs entered Zubeidi's hometown of Jenin that March, Zubeidi insisted the PA had not asked his permission first and proceeded to harass the security chief and fire rounds into the air.[53]

Restoring order had soon become a "national demand," according to Nabil Amr, a parliamentarian close to Abbas.[54] But in order to do that, the new president needed to show his people he was making progress with the Americans and Israelis toward statehood and independence. Abbas couldn't deliver on law and order without gaining popularity through achievements in the peace process. At the same time, he couldn't achieve anything in the peace process without reining in the militias and restoring law and order. He had to succeed simultaneously on both fronts, while also fighting politically with old Arafat loyalists who remained in positions of power.

Thankfully for Abbas, the Americans and Israelis realized his complicated situation. On March 16, Palestinian security forces replaced the Israeli army in the West Bank city of Jericho as Israel transferred control of major Palestinian cities to the PA.[55] A week later, the PA reassumed control of Tulkaram.[56] Within weeks, Ramallah, Bethlehem, and Qalqilya also returned to PA control. In May, Abbas visited Washington for the first visit of a Palestinian president to the White House in five years. Combined, these events created a strong argument on Abbas's behalf that things were moving in the right direction. His first months in office were a time of cautious optimism.

"We will stand with you, Mr. President," Bush told Abbas in May of 2005, "as you combat corruption, reform the Palestinian security services and your justice system, and revive your economy."[57] To that end, Bush announced an infusion of $50 million to fund housing projects in Gaza.[58] Investing money in Gaza made sense, as Israel was moving ahead with its plan to unilaterally withdraw from the coastal enclave. Sharon's disengagement plan, first floated at the end of 2003, was due to happen by the summer of 2005, after it was approved by the Knesset. The Bush administration at first was skeptical of the plan, precisely because of its unilateral nature. White House policy was still in favor of both sides coordinating together. With time, however, the administration changed its attitude and not only expressed support for the Israeli unilateral move but also gave Israel a major diplomatic reward in the form of a letter from the president, recognizing that the future border between Israel and the Palestinian state would take into consideration the changes on the ground in the West Bank.

What this meant, in essence, was that the idea of a land-swap—allowing Israel to annex the large "settlement blocs" close to the 1967 border as long as it compensated the Palestinians with lands from within Israel—was now embraced by the president. Furthermore, the letter could have been interpreted as legitimizing a security barrier Sharon's government constructed between Israel and much of the West Bank in response to the intifada. The Palestinian reaction to this letter was harsh, calling it "the death of the peace process" and accusing Bush of legitimizing the settlements.[59]

By the summer of 2005, however, the Bush letter had become the least of Abbas's concerns. The pictures of Israel pulling its soldiers and evacuating its settlers from Gaza could have been a moment of victory for him and for the PA, but instead they became a recruiting tool for the rival terror faction Hamas. "The unilateral Israeli withdrawal caused a lot of damage to the Palestinian Authority," says al-Ajrami. "For more than a decade, the PA invested in negotiations with Israel, and then when Israel finally withdrew from Gaza, it did so without any kind of negotiations. So obviously, Hamas took credit for the whole thing. They told people to look with their own eyes: Abu Mazen's way of negotiations could barely make the Israelis move a few inches, and yet the armed struggle, the intifada, the bus bombings—all those things caused Israel to run away from Gaza. They presented it as a victory over Sharon, but it was most of all a victory over Abu Mazen for them."[60]

Sharon's insistence throughout 2005, even after Abbas's election victory, on initiating the disengagement plan with only a minimal level of coordination with the Palestinian Authority, remains somewhat of a mystery to this day. David Landau described it in his biography of Sharon as "almost perverse."[61] But some disagree with that characterization. "To say that there was no coordination with the Palestinian Authority during the disengagement is plain wrong," said Dov Weisglass, Sharon's chief of staff at the time. "I personally talked with Abu Mazen about different aspects of the plan. There were also constant communications between security officials on both sides, and we were working on plans for economic initiatives in the future. People who say it was done without coordination have a hard time accepting that it was Sharon, and not their darling Shimon Peres, who eventually took down the settlements. But that doesn't change the facts."[62]

Ashraf al-Ajrami notes that while there were some contacts between the two sides, Israel didn't make even the smallest possible effort to turn the disengagement into a political achievement for Abbas. "Sharon simply didn't believe in an agreement with us. He never did. . . . He wanted to do everything on his own terms."[63]

American officials at the time echo Weisglass's defense of Sharon but add that Abbas was handicapped by Arafat's shadow. The American ambassador to Israel at the time, Daniel Kurtzer, met with one of the top Palestinian negotiators, Saeb Erekat, in January 2004 to explain the merits of the plan. Famous for his proclivity for resigning, the Western-educated Erekat nevertheless became a favorite of his Israeli and American interlocutors and a close advisor to Abbas. He first joined the negotiations team in 1991 at the Madrid conference and would go on to have a role in every major peace negotiation since. "What we wanted to explain to Saeb was the American view that the Palestinians lost nothing by participating in disengagement," recalls Kurtzer. "It was the recovery of territory. It was an Israeli withdrawal. It was a removal of settlements . . . At the end of that meeting I thought Saeb thought that was the way to proceed. But he couldn't get Arafat to agree."[64] The Old Man had refused to participate in disengagement, and Sharon "did not want any discussions with the Palestinians" beyond that. When Arafat died and Abbas became president later, nothing changed in that calculus. Disengagement would proceed.

This didn't mean Abbas didn't have great dreams for Gaza, it just meant he was cut out of the loop. "He wanted to turn Gaza into the Palestinian version of Singapore," says al-Ajrami. "He talked about building a strip of hotels along the coast, and attracting millions of tourists from all over the world."[65] Weisglass also says that, "I don't remember him expressing any fears or concerns about Gaza's future in our conversations during that period. All he talked about was how bright the future would be, how they would turn Gaza into a shining example for the entire Arab world."[66]

Abbas also knew that for Sharon, Gaza was just the beginning. Israel was still committed to the Road Map, and the endgame was still the establishment of a Palestinian state in Gaza and the West Bank. Following the disengagement, pressure from the right caused Sharon to quit Likud and found a new, centrist party called Kadima ("Onwards" in Hebrew). Israel went to new elections, and it was expected that after his upcoming victory Sharon would take the next bold step, this time in the West Bank. But on January 4, 2006, Sharon—who by now was seventy-seven years old—suffered a stroke and went into a coma, from which he never woke up. The peace camp in Israel was now hobbled, and Abbas was left empty-handed. It was the first of many setbacks he would suffer that year.

CHAPTER 7

LOSING PALESTINE

2006–2007

The Palestinian prisoners in Hadarim jail, a high-security prison north of Tel Aviv, could not believe what they were seeing. On January 22, 2006, a seemingly regular Sunday, television crews from leading Arab stations poured into the cell of the most famous Palestinian prisoner in Israel, Marwan Barghouthi.[1] Serving multiple life sentences for coordinating brutal terror attacks during the Second Intifada, Barghouthi was a national symbol for many Palestinians—which is why Israeli authorities usually tried to keep him away from the media. Yet now, out of nowhere, the short, bearded prisoner was given rare permission to speak before the cameras, including a rare interview with Al Jazeera, one of the most popular networks in the Arab world.

The reason Barghouthi was given permission to provide interviews soon became clear. In three days, on January 25, the Palestinian Authority was going to hold its first parliamentary elections since 1996. Fatah and Hamas were competing for control of the Palestinian Legislative Council, the parliamentary body of the PA. In his interviews from prison, Barghouthi urgently pleaded with the Palestinian public to participate in the elections—and to vote for Fatah. He promised that, after securing victory, the ruling party—of which he was a proud member—would reach out to Hamas and try to work together.[2]

In the months leading up to the election, Fatah enjoyed a comfortable lead in most public opinion polls. The party's senior leadership—including Mahmoud Abbas—was certain they were cruising to victory. Yet in the final weeks of the campaign, that assumption was beginning to fade. That's why Barghouthi was recruited for a last-minute "get out the vote" operation with the help of Israeli officials, who agreed to let him speak to the press.

The legislative elections were supposed to be a source of pride for the Palestinian Authority. Only a year after Mahmoud Abbas's inauguration as the new Palestinian president, here were his people once again going to the ballot box, this time to democratically elect their parliamentary representatives. "This is the year of Palestinian elections," Abbas declared in his first speech as president.[3] In an Arab world not known for democracy, Palestinians were a step ahead. If Arafat had been the pseudo-democratic leader, Abbas was going to be the fully democratic one. If Arafat had led the Palestinian national movement with a heavy-handed approach, Abbas was going to be the law-and-order leader.

As part of this rejuvenation, Abbas wanted the inclusion of all Palestinian parties in the political arena. No longer would parties like Hamas, an officially designated terror group in the United States, be excluded from competition. Hamas had boycotted the previous legislative elections in 1996, but its leaders were eager to compete this time around, and Abbas welcomed their participation.

It wasn't so much that Abbas valued inclusivity and compromise, but rather that he thought democratic elections could solve what years of low-intensity military conflict between Hamas and Fatah could not. "If you don't let them into the process they're going to be a spoiler," he told Bush administration officials in October of 2005. "You have to bring them in, defeat them politically, and then you're stronger."[4]

Not everyone in the administration liked the idea. Secretary of State Condoleezza Rice later said the United States "should have insisted that every party disarm as a condition for participating in the vote," but Abbas refused.[5] "Only the participation of all Palestinians would make the election legitimate," Rice recalls Abbas arguing. The International Quartet—a special diplomatic body for dealing with the Israeli-Palestinian conflict that consisted of American, European, Russian, and UN representatives—did actually put out a statement declaring that any party who would participate in the elections would have to hand over its arms to the PA. But that declaration was eventually softened by Abbas out of fear it would "be construed as setting preconditions."[6]

In the run-up to the election, Abbas met with several members of Hamas and assured them he would not force them to disarm in order to participate. Mahmoud al-Zahar, a founder of Hamas, told a local paper that Abbas thought disarming Hamas would lead to a civil war. "I agree with him," said al-Zahar, "because confiscating the weapons of the movement, after all its achievements, is unjustified. Even if it is done under American or Israeli pressure."[7]

Why was the Bush administration, which was waging a war on terror, willing to allow a terror group to participate in democratic elections? In short, because the United States was pushing a democracy agenda in the region. "The Arabs treat you like dirt, we know that," Elliott Abrams, Bush's senior Middle East advisor, recalls the president telling Abbas in their first White House meeting. A Palestinian democracy would send a message to the rest of the Middle East. "We're not going to treat you like dirt. You're on the path . . . you are going to prove that Arab democracy is possible."[8] So, if Abbas was willing to not only accept the United States's prodemocracy agenda but promulgate it, then the United States was willing to take his word on who could participate. "Forced by the Palestinian logic to choose between canceling the elections entirely or allowing Hamas-linked candidates to run," recalls Abrams, "we chose the latter and decided not to have a confrontation with Abbas."[9]

Some within the State Department felt that allowing Hamas to participate without renouncing terror was a major mistake. In the weeks before the elections, Rice held a meeting with her closest advisors about what to recommend to the president. "I said it's a mistake that we're allowing Hamas to run for free," recalls Robert Danin, then the Deputy Assistant Secretary of State for Near Eastern Affairs. Danin argued it was "illogical" for a terror group like Hamas to run for seats in a parliament it rejects.[10] His point was prescient: Hamas was avowedly against the Oslo Accords and the peace process, which were the guiding principle for the PA's very existence. But in Washington, the desire to hold elections outweighed all else, and opinions like his were eventually rejected.

Abbas's initial insistence on allowing Hamas to participate in the

122 THE LAST PALESTINIAN

elections was based on the assumption that Fatah would easily win. "It is he who wanted an election to legitimize himself," says Abrams.[11] The goal of democratic legitimacy and pleasing the United States offset any such fears that Hamas might win. "He believed we'd get some minor percentage," says a senior official in Hamas. "He did not believe that Hamas would get half or even two-thirds of the seats."[12]

Israel had an election of its own to prepare for during the same period. After Sharon fell into a coma, his new centrist party, Kadima, chose the interim prime minister, Ehud Olmert, as its new leader. Olmert ran on a platform promising to do in the West Bank what Sharon had done in Gaza: unilaterally withdraw from most of the territory. The Palestinian election, in that context, wasn't supposed to make too much of a difference: whoever won, Israel planned to carry out its unilateral plans. And yet, it was obviously preferable for Israel to have Fatah entrenching its political power, especially with the moderate Abbas as president, than to have Hamas in control.

Most Israeli intelligence officials expected a Fatah victory, based on public polling information and secret intelligence assessments. One senior Israeli official who was less optimistic, however, was Yuval Diskin, the head of the Shin Bet. Diskin had warned Sharon as early as September 2005 that Fatah's political strength was an illusion and that, on the ground, Hamas was growing more popular by the day.[13] Abbas's political agenda of peace negotiations, coupled with Fatah's dogged perception of endemic corruption, provided an easy campaign target for the "political outsiders" in Hamas. Yet three weeks before the election, a senior IDF intelligence officer told the Israeli press that Hamas most likely had a "ceiling" of around 30 to 40 percent of the population, which it couldn't surpass.[14]

The alarm bells started ringing, both in Ramallah and in Jerusalem, only in the very last stretch of the election. The problem wasn't just that Hamas was running a better campaign with a more disciplined message: it was also that Fatah was completely fractured at the local level. Indeed, the Palestinian legislative elections are essentially a local election, in which every "district" chooses its own members of parliament from the different political lists. While Hamas's candidates ran under one banner, Fatah showed disastrous disunity by having splinter lists in multiple camps, towns, and villages.

The fragmentation was especially severe in Ramallah. "We were supposed to run five candidates there," says Qaddura Fares, a Fatah leader and former Palestinian Authority cabinet member. "Instead, twenty-two candidates ran, five officially with Fatah and seventeen independents."[15] While the party had a clear interest to consolidate votes around a small group of candidates in order to defeat Hamas, each local politician thought only about their own benefits of being elected—thus creating a crowded field that made it easier for Hamas to win.

At the same time, a larger political problem was emerging within the senior ranks of the party. Weeks before the elections, Fatah officials began coalescing around different popular figures. The Central Committee, the highest bastion of power within the party, was largely in favor of Ahmed Qurie, the longtime negotiator, to head the official party list. Others, however, wanted Marwan Barghouthi.[16] A divide turned into a yawning gulf between the camps.

Ten years prior, Fatah candidates for the 1996 elections were largely educated, upper class, and supporters of the Oslo peace process. After the havoc of the Second Intifada, a new strata emerged within Fatah: militants and street fighters. The old guard populated the Central Committee and gravitated toward Qurie, while the new crowd had the support of the street—and pulled for Barghouthi. "I met with Abu Mazen and discussed the list for almost an hour," recalls Fares, a close associate of Barghouthi, "I left very angry with him because it was not clear Marwan would head the list." The message to the Marwan crowd was clear: Abbas, and his bureaucratic loyalists, were in charge. Weeks before the first parliamentary elections in a decade, Abbas was waging a battle against his own party. In response, the Marwan camp launched their own campaign and registered their list. "The Fatah people then saw we were serious, so we launched negotiations and compromised our lists, but Marwan would be the head."[17]

In the post–Second Intifada political landscape, the new militant class within the party was too powerful to ignore. So, Fatah had seemingly merged its old-guard list with Barghouthi's camp, which also included Mohammad Dahlan and Jibril Rajoub, another former security chief.[18] Merging lists meant cutting names, and cutting names meant some party leaders woke up one morning to find they had been cut from the Fatah's final list for parliament. A lot of these individuals didn't take that sitting down, and instead ran against the party individually in their own districts. Thus, instead of unifying the party, merging the lists only further divided it.

In the end, Fatah was dangerously fractured entering the elections. Abbas could not unify the party around a common group of candidates nor prevent rivals and upstarts from running independently. The effect was devastating. In almost every district, Fatah was splitting the vote among itself.

By the time Abbas realized this disaster was about to happen, it was too late to stop it. Fatah's fragmentation, combined with Hamas's strong campaign messages on corruption and its history of armed "resistance," made the unthinkable result of a Hamas victory suddenly very likely. In a desperate attempt to stop this political train wreck, one very senior Fatah official approached the Israelis and asked them to do something that would give the Palestinians an excuse to cancel the elections altogether. "He begged us to do something," recalls Dov Weisglass, Sharon's former chief of staff, who was then working for Olmert. "The best idea we could think of was to shut down polling stations in East Jerusalem, [which would] give Abu Mazen an excuse to cancel the entire election and blame Israel."[19] The senior Palestinian official liked the idea. Yet according to Weisglass, this initiative was rejected by the Bush administration, which was committed to its own agenda of spreading democracy in the Arab world. Weisglass blames the Americans for "telling the Palestinians in very clear words that they shouldn't even think about cancelling the election."[20] White House officials do recall Mohammad Dahlan, a rising star within Fatah and head of the security services in Gaza, leading the effort to postpone the elections. "Dahlan told the Israelis—but initially did not tell us," recalls Abrams, "that he had concluded the elections would be a disaster and must be delayed."[21] Yet this intervention was by itself, too little too late.

Running out of time and options, Abbas quietly prepared for a Hamas takeover of the Palestinian Authority's parliament. Years earlier, Arafat had been pressured into creating a constitutional court to act as a check on the powers of the presidency. Two days before the election, Abbas suddenly sent a note to the Palestinian parliament introducing several changes to the court, namely that the court would no longer be able to "oversee penal measures" against the president and limiting its jurisdiction.[22] In other words, the court was about to become essentially powerless. This was a clear sign that Abbas was preparing for defeat—and for a high-stakes power struggle.

◆◆◆

Nearly 20,000 election monitors turned out to watch 77 percent of the 1.2 million registered Palestinian voters cast their ballots in the West Bank, Gaza, and East Jerusalem on January 25, 2006.[23] According to monitors from the Carter Center and other groups, the elections were largely free and fair and were "considered to reflect the will of the people."[24] Their will, it turned out, had dealt a harsh rebuke to Mahmoud Abbas and his party.

When the final tallies came, it was as if an earthquake had devastated Palestinian politics. Hamas's "Change and Reform" ticket won 74 seats to Fatah's 45 in the 132-seat Palestinian Legislative Council.[25] Fatah not only lost a majority in parliament, it even lost in traditional stronghold cities throughout the West Bank, like Nablus and Tulkaram.[26] There was no silver lining for Abbas.

Fatah's loss can be attributed to two factors: failure to reform and an inability to unify. The first point was Hamas's rallying cry: *Fatah is corrupt, we are not.* The second point—Fatah's internal fragmentation—was ultimately the party's downfall. In many districts, Hamas didn't win a majority; it just won enough votes to beat the competing Fatah lists. "We lost thousands of votes because of the independents" says Qaddura Fares.[27] In Ramallah, Hamas gained over 130,000 votes to Fatah's nearly 115,000, yet independent candidates gained 85,000 votes that were essentially wasted.[28] All Fatah needed to do was win a few thousand more votes, and it would have won the city. Instead, Hamas took four of the five local seats, dealing a huge blow to Abbas in the city that was his de-facto capital. Similar results occurred in multiple districts across the West Bank and Gaza.

In a televised speech the night of the elections, Abbas attempted to do some damage control. "I am committed to implementing the program on which you elected me a year ago," he told Palestinians.

"It is a program based on negotiations and peaceful settlement with Israel."[29] Behind the scenes, his loyalists were in despair. The reasoning was clear: they had bungled it from the start. Abbas's own presidential campaign manager, Mohammad Shtayyeh, admits the party was fractured. "The worst part of that story is that Fatah ran against Fatah. For example, in Salfit [a town in the central West Bank] there were three lists for Fatah and one for Hamas, the three lists got 65 percent, the Hamas list got 35 percent and won, because the 65 percent was divided among three. There was no commitment from Fatah members to the lists of Fatah."[30]

Reformers and critics of Abbas within Fatah place much of the blame on the president. "Abu Mazen led us to this catastrophe," Shukri Radaideh, a Fatah member from Bethlehem, told the press, "He must now resign."[31] Ala'a Yaghi, a Fatah parliamentarian, also holds nothing back in blaming Abbas: "He was the leader of Fatah, and he was the only one culpable. He should have, and he must, taken those positions [to unify the party] that no one else could." Yaghi thinks Abbas should have threatened to expel members of Fatah who ran against the party: "It would have scared them and they would have changed their mind. I'm sure it would have affected [the outcome]. But he didn't make a decision."[32]

Mustafa Barghouthi, who ran against Abbas for the presidency in 2005, thinks Fatah felt no pressure to reform before the parliamentary elections. "The fact that Fatah won the presidential elections made them relaxed," says Barghouthi. "I think they did not have a clue that they were going to lose in the parliament. Had they had a clue, I don't know what they would have done."[33]

Hamas officials recall the 2006 elections with jubilation. "The hands of Fatah, the PLO, and the PA leadership were all tainted with corruption," says Mahmoud Muslih, a Hamas parliamentarian who won in 2006.[34] "The Palestinian public was treated in a contemptuous manner by these Palestinian security agencies. The Fatah militias—the so called Aqsa brigades and others—had side jobs in selling arms and other smuggling monopolies over businesses that created security chaos." Muslih thinks it was a simple choice for Palestinians: "When we put our side and their side on a scale and asked the people to choose, it was obvious who they would choose."

"The Palestinian people were familiar with Hamas's goals and strategies when they voted for us," Hamas leader Khaled Meshaal told a German paper a month after the election.[35] He also pointed to the PA's corruption as a major factor in Hamas's victory. "In the past, international financial assistance was used primarily to pay for the security apparatus and administration of the Palestinian Autonomous Authority," Meshaal explained. "It benefited a corrupt elite, not the Palestinian people. Hamas is in a position to use this money to benefit the Palestinian people, and both the Europeans and the Americans are aware of this."

Fatah officials contend that one of their failures during the election was their inability to separate the party from the PA in the mind of the public. "People who were accusing the PA of things were also accusing Fatah," recalls Yaghi. "We didn't defend ourselves very well. We couldn't separate ourselves from the PA."[36] Hamas officials enthusiastically agreed: "When we talk about Fatah we talk about the PA, and when we talk about the PA we talk about Fatah," says Muslih. "They're one and the same."[37]

Disassociating Fatah from the PA and enforcing party unity were clearly Abbas's responsibilities, but the election was also tipped in Hamas's favor by events that were well outside of his control. The 2005 Israeli disengagement from Gaza had strengthened Hamas's narrative that their path of violent "resistance" produced more tangible results than Fatah's pro-negotiations track. Hamas was able to point to actual results still fresh in many Palestinians' minds. "Somehow, in that moment, everything aligned so that Fatah was at its absolute weakest and Hamas was at its absolute strongest," says Hussein Ibish, a former senior fellow at the American Task Force on Palestine. "Hamas has never been stronger than in that moment, before or since."[38]

Fatah's defeat was a bitter pill for the Bush administration. The administration believed that, if given a chance, the Palestinian public would support more pragmatic forces in an election. Now, Bush was stuck with a result that proved the exact opposite and gave power to Hamas, a designated terror group. There was no chance, given Hamas's extremist ideology, that the Bush White House would cooperate with a government that included terrorists. "You had unanimity in the administration that these [Hamas] guys were bad news," recalls Robert Danin.[39]

Publicly, the White House tried to find a silver lining. "I like the competition of ideas. I like people who have to go out and say, 'vote for me, and here's what I'm going to do,'" Bush told reporters at a news conference two days after the elections. "There's something healthy about a system that does that."[40] Meanwhile, Secretary of State Condoleezza Rice remarked, "We still have every reason for hope and for optimism."[41] On the other hand, the White House was clearly in a bind. In the same press conference, Bush remarked, "I don't see how you can be a partner in peace if you advocate the destruction of a country as part of your platform."[42]

How would the United States proceed with Abbas? "Oddly enough," says Elliott Abrams, his failure caused the United States to "grip him more closely."[43] As Abrams puts it, "[Abbas] seemed to be failing as a leader, which is why he lost the election. But on the other hand, he's all we got. So we cling to him. We have plenty of doubts, but he's all there is."

For the Israeli government, the election results were a massive disappointment. The right-wing opposition, which was against the disengagement from Gaza, could now forcefully argue that Sharon's move had bolstered Hamas. Olmert, a new and untested prime minister, now had to deal with a major crisis on the Palestinian front just weeks after replacing Sharon. For the Israeli center-left political camp, Fatah's political weakness reinforced the difficulty of seeing the Palestinian Authority as a reliable peace partner. As one former Israeli general said at the time, "Americans, Europeans, and moderate Israelis like me wanted to believe that Abbas [and Fatah] were the sole representatives of the Palestinian people, but they were not."[44]

◆◆◆

In the weeks after the election, confusion ensued. How would Abbas, the president of the Palestinian Authority, react to Hamas controlling the PA's legislative body? How would Hamas, a radical Islamist group outside of the PLO and the traditional Palestinian body politic, respond to suddenly having control of the PA's parliament?

Not well. Within days of winning the election, Hamas leader Khaled Meshaal blasted Abbas: "Israel welcomed the coming of Mahmoud Abbas to power a year ago," Meshaal told the BBC, yet, "in spite of that, it did not negotiate with him, didn't take one step towards achieving Palestinian rights."[45] A week later, Meshaal was boldly challenging Abbas. "This is a message to Abu Mazen and other brothers in the [Palestinian] Authority to stop issuing decrees and decisions," he told reporters in Cairo. "We will not deal with them as legitimate."[46]

Abbas was in a panic. Yet rather than reassess and try to understand just how Fatah had lost, Abbas played the blame game and tried to consolidate as much as possible. "Everyone was in shock," says one of his former advisors, yet "there were no attempts at understanding why we lost. Nothing from the office of the president or within Fatah. Instead, the focus was on how to move the powers of the cabinet into the presidency."[47] Suddenly, the man of institutions and democracy in Palestine was not thinking about how to democratically reverse Hamas's gains, but how to preserve control over his institutions.

The electoral defeat was a perfect storm for Abbas. He had never been a grassroots leader of Fatah, had never led a militia nor had to cultivate support at the ground level in Palestinian politics. In losing a public mandate, Abbas didn't have the skills to convince the Palestinian people why he deserved their vote. What the lifelong bureaucrat wanted now was to simply maintain as much control over the government as he could.

In March, Hamas formed a new Palestinian Authority government. Fatah refused to participate in the cabinet, which meant Hamas dominated the ministerial positions. Fatah and its PA loyalists vowed allegiance to the president of the PA, Abbas. Hamas and its cadres pledged itself to the new prime minister of the PA, Ismail Haniyeh, a popular Hamas leader from Gaza. The stage was set for a showdown, and the international community immediately got involved. There was no way the United States would be able to support a government run by a terror group, so they withheld aid. Europe circumvented the PA by funneling cash directly into charities. Israel withheld tax revenues that it collected from Palestinians and was supposed to transfer to the PA.[48] The hope was to strangle Hamas and loosen its grip on power.

Hamas responded by playing to its base. Haniyeh, who grew up in a working-class family and continued to live in the same Gaza neighborhood where he was born, was the complete opposite of Abbas when it came to politics. His first act as prime minister was to turn down the $4,000 monthly salary his predecessor made in favor of $1,500—or what he referred to as just enough to support his family of thirteen children.[49] Hamas had campaigned on reforming Fatah's Palestinian Authority, and the pious Haniyeh was not going to let the people forget that. "We have no doubt we will succeed in shouldering our responsibilities and running Palestinian affairs," he declared. "The people who gave us their trust will not starve."[50]

Still, some Hamas officials wonder if they had prepared adequately for running a bureaucracy. "I think in that time we wanted to participate in the election but not form a government," recalls one former minister of the 2006 Hamas government, who spoke on condition of anonymity. "We were prepared to participate but not prepared to form a government."[51]

One of Abbas's former advisers recalls how Hamas dominated the media fallout from the negotiations: "After a meeting in Gaza, I look outside my office and see the media lined up everywhere. The Hamas delegation promptly goes out to speak so I say to Abbas, we should send a member to get our side of the story out there. His response was 'no, the media will write something biased against us.' So I say to him, 'okay Mr. President, they're going to write something biased against us, but at least we'll get our voice out there.'"[52] Abbas refused to listen, and instead of having a surrogate speak in front of the cameras, chose to release a written statement. The former adviser characterizes this behavior as part of Abbas's outdated "Soviet" style of politics: "There's almost a sense that *Pravda* is still the main source of information and satellite television doesn't exist. That shows you how he viewed the media. He has no appreciation for the more modern ways of conducting politics. It never permeated his thinking."

This tension and constant sense of competition, in turn, paved the way for violence between the two parties. "From the first day after the election, the clashes started," says a former Hamas minister. "I believe both Abu Mazen and Hamas committed mistakes in that time."[53] In May of 2006, policemen loyal to Abbas marched through

Gaza after Hamas deployed thousands of armed militants to the streets. That same month a Hamas cabinet meeting was broken up in Ramallah after Fatah gunmen encircled the building and fired guns into the air.[54] Then Hamas militants marched in the streets— followed a month later by Fatah gunmen setting a Hamas office in Ramallah on fire.[55] By December of that year, gunmen were shooting at PA cabinet officials' cars and lobbing mortars at PA offices in Gaza. A ceasefire was hastily declared after Hamas gunmen killed one of Abbas's bodyguards. A day later, the ceasefire collapsed after a street battle erupted outside of Abbas's house in Gaza.[56] The power struggle had moved from the ballot box to the streets.

Things got even worse in June of 2006 when a group of Palestinian fighters entered Israel through an underground tunnel, attacked an Israeli tank, and kidnapped an Israeli soldier, Gilad Shalit, whom they smuggled back into Gaza. Hamas demanded that Israel release hundreds of Palestinian prisoners in return for Shalit. Israel, in return, launched a massive military operation in Gaza. Then, the IDF effectively laid siege to the Palestinian coastal enclave, creating economic pressure on the local citizens in hope that they, in turn, would pressure Hamas to release the soldier—a policy bound to fail from the start. Instead of turning Gazans against Hamas, it created ever more anger toward Israel—and toward the Palestinian pragmatists in Ramallah who were cooperating with Israel while Gazans were suffering.

Shalit's abduction was bad news for Abbas: it further strengthened Hamas's image as the only Palestinian faction effectively fighting Israel and struggling for the release of Palestinian prisoners—an issue that holds great importance in the eyes of Palestinians. The ordeal was even worse news for Olmert, however. Two months after a lackluster electoral victory, he was now facing his first major security test as prime minister, and the public was not impressed with his performance. Two weeks later, things further deteriorated when two Israeli soldiers were taken hostage on the northern border with Lebanon, leading to thirty-four days of war with Hezbollah, the Lebanese-Shi'a terror organization centered in southern Lebanon. The war effectively killed Olmert's plans for a "second disengagement" in the West Bank. After Israel was attacked over the course of two weeks from two areas that it had unilaterally withdrawn from—Gaza and southern Lebanon—support for unilaterally withdrawing from the West Bank collapsed.

By the end of 2006, Abbas and Olmert were both politically crippled leaders, forced to abandon their own platforms. Abbas had won his election in 2005 promising to establish a state through negotiations with Israel, while Olmert had won a year later by promising to continue in Sharon's footsteps toward ending Israel's control over the Palestinians. Now, however, both lacked the public support necessary to carry out their promises. From this moment on, Abbas's ability to negotiate effectively was neutralized: making concessions to Israel while Gaza was under siege, Hamas was on the rise, and internal divisions were taking over Palestinian politics, was practically impossible. Abbas feared that any moves toward peace would make him look like a traitor in the eyes of many Palestinians.

Hamas saw an opportunity in Abbas's weakness. In January 2007, ahead of a routine trip to Gaza, the PA's intelligence forces discovered Hamas was digging a tunnel beneath the main road to Gaza City. Abbas's motorcade was supposed to use that road on its way to a meeting with Hamas officials. When the local security forces examined the tunnel, they found a startling cache: four large bombs.[57] Amid reconciliation negotiations, Hamas was planning to assassinate the top Palestinian official in the Palestine Liberation Organization, the party head of the largest Palestinian political party (Fatah), and the president of the Palestinian Authority.

"Everyone knew Hamas had their program and their plans to do all sorts of things," recalls a former PLO official, "but to actually have a plot to assassinate Abu Mazen when he visits Gaza, that really threw him off. Before that he was very democratic, [Abbas] was saying 'Hamas is part of our democratic makeup.'"[58] Now, everything had changed. "I know Abu Mazen changed from that moment onwards. He thought: 'if they have the capacity to do this, then I've been completely mistaken.'"

The assassination attempt was a rude awakening. "I think that's where he started to feel paranoid," recalls the former staffer.[59] From that moment on, Abbas would never return to the Gaza Strip. Ironically, he owes his life to a former Hamas official, who alerted him of the attack. PA officials discovered the tunnel after Mahmoud al-

Habash leaked recordings of Hamas officials discussing the attack.[60] Abbas would later reward al-Habash's loyalty. Today he is the PA's supreme Islamic cleric.

In February of 2007, Abbas and Mohammad Dahlan, his long-time rival within Fatah and the head of the PA's security forces in Gaza, flew together to Mecca to meet with Hamas's leaders Ismail Haniyeh and Khaled Meshaal. The Saudis wanted quiet in the West Bank and Gaza and were willing to offer their services as mediators. After three days of negotiations, the two sides produced a document known as the Mecca Agreement. They agreed to reconcile their differences and form a unity government headed by Haniyeh, with a member of Fatah as head of the internal security division.[61]

The document may have been promising, but nothing could stop the path Fatah and Hamas were on. No unity government or ceasefire could resolve the ideological differences driving the enmity between the two parties. The day-to-day operations of governing became impossible. "There was one meeting when I was in Ramallah and Haniyeh was leading the meeting via conference call [from Gaza] and he had to stop the meeting because there were a lot of shots coming at his office," recalls a former Hamas minister.[62] "And on his way home, Dahlan's men wouldn't allow Haniyeh to pass by a checkpoint." Indeed, the prime minister of the Palestinian Authority was not allowed to drive in sections of his territory. Said the former Hamas minister, "I think this is what escalated things to war."

The threat of a Hamas takeover had an unintended effect: it unified Abbas and Dahlan. Both the bureaucratic president and his strongman deputy, as much as they disliked each other, shared an interest in not seeing Hamas take control of the security services. Supported by the White House, Abbas and Dahlan concentrated much of their military power in the PA security bodies devoted to Abbas, including the Preventive Security Service.[63] A military arms race ensued. Hamas formed its own paramilitary brigade, the Executive Force. "We needed that force to maintain law and order," said Hamas's Muslih.[64] Yet by the summer of 2007, these competing armed bodies were in open conflict.

The first battle was in Rafah on the morning of Thursday, June 7, 2007. A gunfight broke out between Hamas forces and PA troops. In the ensuing skirmish, one fighter was killed and several citizens were wounded. By Sunday, clashes were so frequent that an Egyptian military delegation had to intervene to stop the fighting. Local human rights groups estimated that two fighters died and over fifty citizens were wounded.[65] The fighting only further escalated. Hamas forces took a twenty-five-year-old presidential guardsman in Abbas's service and threw him off a fifteen-story building in Gaza.[66] The next day, a Hamas activist was thrown off of a twelve-story building.[67] Things had reached a point of no return.

By Wednesday, June 13, Hamas had started to take control of PA security forces buildings. In southern Gaza, Hamas forces routed PA forces along the Egyptian border and took control of the Palestinian General Intelligence compound in Rafah.[68] On that day alone, at least seventeen Palestinians died. The total, in less than a week, was nearing a hundred dead.[69] The next day, Hamas launched an offensive and drove the remaining members of Abbas's presidential guard out of his compound in Gaza.[70] Looters entered and raided the compound before Hamas's military wing, the al-Qassam Brigades, could secure it.[71] By Friday, June 15, Hamas had clearly won. They captured Abbas's Gaza home, destroyed Dahlan's, and forced members of the PA's Preventive Security Service to flee via fishing boats.[72] Hamas was now in full control of the Gaza Strip.

In Tel Aviv, an emergency security discussion was organized in light of the dramatic events. Israeli intelligence agencies had been warning for months that Fatah was losing its grip over Gaza and that Hamas was showing more and more confidence on the streets, but almost no one had expected Hamas's takeover to be so quick and effective. One senior Israeli official called for intervention on behalf of the PA, explaining that, "We can't just watch this from the sidelines as if it's a [soccer] game between Arsenal and Manchester United."[73] The Chief of Staff of the Israeli military, General Gabi Ashkenazi, corrected the other official: "This is more like a match between Arsenal and Hapoel Ramle," a soccer team long-considered one of the worst in Israel. Eventually, however, Israel refrained from intervening except for opening its border crossings to allow Fatah and PA officials to seek refuge in the West Bank.

"We saw the process as it was happening," says Efraim Sneh, who was Israel's deputy minister of defense at the time. "Hamas was better equipped, better financed, and better organized. They caused a split within Fatah's forces. They isolated Dahlan's people, took care of them first, and then took care of the other Fatah people. If Israel had intervened, we could have stopped it."[74]

Five days later, US ambassador Richard Jones met with the commander of the IDF's Intelligence Corps, Major General Amos Yadlin, for a briefing on the situation. A summary of the meeting from the American side, published years later by WikiLeaks, includes the following sentences:

> Yadlin said the [Israeli defense intelligence] had been predicting armed confrontation in Gaza between Hamas and Fatah since Hamas won the January 2006 legislative council elections. Yadlin felt that the Hamas military wing had initiated the current escalation with the tacit consent of external Hamas leader Khalid Meshaal, adding that he did not believe there had been a premeditated political-level decision by Hamas to wipe out Fatah in Gaza. Yadlin dismissed Fatah's capabilities in Gaza, saying Hamas could have taken over there any time it wanted for the past year, but he agreed that Fatah remained strong in the West Bank.[75]

Yadlin, according to the document, also told Jones that Israel would be "happy" with Hamas taking over Gaza and Abbas declaring a separate entity in the West Bank "because the IDF could then deal with Gaza as a hostile state."[76] Sneh believes that this calculation was why the Israelis remained on the sidelines. Avi Dichter, a former head of Israel's Shin Bet, rejects that interpretation, insisting "It was bad for us that Hamas took over, but we couldn't have done anything about it without being dragged deep into Gaza's mud. That's the whole story."[77]

On June 14, 2007, Abbas dissolved the government and declared a state of emergency. In a speech to the PLO's Central Council, he blamed Hamas for everything. "[Hamas] formulated a plan to split Gaza from the West Bank and to establish an emirate, or a mini-state of extremists and religious fanatics," he told the PLO body. In this moment, Abbas's response to the takeover would dictate his policies for years to come: "There can be no dialogue with these murderers and putschists . . . We have reached a new juncture, and there is no point in calling for dialogues as in the past . . . There will be no dialogue with them under any circumstances."[78]

◆◆◆

In the months that followed, Palestinians struggled to understand just how Hamas had overthrown Abbas and Fatah in the Gaza Strip. "I went to a hospital and met with a Fatah fighter and I asked him how they lost," recalls a former minister at the time. "He just said, 'Hamas was faster than us.'"[79] Hamas was ruthless in its victory. Militants threw Fatah members off the roofs of buildings and engaged in "extra-judicial and willful killing."[80] Dahlan was out of Gaza during the war for knee-surgery (a former senior Israeli official believes this wasn't a coincidence, and that Dahlan realized in advance what was about to happen).[81] Abbas hung the defeat around his head, and Dahlan resigned from his post a month later. The two had quarreled in the past, but losing Gaza in 2007 would be the final straw for their relationship.

Fatah's security officials long understood conflict was inevitable after the elections. Soon after the results, they began warning the Bush administration that coexistence with Hamas was unlikely. In a State Department cable on February 24, 2006, the head of the PA's General Intelligence, Tawfiq al-Tirawi, told US officials that he thought Hamas's political wing would have little control over its military wing in the future, thus paving the way for violence.[82] Ten years later, Tirawi stands by his statements. "The cable is correct," says Tirawi, now a member of Fatah's highest body, the Central Committee.[83] In Tirawi's view, cooperation with a group so ideologically opposed to Fatah's was impossible: "There are people that want a homeland [Fatah], and there is another group that wants a universal program, they want to exploit religion for the sake of spreading their overwhelming authority over the world [Hamas]."

Other PA officials shared this view. Most think Hamas and Fatah were destined to battle, regardless of the elections. Ghassan Khatib, a political independent and minister of planning in the PA during that time, argues that the ideological differences made coexistence impossible: "I blame Fatah very much for the poor way of handling the election; however, I think there's room to argue that no matter what they would do, Hamas was going to take over Gaza in one way or another. Their approach is: the minute we're elected, we will change the system into the Islamic system, and the election we just won will be the last election . . . In my view, Hamas was going to try and take over Gaza regardless."[84]

However, some Fatah officials think Abbas abandoned the PA forces in Gaza before the fight against Hamas. "After the formation of the government by Hamas, the security agencies in Gaza started to weaken," says Yaghi. "Abu Mazen focused on strengthening the presidential guard and left the rest of the security agencies to suffer from lack of attention, arms, ammunitions, salaries, everything. They were living in a dire situation in comparison to the presidential guard. These organizations had to compete with the heavily equipped Qassam Brigades [Hamas] in 2007."[85]

Others accuse Abbas of wanting to lose Gaza. "Abu Mazen, in my opinion, wanted the coup d'etat in Gaza in 2007," says Haytham al-Halabi, a member of Fatah's Revolutionary Council.[86] Halabi echoes a consistent sentiment of the growing cadre of anti-Abbas Fatah members: that Hamas taking control of Gaza gave Abbas a convenient pretext for consolidating power in the West Bank: "He was weak and suffering from the perception that he was placed in his position by the Americans. So, he was fortunate with these two events [in 2006 and 2007], because he was able to gain the support of all the political parties and the Palestinian people because he was the alternative to Hamas and the coup d'etat plotters."

Zakaria Zubeidi, the Aqsa Martyrs' Brigade leader in Jenin who had hoisted Abbas on his shoulders during the presidential campaign, saw a similar convenience for Abbas: "Now Abu Mazen can go to the world and say: We want peace, on the West Bank everything will work out, and nobody will talk to Ismail Haniyeh and his people."[87] Yet, Zubeidi had a dire warning for Abbas: if the peace negotiations fail to produce, as Palestinians thought was the case in the 1990s, Fatah's armed cells could be spoilers for peace in the same way Hamas spoiled the Oslo process by launching terror attacks. "If

Abu Mazen doesn't make progress with peace, we haven't accomplished a thing," Zubeidi told reporters in 2007, "if we see that Abu Mazen is not succeeding, we can destroy him as a leader by means of terror attacks, exactly as Hamas destroyed Arafat through its attacks."

The first time Mahmoud Abbas lost Palestine was in 1948, when he, like hundreds of thousands of his people, was driven out of his homeland by war. As a founding member of the Palestinian national movement, Abbas dedicated most of his adult life to gaining it back. His rise to the position of president signified a temporary yet important victory for Palestinian refugees, who now had "one of their own" sitting in the highest office in Ramallah and negotiating the establishment of their future state.

In June 2007, however, Abbas lost Palestine once again. The civil war in Gaza and the ousting of the Palestinian Authority from the coastal enclave was a devastating setback. Rather than becoming the president of an independent Palestinian state, Abbas had effectively been relegated to a fate something closer to the mayor of Ramallah. Rather than unifying, Palestinians have spent most of the last decade fighting among themselves. Everything after the 2007 war has become either Fatah versus Hamas, Fatah versus independents, Fatah factions versus other Fatah factions, or some variation of all three. And ever since then, Abbas has presided over an increasingly fractured entity.

His response to the defeat in the 2006 parliamentary elections and the fall of Gaza in 2007 revealed more about Abbas's capacity as a leader than any event before or after. When politics becomes more than theoretical, Abbas stumbles. He was not equipped with the skill set to either stave off defeat in 2006 or triumph over Hamas in 2007. Abbas's post–civil war agenda has been focused on one thing: preventing Hamas from taking over the West Bank the way it did in Gaza. Abbas is not alone in this goal. He has been fueled and supported by the United States, Europe, and the Arab world, who all want him to remain in power. After 2007, political consolidation became the primary focus of his presidency.

CHAPTER 8

AN OFFER HE COULDN'T REFUSE?

2007–2008

In the early afternoon hours of September 16, 2008, Mahmoud Abbas arrived for a meeting with Ehud Olmert at the Israeli Prime Minister's official residence in Jerusalem. Olmert was in dire straits: just weeks before the meeting, he announced that he would soon resign from his post as a result of a corruption investigation. His party, Kadima, was scheduled to hold internal elections and choose his successor the day after his meeting with Abbas. But as Olmert greeted the Palestinian president at the entrance to his residence, none of that was on his mind. The meeting he was about to have with Abbas, Olmert believed, would go down in the history books.

Olmert and Abbas had met over thirty times before that day in September and had developed something of a routine in their meetings. At first, they would have lunch with a small group of senior aides. Then, as one regular Israeli participant in the meetings recalled, "Olmert would take out a box of cigars, put his hand over Abu Mazen's shoulder, and they'd walk together to Olmert's study, where they'd sit alone for another fifteen minutes, smoking and drinking espresso."[1] That routine played out once again, as the two leaders left their advisers in the main dining room and moved to a secluded office to talk privately.

When they were alone, Olmert surprised Abbas by laying a map on the table with his plan for the future borders of Israel and the state of Palestine. Abbas had never seen that map before. It included a Palestinian state on approximately 94 percent of the West Bank, with land swaps to compensate for Israel's annexation of a number of prominent settlement blocs. Essentially, it was the closest Israel had come in years to proposing a Palestinian state on land equal in size to the West Bank's entire territory.[2]

In addition to showing Abbas the map, Olmert also offered an unprecedented solution to the question of Jerusalem by suggesting international supervision over the Old City—meaning that neither Israel nor the Palestinians would have sovereignty over the holy area in and around Temple Mount. "It was the hardest moment of my life," Olmert recalled years later, in an interview with Israel's Channel 10.[3] Olmert, the former mayor of Jerusalem, was offering to cede Israeli control over the Western Wall, one of Judaism's holiest sites.

Abbas examined Olmert's map, saying only that it was "very serious."[4] He asked to have a copy of it, but Olmert refused. He said that he would let Abbas keep the map only if he agreed to accept it as the basis for an agreement. "I respected his will not to give it to us," Abbas explained in an interview in 2015.[5] What Abbas didn't respect, however, was Olmert's desperate request that he sign the map "here and now," allowing both of them to then present it to their respective publics as a done deal.

"Mr. President, I beg you, please put your initials on this map," Olmert told Abbas. "Let's make an agreement. Don't give up on this opportunity."[6] Olmert had a plan: it entailed both leaders flying together to the UN headquarters in New York in three days to enshrine his proposed agreement into a UN Security Council Resolution. "After that, we'll invite all the world leaders to come to Jerusalem and stand together," Olmert concluded.

Abbas was skeptical. "How could we sign something that hasn't been given to us and wasn't discussed?" he later explained.[7] Abbas asked for some time to think over the proposal. There were other details in Olmert's offer—issues such as refugees and security—that had to be discussed within Abbas's close circle. The two leaders parted ways with no agreement reached.

On his way back to Ramallah, Abbas asked his senior advisers to gather at the muqata'a for a briefing. What had just happened in Jerusalem was dramatic and deserved further discussion. Just a year earlier, Abbas had suffered the greatest humiliation of his political career in losing Gaza to Hamas. Now, if he accepted Olmert's offer, he would be on the verge of fulfilling the collective dream of his people: a Palestinian state on the 1967 borders, with East Jerusalem as its capital.

The hardest concession that Olmert asked of Abbas was to accept his proposed solution to the refugee problem, which included the return of a few thousand Palestinian refugees to Israel—a small and symbolic amount in comparison to the original Palestinian demand of allowing millions of refugees the "right of return." While that would be a bitter pill for the Palestinian public to swallow, Olmert's offer was forthcoming on many other issues and couldn't be dismissed outright.

As his aides peppered him with questions about the exact details, Abbas asked everyone to be quiet for a moment so he could draw up the map Olmert presented to him—as he remembered it—on a piece of paper.[8] The result wasn't as precise as the original, but it captured the essence of the Israeli offer.

According to Abbas's recreation of the map, Israel was supposed to annex three settlement blocks: one around the settlement of Ariel in the northern West Bank, another in the settlement suburbs of Jerusalem, such as Ma'ale Adumim, and a third in Gush Etzion, an area tucked between the 1967 border and the Palestinian city of Bethlehem. To compensate the Palestinians for these annexations, Olmert offered to give the PA agricultural lands in four regions of Israel that bordered either Gaza or the West Bank. In addition, Israel agreed to the construction of a highway between Gaza and the West Bank, which would run through Israeli territory.[9]

In Jerusalem, meanwhile, Olmert and his advisers were waiting for the phone to ring. With Olmert's official resignation looming in a matter of days, there was no time to waste. Olmert hoped Abbas would act quickly in convincing the Palestinian leadership to accept the offer. But when Saeb Erekat finally called the next morning, it wasn't to set up a meeting. Instead, Abbas's top negotiator informed the Israeli government that Abbas would be traveling to Amman that day for a prescheduled event, which was why any follow up meeting would have to wait.[10]

"I got a call that Abu Mazen forgot he needs to be in Amman on that day, and they asked to delay the meeting," Olmert recalled years later. "Ever since then, I haven't met with Abu Mazen again. I kept the map."[11]

◆◆◆

That meeting in September 2008 was the last one between Abbas and Olmert. It came after hundreds of hours spent negotiating together in what Abbas later called "the most serious negotiations" between Israel and the Palestinians since the signing of the Oslo Accords in 1993.[12] In subsequent years, both Olmert and Abbas declared in public that they came very close to reaching an agreement and that if it weren't for Olmert's early departure peace could have been achieved. Not everyone who was involved in these talks, however, agrees with that characterization. A number of prominent Palestinian, Israeli, and American officials agree that, while there was indeed a lot of goodwill shared by the two leaders, their respective political situations made it almost impossible to reach an agreement.

The process began in December 2006. The two weakened leaders—Abbas tainted by Fatah's loss in the election and Olmert by the war in Lebanon—met for the first time on a Saturday evening in Jerusalem, after weeks of failed attempts to organize such a meeting. "I kept sending him messages that I want to meet, and every time we'd get a call from Erekat saying—sorry, something happened here or there, and the president can't come to Jerusalem," Olmert recalled in a 2015 interview. "Eventually, we set up a meeting for December 23, but a day before, he called me to explain that he won't be able to come, because he had to urgently go to Gaza."[13]

Olmert, according to his own telling, replied to Abbas's cancellation with feigned offense. "Mr. President, I understand you've decided to insult me," he chastised Abbas. "You have a right to do so. But why are you insulting my wife? She's been on her feet for a whole day now, cooking the foods we were told you like to eat. What should I tell her now?"[14] This, according to Olmert, was what convinced Abbas—a notorious family man—to alter his plans and finally go to Olmert's residence in Jerusalem.

"I don't want to change the nature of your country," Abbas told Olmert when the two of them sat together for dinner the following evening. It was a reference to the "right of return" of Palestinian refugees, and it pleasantly surprised Olmert.[15] Abbas had an established reputation as a moderate leader, but even that had not prepared Olmert to hear such a conciliatory stance on refugees from the leader of the Palestinians. Indeed, Abbas realized Israel could never agree to be flooded by hundreds of thousands of Palestinian refugees in a future peace agreement. "He told me that on the refugees, he needed a gesture," Olmert later explained.[16] A gesture, unlike a full acceptance of "the right of return," was something Israel could, under the right conditions, definitely deliver.

Abbas and Olmert agreed to proceed with negotiations toward a final-status agreement, in which all the issues would be on the table. For Olmert, this was somewhat of a policy shift: he had abandoned his plans for unilateral Israeli withdrawals, and instead adopted the Labor Party's old negotiations platform. This new position was a result of the Israeli public's reaction to the Shalit abduction and the Lebanon war, which killed any support for further Israeli withdrawals without guarantees from the other side. Unilateralism was dead, but Olmert was still determined to end the Israeli-Palestinian conflict, and he would now try to do so through a negotiated agreement.

The two leaders agreed to appoint Ahmed Qurie and Israel's foreign minister, Tzipi Livni, as the heads of their negotiation teams. Olmert at first resisted the idea, asking Abbas if it wouldn't be better to keep the entire negotiations strictly between the two leaders—to which Abbas replied that, politically, he needed Qurie to be involved.[17] Qurie began meeting regularly with Livni, a former member of Likud who, over time, had gravitated to Israel's center-left camp. Yet despite the existence of this negotiation track, it was clear to everyone involved that the real negotiations were happening between Abbas and Olmert directly.

Throughout 2007 and early 2008, very little progress was made. Abbas and Olmert kept a friendly relationship for most of the time, but that was not enough to overcome their different positions and the obligations created by their dismal political situations. Abbas's ability to seriously negotiate a peace agreement—already limited following the 2006 election loss—took a huge hit after the Gaza coup in the summer of 2007. After suffering the worst political, and subsequently military, defeat in the history of Palestinian politics, Abbas and the Ramallah crowd found their ability to be flexible handicapped. Merely months after having their mandate halved, Abbas and his Fatah allies could not appear to their rivals and constituents to be too eager to make concessions.

"After one of the meetings, a number of advisers from our side sat down with Abu Mazen's staff and we did a follow-up discussion on what was discussed with the leaders," Tzipi Livni recalled years later. "At some point, the Palestinians said: 'Abu Mazen didn't agree to what you just said.' I immediately said: 'actually, he did.' So then the Palestinians asked: 'did he say yes?' I thought about it for a moment and said: 'he didn't, but he made a mum sound and nodded his head.' So Saeb Erekat said: 'that's not how he says yes, that's how he prays.' We all burst out laughing." Livni left the meeting with an important takeaway: Mahmoud Abbas always wanted to keep a degree of deniability: "For me, it was an important lesson about Abu Mazen."[18]

Back in Washington, former negotiators and current administration officials were still grappling with the repercussions of Hamas's takeover of the Gaza Strip. Veterans of the peace process, especially, were skeptical of any progress while the terror group controlled half of the Palestinian territories. "All this is a fantasy unless internal Palestinian divisions are healed," noted Camp David veteran Robert Malley.[19] "If you don't control the guns and a monopoly on force, people don't respect you," commented Aaron David Miller, a veteran Middle East expert in the Clinton and Bush administrations. "Will an Israeli prime minister make existential concessions to a man who doesn't control the guns?"

In the final years of his second term in office, Bush was desperately looking for palpable foreign policy achievements. The main pillar of his Middle East policy—the war in Iraq—was increasingly unpopular in the United States. Bush's foreign policy was viewed at home and abroad as creating a source of violence and instability across the region. In 2006, the White House commissioned the Iraq Study Group to analyze the war and the administration's wider Middle East policy. The group concluded that the "United States cannot achieve its goals in the Middle East unless it deals directly with the Arab-Israeli conflict and regional instability."[20] The prevailing takeaway, for the Bush White House, was the simple concept of "linkage": solve the Israeli-Palestinian conflict and dealing with the region's other maladies would become easier.

Inside the White House, a robust discussion erupted over just what to do regarding the conflict. On one side was Secretary Rice, who remained committed to promoting the peace process and trying to reach an agreement, despite Abbas and Olmert's sliding political standings. "In the early years of the Bush administration, the time had never seemed right for an international conference," recalled Rice.[21] But after the intifada, elections, and Hamas's takeover of Gaza, she was convinced that "Abbas needed an agreement with Israel." Bush, in Rice's retelling, "was immediately skeptical but not hostile to the idea." On the other side were a number of officials in Bush's National Security Council, most prominently Elliott Abrams, who saw very little chance of success in negotiations. "This diplomacy will not work unless and until the security situation improves," Abrams recalls telling Stephen Hadley, Bush's national security advisor. "Yet we're concentrating not on that issue but on the location, the banners, and the program for our conference."[22]

Bush, nearing the final year of his presidency, eventually chose to proceed with Rice's plan for an international peace conference. Just seven years prior, his predecessor had warned him against getting too invested in the Israeli-Palestinian conflict. Now, with two unpopular wars in Iraq and Afghanistan, Bush's own commission had concluded that solving the conflict would unlock broader stability in the region.

In November of 2007, almost a year after Abbas and Olmert's first meeting, the President's grand conference got underway in Annapolis, Maryland. Dozens of dignitaries from foreign countries, including a number of influential Arab states, were in attendance. The parties released a broadly worded text at the end reaffirming their commitment to ending the conflict and making "every effort to conclude an agreement before the end of 2008."[23] What followed that statement was something akin to theatrics. Everyone issued encouraging declarations, but mere weeks after the conference ended, it was clear that the peace process wasn't going anywhere. Abbas and

Olmert were both too weak to deliver actual concessions, and the Bush administration—despite its eagerness to solve the conflict—had bigger crises to address.

Still, Bush told the Israeli daily *Yediot Aharonot* two months later that he believed it was possible to reach a final-status agreement during the last year of his presidency. "I'm an optimistic guy," he explained, but offered no specific way forward to reflect that optimism.[24] Abbas and Olmert would continue holding their talks, yet over a year after they had started nothing concrete had emerged. Time wasn't on the side of any of the three leaders.

Ever since the 1990s, whenever Abbas was busy holding talks with Israel, so were his two longtime advisers, Hussein Agha and Ahmad Khalidi. During the Oslo years, they worked on the "Beilin-Abu Mazen" channel. Before Camp David, they were involved in an attempt to set up a secret channel in London. Now, as Abbas was talking to Olmert, the two London-based academics were again holding a quasi–back channel with a group of former Israeli officials, all of whom had ties to Olmert.

The meetings took place in Spain, under the auspice of the Spanish government. On the Israeli side, the participants were Giora Eiland, a former IDF general and national security adviser to Sharon; Yoram Raved, a prominent lawyer who was a close adviser of Sharon's and played an important role in the foundation of Kadima; and Gidi Grinstein, the head of a Tel Aviv think tank and a former adviser to Ehud Barak.

The meetings in Spain began in 2006 and were organized by Shlomo Ben Ami, Israel's former foreign minister, who was by then working for the Toledo International Center for Peace. Ben Ami wanted to help create a back channel where influential people close to Olmert and Abbas could trade thoughts, ideas, and perhaps also messages. That's how the group containing Agha, Khalidi, Raved, Eiland, and Grinstein came together.[25]

"We met every few weeks, usually for an entire weekend," recalls one of the Israeli participants. "After each 'round' of talks, we'd imme-

Palestinian leader Yasser Arafat shakes hands with Israeli premier Yitzhak Rabin at the White House with Bill Clinton in 1993. (*Vince Musi / The White House*)

Mahmoud Abbas and Yossi Beilin at the time of their back-channel negotiation: the Beilin-Abu Mazen Agreement. The details of this negotiation would leak shortly before the 1996 Israeli election. (*The Israel Internet Association via Pikiwiki, Dr. Yossi Beilin*)

Mahmoud Abbas, George W. Bush, and Ariel Sharon at the Red Sea Summit in Aqaba in 2003. Abbas's speech, in which he thanked the Americans and Israelis, would lead to Arafat calling him a traitor at home. (*Paul Morse / The White House*)

Ehud Olmert, Condoleezza Rice, and Mahmoud Abbas in 2 negotiations with Olmert "the most serious" since the days of Oslo. (*Matty Stern, US Embassy, Tel Aviv*)

Olmert, Bush, and Abbas at the close of the November 2007 Annapolis conference. The conference ended on an optimistic tone, but very little changed on the ground in the coming months. (*Chris Greenberg / The White House*)

Abbas and President Barack Obama in the Oval Office in May of 2009. Palestinian officials put great stock in the new president, boasting that Abbas was among the first to receive a call from Obama. Ultimately, Abbas would become disappointed with Obama. (*Pete Souza / The White House*)

Israeli premier Benjamin Netanyahu, US secretary of state Hillary Clinton, Mahmoud Abbas, and special envoy George Mitchell at a meeting in Sharm El Sheikh in 2010. The two leaders spent the next six years blaming each other for the stalemate in the peace process. (*US Department of State*)

Mahmoud Abbas and US secretary of state John Kerry meet in Bethlehem in March of 2013. Kerry launched his ambitious peace talks four months later. Abbas agreed to enter the negotiations but had very little hope that they would succeed. (*US Department of State*)

Obama and Abbas share a moment during their tour of the Church of the Nativity in Bethlehem in March of 2013. (*Pete Souza / The White House*)

By July of 2014, Abbas had walked away from a peace offer from President Obama, joined fifteen international organizations, and signed a reconciliation agreement with the terror group Hamas. John Kerry's hopes for negotiating an agreement had dissolved. (*US Department of State*)

Abbas and Kerry met again, in 2016, ahead of the UN General Assembly. Three months later, the United States would abstain on a UN Security Council vote on Israeli settlements. It would be the Obama administration's first abstention on a resolution involving Israel. (*US Department of State*)

Abbas, with his top negotiator Saeb Erekat and foreign minister Riyad al-Maliki, meet with Russian president Vladimir Putin in 2016. Abbas studied in Russia in the 1980s and was considered back then the PLO's point man to the Soviets. (*www.kremlin.ru; Licensed under CC BY 4.0 International*)

diately send a detailed report of the conversation to Olmert's office, as well as to Livni and to the head of the Shin Bet, Yuval Diskin."[26]

The Israeli summaries of the meetings usually left out the positions of the Israeli participants in the talks, instead focusing on what Agha and Khalidi were saying. "This wasn't a negotiation channel," explains one of the Israelis. "We didn't try to negotiate an agreement. These were informal exchanges of ideas. We spoke strictly for ourselves, and so did Agha and Khalidi."[27] The ideas offered by Agha and Khalidi, however, surprised their Israeli counterparts, as is evident by the summaries they sent back to Jerusalem.[28]

In a January 2007 session—two weeks after Abbas and Olmert's first meeting—the Israeli report quotes Agha and Khalidi warning that a peace agreement was very unlikely to come out of the renewed negotiations.[29] Gidi Grinstein, who was the Israeli side's "note taker" during the discussion, emphasized in bold letters that: "The Palestinian side doesn't believe Abu Mazen can lead a substantial agreement with Israel and is likely to fail in doing so."[30] Agha and Khalidi, according to their Israeli counterparts, warned that under the current political situation in the Palestinian Authority, it was impossible for Abbas to generate enough public support for a comprehensive peace agreement.[31]

At a subsequent meeting, the Israeli summary included this startling conclusion from Agha and Khalidi: "Abu Mazen can't [sign an agreement], even if he wants to. Any agreement will become an instrument for internal political struggle, and even a unity government with Hamas won't put aside the disagreements between Fatah and Hamas on diplomatic decision-making."[32]

Here were two close confidantes of Abbas—his most trusted secret negotiators, who had worked with him on the Beilin-Abu Mazen agreement in 1995—telling their Israeli counterparts that Abbas's political situation at home has made it impossible for him to sign a peace deal with Israel. To the Israeli participants, it was shocking to hear this while Abbas and Olmert were holding negotiations about a possible peace agreement.[33]

"The gaps on the final-status issues are wide and cannot be bridged at this moment," the Israeli minutes conclude after one of the meetings in late 2007, half a year after the Gaza coup. "But even if it was possible to reach an agreement between Israel and Abu Mazen, there is no one who can fulfill it on the Palestinian side."[34]

According to the Israeli summaries of the meetings in Spain, Agha and Khalidi explained that instead of trying to negotiate a final-status agreement, Israel should unilaterally, albeit gradually, withdraw from parts of the West Bank.[35] The term they used was "de-occupation," meaning a gradual handing of territories and responsibilities to the Palestinian Authority, including the evacuation of certain isolated settlements. This course of action, if carried out in cooperation with the Palestinian Authority, was "the only one that can succeed," Agha and Khalidi are quoted as saying in the Israeli summary of one of the last meetings of the back channel.[36] The logic behind their position was that an independent Israeli plan could skip over the Palestinian political constraints on Abbas and, if managed correctly, could even boost Abbas and the PA at the expense of Hamas.

This kind of plan was somewhat similar to what Olmert had presented to Israeli voters before his decisive victory in the March 2006 elections. It was also the founding idea behind Kadima, the political party created by Sharon after he decided to quit Likud. Yet by 2007 and 2008, Olmert was no longer sold on his own plan. The coup in Gaza, the war in Lebanon, and the Gilad Shalit abduction had dramatically lowered the levels of support for such a move within Israeli society. The Israeli right wing claimed that these events proved that any Israeli withdrawal was a dangerous mistake, while the left wing countered by saying that a negotiated peace agreement—like the one Israel signed with Egypt before evacuating all its settlements from Sinai—was always preferable to unilateral steps. The steps offered by Agha and Khalidi—according to their Israeli interlocutors—would become the road not taken in the Olmert years.

Back in Ramallah, Palestinian officials were worried about how much it would cost Abbas to enter into a new US-led initiative. "A lot of the talk at that time was on how Abu Mazen could go along with the Annapolis process and ensure something palpable came out of it so he could make a dent in the Palestinian people's skepticism," recalls an official in the PLO's negotiations department at the time.[37] Hamas was threatening Abbas's position at home, but they weren't alone. Other terror groups, like Hezbullah, had secured the release of 401 Palestinian prisoners years prior for the remains of three Israeli soldiers and a captured civilian.[38]

"This was one of Saeb's main talking points [at the time]," recalls the Palestinian official. "He'd say: 'I've been negotiating the release of Oslo prisoners for seven years and got nowhere, and Hezbullah abducts three soldiers in Lebanon and they get 400 Palestinian prisoners released. So how are Palestinians going to believe that violence doesn't get them results?'"[39] For Abbas, the risk of negotiating without getting anything was great: "This kind of tangible outcome does not escape the Palestinian public."

In May of 2008, Bush was scheduled to arrive to the region for his second visit since becoming president, and the administration was hoping that perhaps this visit could be used for finally creating a breakthrough. Two weeks before Bush's arrival, on Saturday, May 3, Rice came to see Olmert in Jerusalem, to discuss what could be done on the peace process front. Rice wasn't overly enthusiastic, but she did think both parties were "trying very hard." Olmert, however, surprised her by going beyond that and unveiling for the first time the peace offer he would later present to Abbas. "This is unbelievable," recalled Rice. "Am I really hearing this?"[40]

The next day, Rice took Olmert's proposal to Abbas. In a dining room next to Abbas's office, Abbas listened to Rice's relay of Olmert's proposal and "started negotiating immediately." Olmert had proposed to Rice a Palestinian capital in East Jerusalem and approximately 94 percent of the West Bank, with land swaps, but he was not willing to allow more than a few thousand Palestinian refugees to return. According to Rice, Abbas resisted: "I can't tell four million Palestinians that only five thousand of them can go home."[41] Still, Abbas was willing to meet one on one with Olmert.

Olmert's critics in Israel, from the right and left alike, point out that twenty-four hours before his meeting with Rice Olmert suffered a major blow when the Israeli police investigated him for the first time—and on very short notice—about one of his corruption cases. According to his opponents' telling of the events, Olmert basically understood on May 2 that his time in office had run out (he would resign four months later). Astonishingly, he rushed to present his far-reaching peace proposal to Rice, literally the next day.[42]

Olmert has strongly rejected this characterization of his meeting with Rice, claiming in a number of interviews over the years that he was preparing to present his peace plan to Rice long before his surprise investigation.[43] He has also hinted that instead of the police investigation being the reason for his sudden embrace of this plan, it was in fact his willingness to take brave steps for peace that caused his political opponents to conspire against him and bring down his rule. Abbas, in a rare public statement he made on the issue in 2011, seemed to adopt this version, stating, "History will reveal the truth about Olmert's disappearance from public life in Israel and the disappearance of agreements that Israel was supposed to sign."[44]

In August, three months after Rice first described Olmert's offer to Abbas, the Palestinian Authority president's spokesman denied that a serious offer had been presented to the Palestinians.[45] Instead of rushing to discuss the offer, both leaders took their time, for reasons that people close to them have failed to convincingly explain. Only in September, four months after Bush's visit, did Olmert finally present his map to Abbas in Jerusalem.

Throughout this period, the Palestinian leadership received mixed signals from the Israeli side. Senior ministers in Olmert's cabinet—according to Palestinian sources—told Abbas not to sign any deal with Olmert, since he was on his way out. "There was so much whispering in our ears by Israelis—Olmert is over, don't take him seriously, it's not going to be binding," recalled Erekat years later. "These messages had a great effect on us."[46] Rice wrote in her memoirs that these messages came from "some of Olmert's closest advisors,"[47] a possible reference to Livni, who strongly denies that she told Abbas to wait. "She may not have sent that message," recalls Abrams, "but they received it."[48]

Five days after he showed Abbas the map, Olmert officially resigned from his post as prime minister. Yet, according to Israeli law, he would govern the country for another five months, until the scheduled election—between Livni and a resurgent Benjamin Netanyahu—would determine his successor. It was during these five months that Abbas still could have given him an answer to his peace proposal and yet did not.

According to Abrams, when Abbas met Bush at the sidelines of the UN General Assembly that September, the President encouraged Abbas to continue talking to Olmert for the sake of making some sort of progress on the ground, but told Abbas that "there was no deal coming."[49]

Bush did try, however, to convince Abbas and Livni to both publicly commit to Olmert's peace plan. He even wanted Livni to run on it in the elections. Stephen Hadley, his national security adviser, told the *New Republic* in 2013 that Bush told Livni, "You'll never get to the right of Netanyahu, so you might as well run to his left with something to run on."[50] Livni, however, concluded that running on a platform that included the partition of Jerusalem and a return of thousands of Palestinian refugees into Israel would constitute political suicide. When she met Abbas two months later, they discussed some ideas about promoting the peace process if and when she became prime minister, but according to her account never mentioned Olmert's offer.[51]

Like Livni, Abbas also wasn't ready to commit to the Olmert offer. According to his explanation, it wasn't because he didn't like the offer, but rather, because his contacts with Olmert ended once the prime minister officially resigned. "Everything stopped," Abbas explained in a TV interview in 2015. "He was taken to serious investigations and we stopped talking. If the negotiations had continued for another five or four months, perhaps we would have reached understandings on all the core issues. After he [Olmert] left office, I didn't see him again. He left and we waited for somebody to be elected, and here we are."[52]

Though Livni received a plurality of votes, she could not form a coalition. Netanyahu could, and in February of 2009, he returned to power, exactly a decade after his election loss in 1999. Before the elections, Netanyahu made it clear that he would not commit to any offers made by Olmert during his talks with Abbas, and that under no conditions would he dismantle a single Israeli settlement in the West Bank. The Olmert years were over.

✦✦✦

Why did Abbas not respond to Olmert's offer? Was it a mistake to ignore it? Or was it simply an obvious, inevitable decision? What would have happened if he had said yes, flown to the UN with Olmert, and pronounced an end to the conflict? Both Palestinians and Israelis have starkly different answers to those questions.

On the Palestinian side, a clear consensus has emerged in recent years. As more details have leaked from the talks, Palestinian officials think Abbas made the right decision in not saying yes or no to Olmert's offer. Palestinians feel Olmert was not serious in his offer, and that had Livni succeeded Olmert she would have been able to negotiate a peace deal while actually enjoying a public mandate. "To us, Livni always came across as a much stronger leader than Olmert," recalls an official in the Palestinian negotiating office at the time. "Abu Mazen was careful . . . he wanted to know if this process was serious. So when he asked for the map, and Olmert said no, he knew this guy wasn't really serious."[53]

American observers are likewise skeptical of Olmert's offer. "By that point Olmert was manic, and manic for a reason: he was just about to lose his job," recalls former ambassador to Israel Daniel Kurtzer. "So the idea that he had told Abbas to just sign, and that he could only look at the map and then draw it on a napkin, was really quite ridiculous."[54] Aaron David Miller echoes this sentiment: "You had a set of conversations between Abu Mazen and Olmert, but these were not real negotiations that generated the kind of texts that led to agreements."[55]

In Israel, a different narrative of the Abbas-Olmert talks has emerged over the years. Right-wing Israeli politicians, chief among them Netanyahu, have used Abbas's behavior during the last months of Olmert's reign to claim that Abbas isn't a true partner for peace. "Abbas ran away from Olmert" has become a standard talking point for politicians from Likud.

However, Yair Hirschfeld, the Oslo negotiator who usually speaks very positively about Abbas, also says that the decision to ignore Olmert's offer was "a great mistake." He says that Olmert sent clear messages to Abbas that "he was willing to continue negotiating the exact details of the agreement." According to Hirschfeld, "Abbas had the choice to say—this part yes, this part no—but he chose not to do that."[56]

Others in Israel reject this interpretation and claim that it was ludicrous to expect Abbas to rush into an agreement with a prime minister who was essentially on his way to prison. Amit Segal, a prominent Israeli journalist, wrote in 2015 that "the Palestinian President acted wisely when he didn't accept the offers of the investigated prime minister. He understood that Olmert, like a general who has lost in battle, [was] moving imaginary divisions. He had no ability to pass such a far-reaching agreement."[57]

Mahmoud Abbas's true intentions are hard to know. His supporters and detractors can point to their own interpretations to support their own conclusions on Abbas. Yet a careful examination of the talks with Olmert reveals a simple observation about Abbas: like most world leaders, he is first and foremost a politician. His ability to take fateful and brave decisions is forever limited by politics.

At nearly every point in Abbas's life, when his political ideology was challenged by a political reality, he ended up submissive to the latter. In 1995, it was the harsh reaction from his peers to the Beilin-Abu Mazen agreement that forced Abbas to distance himself from his own agreement. Over a decade later, when Olmert proposed a new peace agreement, it was his weakness following the loss of Gaza—and Olmert's weakness after the loss of his mandate as a prime minister—that prevented Abbas from even responding.

Yet even if Abbas had said yes to Olmert's offer, his political reality is such that the proposed agreement would remain simply a hypothetical thought experiment for the half of his constituents who live under Hamas's rule in Gaza. Unlike Arafat, who could have theoretically signed an agreement and imposed it on the West Bank and Gaza, Abbas cannot.

This is part of the tragedy of Mahmoud Abbas. He ascended to the peak of Palestinian political power on a platform of peaceful negotiations and within two years had his legitimacy halved. The political price he would have had to pay for an agreement at the start of his presidency was suddenly insurmountable by the end of 2007.

The "Spanish Backchannel" revealed what the Israelis and Americans had failed to grasp at that point: the man who lost Gaza will find it almost impossible to sign a historic compromise on Jerusalem.

CHAPTER 9
BETWEEN BARACK AND BIBI
2009–2012

January first is typically a day of celebrations in the West Bank, as it marks the anniversary of Fatah's first-ever armed attack against Israel: an ill-fated raid on a strategic water facility in 1965.[1] The occasion is marked by parades and concerts in most major cities. The first day of the year 2009, however, brought Palestinians no reason for celebration. Instead, it was a day of grief, as a devastating war was raging in Gaza.

Officially called "Operation Cast Lead" by the Israeli military, the war began on the morning of December 27 when Israeli jets struck more than a hundred targets across Gaza.[2] The Israeli attack was not a complete surprise to observers. The situation in and around Gaza was very tense in the weeks leading up to the operation, with Hamas shooting dozens of rockets into Israeli towns and villages across the border. Still, the magnitude and swiftness of Israel's actions were unprecedented. Over the next three weeks, more than a thousand casualties were reported in Gaza, and over five thousand people were injured.[3] On the Israeli side, ten soldiers and three citizens were killed during the fighting, almost half of them by accidental friendly fire. "Cast Lead" was a clear demonstration of Israel's force—and of Hamas's failure to even compete with Israel on the same level.

Mahmoud Abbas could do nothing but look on helplessly from the sidelines. He issued a statement from the muqata'a condemning Israel's actions as "barbaric" and threatened to walk away from peace talks with the Jewish state, but his words were empty.[4] Both the Olmert government in Israel and the Bush administration in the

155

United States had just a few weeks left in office. No one was planning any bold moves toward peace in that short timeframe. "The
longer the conflict endures," wrote Palestinian political commentator Mohammad Yaghi, "the more Abbas will lose credibility among
Palestinians."[5]

Indeed, as much as Hamas was humbled militarily by Israel, its
fighters were still glorified among the Palestinian media and general
public. For Mahmoud Abbas, that was part of what made the war so
damaging. As Arab television networks across the region were broad-
casting wall-to-wall coverage of the war in Gaza, his American-trained
security forces were maintaining order in the West Bank by prohib-
iting Palestinians from carrying out terror attacks against Israel.

In Palestinian politics, a number of criticisms have haunted Abbas
for years. In the 1990s, it was the constant refrain that he was too
willing to compromise. During the Second Intifada, he was hounded
for his aversion to terror. Yet no accusation had hurt Abbas more
than his depiction by Hamas, and even by some within Fatah, as a
"collaborator" with Israel. It's one of the most sinister labels that can
be attached to a Palestinian figure, and if verified by a court of law in
either Gaza or the West Bank, can even lead to a death sentence. As
the body count was growing in Gaza, this was the adjective used by
Abbas's opponents to describe the Palestinian president.

Security coordination with Israel has always been a double-edged
sword for Abbas. It's deeply unpopular among Palestinians, but it
also is crucial to mitigating threats to his rule from groups like Hamas
in the West Bank. It is, essentially, a choice between popularity and
survival. Abbas has always chosen the latter, paying a steep price on
the former.

Abbas was well aware of this criticism gaining traction, which is
why he desperately wanted to stop the war. A former senior Israeli
official recalls how "[Abbas] kept sending messages to us that he's
afraid that Hamas will only get stronger as the war goes on and on.
He is always afraid that violence empowers Hamas, like it empowers
the right wing in Israel."[6] In the middle of the fighting, says this
senior Israeli official, "all the channels with him were shut down,
when he understood that his pleas aren't making a difference and
that no one is counting his opinion."

By the time a ceasefire was reached and the war was over on January 18, the damage to Abbas was already done. "The shaky legitimacy of Abbas's government in Ramallah . . . appears to have grown shakier still," wrote former PLO official and Palestinian academic Rashid Khalidi.[7] Hamas emerged from the conflict with Israel bloodied, but intact. That, in and of itself, was a victory for the terror group in the eyes of the people. Hamas officials could tell everyday Palestinians that they, not Abbas, were upholding Palestinian "resistance." Abbas looked weak and, to some Palestinians, even treasonous.

In Israel, meanwhile, Netanyahu was about to return to the prime minister's office after Olmert's resignation and Livni's inability to form a coalition. On the campaign trail, Netanyahu had touted his right-wing approach as a way forward. For Abbas, it seemed like things would only get worse over the next months. But then came a surprising phone call from Washington—and with it, a sense of new opportunities.

Barack Obama's victory in the 2008 US elections was greeted with excitement in the Palestinian Authority. Here was a president who was born to a Muslim father, spent time as a child in a Muslim country, and took part as a young politician in pro-Palestinian activities in Chicago.[8] Viewed from Ramallah, this was a possible advantage.

Yet even those in Palestinian circles with the rosiest views of Obama did not expect what happened in the waning hours of Thursday, January 21, 2009. It was Obama's first day in office, and when he began a round of calls to leaders around the world, among the first ones to receive a phone call was Mahmoud Abbas.[9] Obama wanted to discuss the situation in Gaza and to reassure Abbas that his administration would act quickly on the peace process.

The substance of the conversation was encouraging, but the fact that Obama had called Abbas on his first day in office was truly significant. Though American officials later insisted that Abbas was not the first world leader to receive a call from Obama, Palestinian officials still gloated as if it was the case.[10] Nabil Abu Rudeineh, Abbas's veteran spokesperson, proudly told the international press that

Obama specifically told Abbas at the beginning of the conversation: "This is my first phone call to a foreign leader and I'm making it only hours after I took office."[11] In Ramallah, the symbolic value was clear.

Palestinian negotiators have long questioned the United States's role as arbiter of peace talks with Israel. "The US has never been a reliable honest broker," remarked Fatah leader and former top nego-tiator Nabil Sha'ath in 2016. "It is a strategic ally of Israel. Period."[12] Having an American president seemingly so sympathetic to the Pal-estinians was a sign of change. Additionally, Abbas thought that Obama could perhaps also help him in his power struggle against Hamas. As Yasser Abed Rabbo explained at the time, "The speed of the call is a message signaling to all concerned parties that the Pales-tinian people has one address and that's president Abbas."[13]

Four months later, an excited Abbas came to see Obama at the White House. It wasn't their first meeting: the two had met in Ramallah during Obama's international tour at the height of the 2008 campaign.[14] The meeting on May 28, 2009, however, was their first since Obama entered office. Despite the fact that Obama was seen as a breaker of foreign policy traditions, much of his conversa-tion with Abbas was actually about continuity: he emphasized the importance of Bush's Road Map, which both Israel and the Palestin-ians had to implement, and also talked with Abbas about continuing a successful training program for the Palestinian security forces led by US General Keith Dayton.[15]

Abbas's arrival at the White House happened only a week after Obama hosted Netanyahu. That meeting was much more tense and uncomfortable. The main problem, at least in the eyes of Obama, was that Netanyahu refused to officially commit to the two-state solution, which wasn't mentioned in the platform of his government. Trying to downplay the importance of the peace process, Netanyahu instead offered a plan for "economic peace" with the Palestinian Authority.[16]

Obama was fine with enhancing economic cooperation, but he wasn't going to let Netanyahu shun the two-state solution as the basis for any future discussion. At his press conference with Abbas, Obama stressed the urgency of diplomacy from his perspective. "I think that we don't have a minute to lose," he said, "but I also don't make deci-sions based on just the conversation that we had last week. . . . Prime

Minister Netanyahu has to work through the issues in his own government."[17]

After being asked by a journalist if he had a specific timetable for the establishment of a Palestinian state ("President Bush hoped that you would have a Palestinian state by the time he leaves office. It didn't happen."[18]), Obama replied, "I have not put forward a specific time-table. But let me just point out, when I was campaigning for this office I said that one of the mistakes I would not make is to wait until the end of my first term, or the end of my second term, before we moved on this issue aggressively. And we've been true to that commitment."[19]

That commitment became clearer a week later, when Obama flew to Cairo and gave his first major address to the Arab world. It was arguably the most important speech of his first year in office. On the Palestinian issue, Obama's words were stronger than those delivered by Bush and Clinton. "America will not turn our backs on the legitimate Palestinian aspiration for dignity, opportunity, and a state of their own," Obama declared.[20]

In Ramallah, Palestinian officials were overjoyed at the new American tune. Abbas's spokesman called the speech "very encouraging," and a "new start and different American policy." Saeb Erekat, the chief Palestinian negotiator, similarly called it a "very important speech."[21] For the embattled PA officials in the West Bank who had just endured a surge in Hamas's popularity, an American president saluting the peace process from a neighboring Arab country was a welcome boost.

In Jerusalem, Israeli officials greeted the speech with gritted teeth. If, after his meeting with Obama in May, Netanyahu thought he would be able to drag his feet on accepting the two-state solution, Obama's speech made it clear that the road ahead would be difficult.

Cornered, Netanyahu took the stage at Israel's Bar-Ilan University eleven days later to deliver a speech of his own, in which he publicly accepted—for the first time in his life—the concept of a Palestinian state existing side by side with Israel. Netanyahu had privately discussed different plans for the partition of the land many times before, but his public position always remained steadfastly opposed to territorial compromises. The Bar Ilan speech marked an important change.

In his speech, Netanyahu offered a very specific formula, describing a desirable outcome as a "demilitarized Palestinian state side by side with the Jewish state."[22] While Palestinians could theoretically accept the first part of Netanyahu's equation—a demilitarized state that would not have an army—it was the second part that made his speech more of a headache than a relief. Netanyahu adopted a demand previously floated by Tzipi Livni during the Annapolis talks that under any final-status peace agreement the Palestinian side should recognize Israel as a "Jewish state."[23]

It's a demand that has vexed Palestinian negotiators for years. Saeb Erekat's internal memos in 2007 repeatedly complained that Israel's peace agreements with Egypt and Jordan included no such reference—yet Israel was presenting this demand to the Palestinians.[24] "I will never recognize Israel as a Jewish state," Erekat told Al Jazeera in 2014. "What the Israelis want me to do when I recognize Israel as a Jewish state, they want me to change my narrative, my history, my religion. . . . No force on earth will . . . make me change my narrative."[25]

One of the most influential people in Netanyahu's life was his father, Ben-Zion Netanyahu, an old guard Likud supporter who vehemently opposed any territorial compromises. Two days after the Bar Ilan speech, the elder Netanyahu told Israel's top-rated news broadcast that his son didn't actually mean what he said: "He put out conditions that they will never accept. Benjamin knows what he is doing."[26] Saeb Erekat seemed to agree: "[Netanyahu] announced a series of conditions and qualifications that render a viable, independent and sovereign Palestinian state impossible."[27]

Obama had appointed former senator George Mitchell, who was known for his involvement in the peace talks that yielded a successful agreement in Northern Ireland a decade earlier, to be his special envoy to the Middle East peace process. Jumping between Jerusalem, Ramallah, and Arab capitals, Mitchell made clear that America wanted to launch peace talks as soon as possible. His priority was getting Israel to halt settlement construction. In November 2009, Netanyahu acquiesced, and agreed to a ten-month freeze. The White House believed this would help create an atmosphere of trust between the two sides.

The stage was now set for another round of peace negotiations. There was only one question left to answer: would Mahmoud Abbas participate?

◆◆◆

Palestinian officials like to say that when George W. Bush was president he once told Abbas that the key to successful governing was a strong political base of support.

"I am strong because I have a strong party behind me," was the quote attributed to Bush by a number of Palestinian sources.[28] Whether or not the president actually said it, Abbas nevertheless took the advice to heart. That's why the question of his ability to reenter negotiations with Israel—this time, with Netanyahu holding power in Jerusalem and Obama sitting in the White House—was first and foremost a political one. After losing his parliament in 2006 and half his territory in 2007, Abbas couldn't take any risks. That was why, in the middle of 2009, he did something Arafat had never done in his time as president of the Palestinian Authority: he held a conference for Fatah.

Fatah conferences operate the way major political party conventions operate elsewhere in the world. Local branches are mobilized, delegates are selected, a conference is held, and a new leadership is elected or an existing leadership reconfirmed. In the case of Fatah, it's a seismic event: local elections for delegates become heated contests, Fatah cadres march in the streets, and candidates court allies and voters alike with promises and pledges. According to the party's bylaws, a conference is supposed to happen every five years.[29] Before 2009, however, the last conference had been in 1989.[30] Abbas, in other words, was about to convene the first conference since the creation of the Palestinian Authority in 1994. It was going to be his coronation.

Since Abbas's rise after the death of Arafat there had been a slight dispute within the Fatah party. On a purely technical level, Abbas ran in the 2005 presidential elections as Fatah's candidate for presidency. But while his control of the party was de facto, other leaders took swipes at his legitimacy. One of them was Fatah secretary general Farouq Qaddoumi, another cofounder of the party, who rejected the Oslo Accords and stayed in Tunisia after the foundation of the Palestinian Authority. Qaddoumi blasted Abbas at every turn and even prevented him from convening Fatah's highest body for a year and a half after Arafat's death.[31] When preparations for the conference got underway, Abbas made sure he would hold it in the West Bank, where Qaddoumi (and Abbas's other rivals) could not attend. In May of 2009, Abbas announced the conference would start on Yasser Arafat's birthday, August 4, in the West Bank city of Bethlehem.[32] Qaddoumi and the Fatah leadership abroad were out of luck.

"On the first day, the atmosphere was celebratory and Abbas was king," wrote a delegation observing the conference from the International Crisis Group (ICG).[33] Abbas opened the conference, held at a school near Manger Square in the heart of Bethlehem, with a long speech, admitting, "we have made mistakes," and vowing a "new start."[34] Then Abbas was confirmed as the *ra'is al-haraka*, president of the movement, by public applause. It was an election by acclamation, and a relatively new title: Arafat had been billed as the "commander-in-chief," but Abbas would simply be called the leader of the movement.[35] Some delegates were less than thrilled with the electoral process. "He became head of Fatah just through acclamation," complained Haytham al-Halabi, a Fatah leader from Nablus, "through applause only!"[36]

Abbas defended his platform of negotiations while also attempting to placate some of the militant members of his base. "It is the right of people to say . . . these negotiations are in vain, but there is still a glimpse of hope and we have to continue this way, for the interest of the people," he told the nearly two thousand delegates in attendance. "Although peace is our choice, we reserve the right to resistance, legitimate under international law. . . . We are not terrorists, and we reject a description of our legitimate struggle as terrorism. This will be our firm and lasting position."[37]

Having reaffirmed his stake as the movement's leader, Abbas then sought to rehabilitate the two largest organs within Fatah: the Central Committee and the Revolutionary Council. Long sidelined in the Palestinian Authority era, Abbas saw a benefit in revitalizing these bodies after the defeat in 2006 and subsequent civil war. The Central Committee, a body of twenty-two members, acts as the highest decision-making body within the group. The Central Committee approves or vetoes proposals from the Revolutionary Council, an internal parliamentary body with over a hundred members. When neglected, both bodies lack any real power; when activated and filled with loyalists, they add a weight and legitimacy to executive decisions. Abbas craved this legitimacy.

But filling the two bodies proved controversial. For one, numerous delegates accused Abbas of deploying PA presidential guard troops to the hall to influence voting. "The number of presidential guard troops were more than the number of participants," recalled al-Halabi. "They were looking over everyone's votes. They were telling people how to vote."[38] ICG reports that one delegate encountered a PA presidential guardsman pointing to a candidate on their ballot and saying this was "the president's man."[39]

Also irking delegates was the way the leadership bodies were elected. During the counting of ballots for the Revolutionary Council, Abbas abruptly ordered counting halted one day. "They were counting and started seeing some names that were not desirable for the president," recalls al-Halabi. "The next day they started counting ballots and we saw new names in there."[40] Those Abbas endorsed, including his negotiator Saeb Erekat and his campaign manager Mohammad Shtayyeh, found themselves newly-appointed leaders of Fatah. Those Abbas opposed, or neglected, found themselves out. Abbas also chose to settle an old score with Ahmed Qurie, his long-time deputy who became somewhat of a challenger to him in the Oslo years and now suddenly found himself out of the highest body in the party.

"He wanted Abu Ala'a (Qurie) off," recalls al-Halabi. "He worked really hard against him."[41] Qurie wasn't about to capitulate, either, insisting that "from the outset" the elections "did not meet the minimum principles of transparency." Abbas retorted that for "those who were unlucky in this election, that's democracy."[42] The two top negotiators in the Arafat era were still at each other's throats years after the Old Man had passed.

Still, other members of Fatah were happy with the conference. "I think the conference is some kind of rebirth for Fatah," said Jibril Rajoub, a member of the Central Committee.[43] Polls showed the Palestinian street largely agreed. Three months before the conference,

Fatah led Hamas in the polls by a margin of eight points (41 percent to 33 percent). A week after the conference, that margin had doubled to sixteen points (44 percent to 28 percent). Four months after the conference, that margin remained at sixteen points (43 percent to 27 percent).[44]

The 2009 conference was the beginning of Abbas's autocratic age. The civil war in Gaza sparked a paranoia in his mind, and that paranoia drove him to become obsessed with solidifying his control over the party and the West Bank. The Fatah conference was the perfect vehicle for him. It allowed him to play politics the way he preferred: quietly and behind the scenes. Through a combination of private dealings and public muscle flexing, Abbas was able to influence the balloting process in a way that favored his rule. From this moment on, Abbas's primary focus as president would be consolidating his grip on power.

A few days after the conference ended, Abbas took his newfound authoritarianism a step forward: he invoked emergency protocols within the PLO and ushered in his allies in a meeting of the body's parliament, the Palestinian National Council.[45] The purpose of this meeting was to appoint a number of Abbas's loyalists to key positions in the organization. Abbas made it clear: in the post–civil war political environment, there was no place for internal dissent within the PLO or Fatah.

Abbas's focus on consolidation of power would set him on a collision course with the other political forces in the West Bank. Chief among them would be the independents, including the prime minister of the PA, Salam Fayyad. The partnership between Abbas and Fayyad was, on its surface, one of the most successful in Palestinian politics: Fayyad was a respected economist, who had previously held senior positions at the World Bank and the IMF, before becoming the PA's finance minister when Abbas was prime minister. Fayyad held that role for three years, becoming a favorite of the Bush administration, both for his strong support of clean and efficient governance ("He really talked our language," recalled Elliott Abrams[46]) and for the fact that he held a doctorate in economics from the University of Texas, which endeared him to the Texan president.

Fayyad ran as an independent candidate in the 2006 legislative elections. During the campaign, he joined other political parties in portraying himself as different from the old guard of Fatah. He was initially rewarded by the Palestinian public, winning a seat in parliament. Yet after the civil war in 2007, Abbas needed Fayyad back in office, this time as both finance minister and prime minister. The Palestinian Authority was in a deep crisis, and Fayyad, with his strong contacts in Washington and his financial expertise, seemed like the right man to help Abbas pull it out of the mud. The problem was that Fayyad had no plans to simply serve Abbas's agenda. He strongly believed that the Palestinian Authority was in need of serious reforms, a notion that Abbas didn't necessarily support.

In 2009, shortly after the Fatah conference, Fayyad launched a bold new plan for preparing the PA for statehood. "Fayyadism," as *New York Times* columnist Thomas Friedman dubbed it in a flattering column, was "based on the simple but all-too-rare notion that an Arab leader's legitimacy should be based not on slogans or rejectionism or personality cults or security services, but on delivering transparent, accountable administration and services."[47] Israeli president Shimon Peres compared the Palestinian prime minister to Israel's founding leader, David Ben Gurion, who had insisted on building state institutions before actually establishing a state.[48] Fayyad unveiled his program on a Tuesday morning in late August 2009, giving it a clear and ambitious headline: "Ending the occupation, establishing the state."[49] The end goal was independence within two years, and the way to get there, according to Fayyad, involved a painstaking process of cleaning, reforming, and reorganizing key elements of the Palestinian government and institutions, so that when a final-status agreement with Israel was finally signed, the new "state of Palestine" would be ready.

Washington welcomed Fayyad's bold plan. The American consul general in Jerusalem, Jake Walles, called it a "concrete plan" and noted that Fayyad had produced a "lot of progress in the West Bank" already.[50] Inside Fatah, however, not everyone was as enthusiastic. Fayyad's plan meant, in effect, that corruption and nepotism—which were rampant and deeply ingrained in Ramallah atmospherics—would no longer be tolerated. Since the PA was founded by Fatah members in 1994 it had been a cash cow for senior party officials. In attempting to clean it up, Fayyad was on a collision course with the largest Palestinian political party—of which Abbas was the leader.

After Fayyad's plan came out, he and Abbas would feud frequently. Fayyad would threaten to resign numerous times in his tenure. As the United States and Israel grew to adore Fayyad more and more, Abbas began to view him as a threat. He would become so obsessed with his deputy challenging his rule that he would attack anyone associated with Fayyad's reform movement. At one point, Abbas ordered Fatah subordinates to protest against Fayyad's economic policies outside his offices.[51] In another instance, Abbas loyalists in his party published a letter calling on the president to fire Fayyad.[52]

The tragedy of Abbas's fight with Fayyad was that it echoed the very struggles he had had with Arafat a decade earlier, when he was prime minister and the Old Man stopped him from pursuing reforms for transparency and good governance. Now, when Fayyad was trying to do the same thing, Abbas resisted simply to stay in power. Palestinian civil society was starting to suspect another dictator emerging. As one frustrated Fatah member put it later, "We used to call Arafat a dictator, but compared with Abu Mazen, Arafat was a champion of democracy."[53]

As much as Fayyad and the disparate Fatah apparatchiks were a headache for Abbas, the biggest thorn in his side remained Hamas. In 2009 and 2010, as Israel was beginning the settlement freeze, Hamas was on the offensive in the war of public opinion. Having reclaimed the narrative as leader of the "resistance" following Cast Lead, the Islamist group was waiting for the right opportunity to deal a decisive blow to its rival in Ramallah. The opening for that arrived, unexpectedly, in October 2009.

Shortly after the end of the war in January 2009, the UN set up a "fact finding mission" to research the causes and repercussions of the conflict. The mission was headed by South African judge Richard

Goldstone, whose team worked for months before releasing a deeply flawed and controversial report in September of that year. The report accused the IDF of "grave breaches of the Fourth Geneva Convention in respect of willful killings and willfully causing great suffering to protect persons."[54] While Hamas was also criticized for "serious violations of human rights"[55] and shooting rockets into civilian areas in Israel, Israeli officials complained that, overall, the report was slanted against them. The fear in Jerusalem was that Goldstone's harsh conclusions would lead to international lawsuits against Israeli officers.

On October 2, the UN's Human Rights Council was expected to pass a resolution supporting the report's conclusions. Despite attempts by Israel and the Obama administration to stop the resolution from reaching a majority, it became increasingly clear that it would easily pass. That was why when the Palestinian representative to the Council suddenly announced that the PA wouldn't object to postponing the vote by six months an earthquake ripped through the diplomatic community and the Palestinian street. Why, asked many observers, would the Palestinian Authority resist an immediate vote on a resolution that would put Israel in diplomatic purgatory and possibly deter it from using force in any future conflict in Gaza?

Rumors gripped the Palestinian press in the ensuing days. One news agency reported that Israel threatened Abbas by informing him that if he didn't stop the vote from taking place, it would release a recording of him celebrating Hamas's losses during the fighting (no confirmation to this report was provided by any Israeli source).[56] A more serious report appeared in the Israeli paper *Ha'aretz*, detailing how the head of the Shin Bet, Yuval Diskin, told Abbas about a list of economic sanctions Israel would enact against the PA if it didn't back out of the Goldstone vote. One of those threats was to revoke the license of *Wataniya*, the second-largest telecommunications company in the West Bank in Gaza (and a firm with multiple reported financial connections to Abbas's sons).[57] One Palestinian source told the paper that Diskin's message to Abbas also included a more menacing threat: if the vote went through, Israel would turn the West Bank into a "second Gaza."[58]

Pressure from the United States also played a factor in Abbas's controversial decision. On the day the vote was supposed to originally take place, Saeb Erekat met George Mitchell in Washington, DC, where the American peace envoy asked him to "refrain from pursuing or supporting any initiative directly or indirectly in international legal forums."[59] Whether it was the American or Israeli pressure that ultimately swayed Abbas from supporting the vote on the report, the perception of outside influence hurt him domestically.

The response was harsh. Hamas officials made sure the Palestinian public knew of Abbas and the PA bowing to Israeli pressure. Some accused him of committing "national treason," while others demanded he "apologize to the Palestinian people."[60] Fatah members also agonized over Abbas's decision. "The consent to defer the vote had cost us dear," said one Fatah official, "we'll need years to fix this mistake."[61] Even the Arab-Israeli party Balad contemplated calling for Abbas's resignation over the affair, an unprecedented move in the relationship between Arab-Israeli politicians and the Palestinian Authority.[62] Indeed, Abbas was under fire on all sides. "Even the average man in the street thinks Abu Mazen has given up the rights of the victims and given up on pursuing Israeli war criminals," said Shawan Jabarin, a human-rights monitor in Ramallah.[63]

On October 7, Abbas changed course. The president "was misled," one Palestinian official told reporters.[64] Other officials apologized profusely, while Abbas announced the creation of a new committee to investigate the incident.[65] But that wasn't enough to satiate his rivals. Hamas's Khaled Meshaal pounded Abbas, accusing him of "saving Israel" by succumbing to American pressure.[66]

Eventually, Abbas had no choice but to make another push for the resolution, which easily passed on October 16. Only six countries—including the United States—voted against it.[67] The two weeks between the original date of the vote and the day it actually took place were a living hell for the Palestinian president. The timing of the Goldstone controversy was simply awful for Abbas, as it happened at the exact same time that Mitchell was convincing Netanyahu to accept the settlement freeze. This meant peace talks were much more likely to be renewed, and that Abbas would once again enter them from a position of profound political weakness.

On the Israeli side, the man Netanyahu put in charge of the negotiations was Yitzhak Molcho, his trusted personal attorney. Molcho was a veteran Netanyahu loyalist who had known Netanyahu ever since childhood and had been involved in talks with the Palestinians since his first term in office in the 1990s. Yet progress at these talks was scarce. The two parties mostly negotiated *about* negotiations, fighting tirelessly over the terms and conditions of the talks, instead of making progress on the substance of a possible agreement. And Abbas wasn't making things any easier: from the start, he declared that he wanted the talks to begin from the same point where he and Olmert had stopped their negotiations in 2008. Netanyahu refused, pointing out that Abbas never accepted Olmert's offer back when it was presented to him. He also accused Abbas of spreading incitement against Jews and refusing to recognize Israel as a Jewish state. It took nine months for the Obama administration to just get the two leaders to meet, and by that point Israel's ten-month settlement freeze had almost expired. Abbas and Netanyahu met a second time, under the auspices of the Egyptian government, in mid-September 2010, but once again couldn't overcome their disagreement about the most basic question: what the parameters for negotiations should be.

Israel's settlement freeze was set to expire on September 26, 2010. As the date approached, the administration made a last-minute attempt to convince Netanyahu to prolong the freeze by another two to three months, hoping that such a period of time would allow for a real breakthrough in the peace talks.[68] Netanyahu, however, was under pressure from the right-wing parties in his coalition to immediately renew building permits in the West Bank once the ten-month period expired. Abbas, meanwhile, was showing no signs of flexibility in the negotiations, making it easier for Netanyahu to reject the idea of prolonging the freeze. On September 26, the talks were officially over.

A year removed from the Fatah conference, Abbas's decision-making process had become entirely domestic. Every Israeli and American overture was met by Abbas with one question: *How does this impact my survival at home?* In the past, it had been one of several questions that Abbas asked himself. Now, it seemed to be the only thing on his mind.

✦✦✦

With 2010 drawing to a close, it was clear Mahmoud Abbas and Benjamin Netanyahu were not remotely close to reaching a peace agreement. Negotiations were moribund and Abbas was now demanding Israel reinstate the settlement freeze as a precondition for any resumption of peace talks. The Obama administration, while publicly refusing to give up on the issue, was forced to kick it down the list of policy priorities in the Middle East as the region erupted.

It started roughly 1,500 miles from Jerusalem, in the small Tunisian town of Sidi Bouzid, where a young fruit vendor named Mohammad Bouazizi lit himself on fire on December 10, 2010. After local authorities confiscated his goods and equipment and humiliated him in front of his colleagues, the twenty-six-year-old doused himself in gasoline in the middle of the road and in town and bellowed, "How do you expect me to make a living?"[69] Bouazizi's death inspired protests in Tunisia that soon engulfed the region with breathtaking speed. The protests in Tunisia ousted longtime leader Zine el Abidine Ben Ali the following month. Massive protests then erupted in Egypt, Syria, Yemen, Bahrain, and Libya. Tens of thousands of Egyptians took to Tahrir Square in central Cairo and within weeks toppled Hosni Mubarak, who had ruled Egypt for nearly thirty years.

Watching all of this from the muqata'a with a sense of trepidation was the embattled leader of the Palestinian Authority. Abbas had nothing close to the resources available to leaders like Ben Ali, Mubarak, and Qaddafi—after all, his own security forces hadn't even been able to hold on to Gaza four years earlier. If this could happen to such strong leaders, who had ruled their countries for decades with an iron fist, Abbas feared it could happen to him as well. Corruption and heavy-handed governance had brought millions across the Middle East out to the streets, and there was no shortage of those two features in Abbas's government.

One poll commissioned in March 2011 found that 92 percent of the Palestinian public sympathized with the protestors in what by then was being called the "Arab Spring." In the same poll, nearly 50 percent of Palestinians in the West Bank and Gaza felt there was a need for similar protests in the West Bank.[70] All of this spelled one word for Abbas: danger. Compounding his fear was the knowledge that if protests did break out, popular and influential news outlets like Al Jazeera would, in all likelihood, give the protestors a large platform (as they had in Egypt and Tunisia).

Abbas had a nominally positive relationship with the Qatari royals who owned Al Jazeera, but by 2011 the small but rich Gulf country had become more supportive of Hamas and other Islamist forces in the region. His suspicion of the Qataris and their news network was confirmed in January 2011 when Al Jazeera published the "Palestine Papers," a collection of over a thousand leaked documents from inside the Palestinian negotiating department. It was a bombshell. The Papers included emails, minutes, and negotiating materials from the PLO's Negotiations Affairs Department (NAD), all revealed to the Palestinian public for the first time. After years of opacity, Palestinians were suddenly given insight into the compromises the PLO had made on issues such as Jerusalem and refugees in past negotiations.[71]

For example, in one meeting in October 2009 between Erekat and Obama's special envoy for peace, Senator George Mitchell, the issue of refugees came up. "Palestinians will need to know that 5 million refugees will not go back," Erekat told Mitchell. "Also the number returning to their own state will depend on annual absorption capacity. There will be an international mechanism for resettling in other countries or in host states, and international mechanism for compensation. All these issues I've negotiated."[72] It was a stunning revelation from the top Palestinian negotiator. For years, Palestinian officials had told their publics that all, or most, of the refugees and their descendants from 1948 would be able to fulfill the "right of return." Now, here in negotiations with the top American official on the peace process, was the chief Palestinian negotiator dismissing the issue.

In another June 2008 meeting between Palestinian, Israeli, and American negotiators as part of the Annapolis process, Erekat again made a shocking concession, this time on Jerusalem. "It is no secret that on our map we proposed we are offering you the biggest Yerushalayim [Hebrew for Jerusalem] in history," he told Israeli negotiator Tzipi Livni.[73] Ahmed Qurie, in another meeting that month, elaborated on Erekat's comments. "We proposed that Israel annexes all settlements in Jerusalem except Jabal Abu Ghneim [also known as Har Homa, a settlement in southern East Jerusalem]," Qurie told

Livni. "This is the first time in history that we make such a proposition; we refused to do so at Camp David."[74]

The public feedback was overwhelmingly negative. "Abbas is in a very hot spot. He owes the Palestinians an explanation," Bassem Ezbeidi, a professor at Birzeit University in Ramallah, told reporters.[75] Saeb Erekat attempted to defend himself and called the reports "lies and half-truths," but that didn't stop him from offering his resignation (something Erekat has come to do once every few years, never actually retiring from his eternal role as Abbas's top negotiator.)[76] Yasser Abed Rabbo, the longtime member of the PLO's Executive Committee, accused Al Jazeera of engaging in "media games . . . to trick and mislead the simple citizen."[77] Many Palestinians were skeptical of the Abbas team's defense. According to polls at the time, the public was split almost evenly on whether or not the Palestinian negotiation positions were consistent with national goals.[78]

"One of the things that came out of the Palestinian Papers was the reality of the negotiations," says Nizar Farsakh, a former general director of the PLO's delegation to the United States. "As far as the Palestinians were concerned, negotiations were a black box. No one knew anything. Then they come out, and the way Al Jazeera portrays it, it looked like the most treacherous of activities."[79]

Abbas was at one of the lowest political points of his career. He needed to reinvent himself as a leader, and fast. Having lost his public mandate in the 2006 elections and the 2007 civil war, his credibility as a reformer in lashing out at Fayyad, and his promise to deliver for his people through the moribund peace process, it was hard for him to explain to the Palestinians why he deserved to be their leader.

The answer he came up with was based on an alternative policy that he unveiled in 2011. It was under preparation in the months and years leading up to the Palestine Papers scandal, but became more urgent once the scandal erupted. This new strategy was all about circumventing the peace process in favor of internationalizing the conflict.

The calculation was simple: shift the conflict to the international community by gaining recognition in international bodies. These symbolic recognitions abroad could translate to palpable support at home. Officially called "Palestine 194" in Ramallah, the plan was simple: get the international community to recognize the "state of Palestine" as the 194th member of the United Nations. Appealing to the various Palestinian parties fed up with the peace process, Palestinian officials had created a target list of organizations, conventions, and treaties to ascend to, in addition to seeking bilateral recognition from countries across the globe. "In terms of power," wrote a group of senior Fatah officials in a newly formed group, the Palestine Strategy Group (PSG), in 2011, "Arab, regional and international support [are] the main 'balancer' or 'equalizer' against Israeli military preponderance. . . . International legitimacy is in the long run a more potent force than military power."[80]

Palestinian officials envisioned the 194 campaign as the natural successor to the PLO's attempts to internationalize the Palestinian issue in the 1970s under the leadership of Arafat. In 1974, Yasser Arafat extended his hand (while reportedly holding a sidearm holster) during a speech before the UN General Assembly and warned the international community to "not let the olive branch fall from my hand."[81] Later, in 1988, Arafat again addressed the General Assembly, where the Palestinian mission was upgraded to the status of an "observer entity," marking a small moral victory.[82] In the late 1990s, when the Oslo process seemed to fall apart, Arafat once again toyed with the idea of deserting the peace process and pursuing unilateral recognition of a Palestinian state, but eventually was pressured by the United States to return to negotiations.[83]

Now, with the collapse of the 2010–2011 peace talks and protestors overthrowing leaders in the region, Abbas was in a corner. Under fire for the Palestine Papers and facing the prospect of angry masses in Ramallah, Abbas was ready to revive the international campaign. If Arafat had used internationalization as a threat, Mahmoud Abbas was going to use it as a means of survival. It would become his main justification for staying in power and his biggest political commodity to present to his people.

It was the ultimate tool for Abbas. The internationalization of the conflict enabled him to deflect public criticism from the PA, replace the peace process as a means of giving people hope for a better future, turn attention away from internal political problems, and create a "narrative of struggle" against Israel. He could do all this without resorting to violence, which Abbas still considered wrong and politically misguided.

The first thing Abbas did was accelerate a vote on Israeli settlements at the UN Security Council in February 2011. Cosponsored by over 120 of the UN's member states, the resolution called on Israel to cease "all settlement activities in the occupied Palestinian territory."[84] It was forceful language, and a direct challenge to Israel. The night before, Obama called Abbas and tried to convince him to halt the vote. "He said it's better for you and for us and for our relations," Abbas recalled.[85] Then, when Abbas refused to budge, Secretary of State Hillary Clinton called and did the same for a half hour. But Abbas wasn't about to listen to an administration he saw as unsupportive of regional leaders. Despite the administration's appeals, he was determined to move forward with the resolution.[86]

In the end, the United States defied the fourteen other Security Council members who voted in favor of the resolution and cast the first veto of the Obama administration. "Every potential action must be measured against one overriding standard: will it move the parties closer to negotiations and an agreement?" said Ambassador Susan Rice, defending the decision. "Unfortunately, this draft resolution risks hardening the positions of both sides."[87]

Even without the settlements resolution, however, Palestine 194 was well underway at that point. Abbas had launched the opening salvo in a broad, popular, internationalization campaign. What he had started at the Fatah conference in 2009 was sped up after the Arab Spring. He needed to present himself as proactive and revolutionary to both satiate his people and stunt any public criticism. This was the easiest and safest way for him to do so. Polls in 2011 showed 83 percent of Palestinians supported the leadership in going to the UN to obtain recognition of a Palestinian state.[88]

The 194 campaign gave Abbas something he had never truly enjoyed: near-unanimous political support. Rivals from just about every other political party supported him. So, in May 2011, he formally escalated the campaign in the pages of the *New York Times*.[89] He called on the international community to support his campaign, insisting it was genuine:

We go to the United Nations now to secure the right to live free in the remaining 22 percent of our historic homeland because we have been negotiating with the State of Israel for 20 years without coming any closer to realizing a state of our own. We cannot wait indefinitely while Israel continues to send more settlers to the occupied West Bank and denies Palestinians access to most of our land and holy places, particularly in Jerusalem.[90]

On October 31, 2011, shouts of "Long live Palestine!" rang out in French at the Paris headquarters of the United Nations Educational, Scientific and Cultural Organization, also known as UNESCO. The Palestinian Authority, in a step toward international recognition, had officially been accepted as a full member in the UN's body for international cultural exchange.[91] In Ramallah, the vote to grant them membership was seen as an endorsement of the 194 campaign. The PA's diplomat in Geneva declared that the Palestinians were looking "to move for full membership on the other UN agencies."[92] With newfound international recognition, Abbas turned his attention to securing a resolution on statehood at the UN Security Council. "We are going to the Security Council," Abbas had announced on television earlier that month. "We need a state, a seat at the United Nations."[93]

But getting one would prove too difficult in 2011. Shortly after the UNESCO vote, Israel withheld the tax revenues it collects (and then redistributes) for the Palestinian Authority, as it warned it would. With its budget cut, the PA hobbled toward the Security Council before it became clear that Palestinian allies on the council, including France, were likely to abstain on a vote.[94] Pressure from the Obama administration had taken hold, and after the Palestinians joined UNESCO the United States immediately cut funding to the organization. Abbas then called off the vote on Palestinian statehood at the UN Security Council.[95] He had failed, but he had set a precedent in the conflict: he could internationalize the Palestinian cause.

◆◆◆

Abbas's international diplomatic victories were first and foremost an attempt to strengthen his standing at home. The problem for Abbas was that for as much as his political allies and loyal state-media outlets cheered for his international "achievements," these were still largely just symbolic. Accession to UNESCO—and other such international organizations—were not going to change the reality on the ground for many Palestinians, and they were certainly not going to impact one of the more emotive issues in the Palestinian political psyche: the status of Palestinian prisoners in Israeli prisons.

This is where Hamas held a major advantage. In October of 2011, they reached an agreement with Israel to release Israeli soldier Gilad Shalit (whom they had captured in 2006) in exchange for the release of over a thousand Palestinian prisoners. To the obvious pride of his captors, Shalit became the most "expensive" Israeli prisoner of war in the country's history. The Shalit deal was especially humiliating for Abbas, since a number of the prisoners demanded by Hamas were either Fatah members or residents of the West Bank, individuals Abbas could not release himself. Hamas's message to the Palestinian public was clear: not only were they the only group who managed to get Israel to release over a thousand prisoners, they were even helping the weakened Fatah party "along the way."[96]

Netanyahu pursued the Shalit deal against the advice of a number of his most senior security and intelligence officials, who warned that the deal would embolden Hamas and weaken the more moderate Palestinian Authority. By signing the deal, Netanyahu also reversed his own positions: in the 1990s, he had penned a best-selling book urging leaders to not negotiate with terror organizations.[97] But politics changed that. One of the main reasons for agreeing to the Shalit deal, according to one of his top aides, was a wave of protests sweeping Israel over the state of the economy and the housing crisis, which drove hundreds of thousands of Israelis to the street. In Netanyahu's view, releasing Shalit was a way to satiate a rancorous public.[98] This deal would hurt Abbas's standing at home immensely, yet again.

Looking back, the four-year period between Olmert's offer in 2008 and the end of Obama's first term in 2012 was a long period of disappointments for Abbas. In these years, Abbas's response to the crushing defeat in the legislative elections and subsequent civil war with Hamas shaped his governing style for the rest of his time in office. These moments demonstrated both the limits and the extent of his power as leader of the Palestinians.

The Fatah line that the 2007 civil war actually *helped* Abbas because it allowed him to gain total control over West Bank politics only offers part of the truth. Abbas was able to focus on the West Bank, and indeed consolidate his grip on politics there in the 2009 Fatah conference, but, still, something had clearly changed during Obama's first term. Losing Gaza, coupled with the resurgence of Netanyahu and Abbas's increased disappointment with the United States, had shifted Abbas's priorities. Survival was now the sole goal of his rule—much more than peace and statehood.

Abbas now had only one option to remain relevant, and that was to double down on the international strategy. Faced with familiar rivals in Gaza and a longtime adversary in Israel, Abbas needed something to win back some modicum of public support. He had found it in the Palestine 194 campaign, but would it be enough?

CHAPTER 10
NEGOTIATOR NO MORE
2012–2014

"Where is George Bush?" Mahmoud Abbas asked, before cracking a wry smile. It was the winter of 2012, and a group of Israeli peace activists were visiting Abbas in the muqata'a. In the meeting, Abbas confessed that after almost four years of working with Barack Obama, he now actually longed for the American president's Republican predecessor. "We miss Bush," another Palestinian official present at the meeting explained to the Israeli guests, who were genuinely surprised.[1] On the surface, Obama was seen as more sympathetic to the Palestinians than Bush. Yet after Obama's failed attempt at peace talks in 2010–2011, the United States had effectively withdrawn, and Ramallah was disappointed. At least under Bush, Palestinian officials noted, Israel had accepted the Road Map and even dismantled some settlements.[2]

After the 2010–2011 peace talks collapsed, but especially after the Arab Spring engulfed the region, the White House had little incentive to invest much beyond rhetoric in the Israeli-Palestinian conflict. For Obama, there were just too many other crises in the region. Obama continued to talk about the issue—in May 2011 he even feuded with Netanyahu over a speech in which the president referred directly to the 1967 borders (with mutually-agreed land swaps) as the basis for a future partition of the land—but it was all talk. On the ground, nothing had changed for the Palestinians.

The Obama administration had reached the conclusion that both Netanyahu and Abbas were not ready for a final peace agreement, and that until they changed their minds—or were replaced—

there was no point in trying. For Abbas, this American withdrawal from the conflict was disappointing on one hand, but it also gave him a tacit green light to proceed with his internationalization campaign abroad, and to increase his consolidation of power at home.

As 2012 drew to a close, a wave of angry protests washed over the West Bank. Protestors hit the streets in Nablus, Bethlehem, and Hebron as they threw shoes at pictures of Prime Minister Salam Fayyad.[3] Corruption stories swirled on social media. Palestinians in Hebron and Bethlehem railed against the PA for soaring economic costs.[4] Fatah goaded some of these protests on; others were organic. Abbas needed to divert attention from his situation at home—and the easiest place to do so was the UN General Assembly.

On September 27, he announced that he had begun "intensive consultations with various regional organizations and Member States aimed at having the General Assembly adopt a resolution considering the State of Palestine as a non-Member State of the United Nations."[5] He promised the Palestinian public he would work hard to turn this statement into a reality.

Two months later, he delivered.

"The General Assembly is called upon today to issue a birth certificate of the reality of the State of Palestine," Abbas declared from the podium at the UN headquarters in New York.[6] A standing ovation ensued. Crowds watching the speech in Ramallah erupted. The date of the speech—November 29—was a highly symbolic one, since it was the date on which the UN voted in 1947 to accept the "partition plan," paving the way for the foundation of the state of Israel.[7] After Abbas finished speaking, the votes were counted: 138 countries in favor, 9 against (including the United States), 41 abstentions. Palestine was now a non-Member Observer State in the United Nations, putting it roughly on par in status with the Vatican.[8]

On the Palestinian Authority's official media outlets, jubilation ensued. Hundreds of Palestinians poured into the streets in Ramallah to watch Abbas's speech.[9] But for many Palestinians, the victory was symbolic yet sobering. "People here know that when they wake up on Friday they'll still be living under an Israeli occupation," remarked one reporter in the West Bank. "What they do hope is that when it comes to negotiations with Israel, the fact that Palestine might be able to refer Israeli officials to bodies like the International Criminal Court (ICC) could put pressure on Israel."[10]

Abbas's victory at the UN prompted condemnation from Netanyahu and his government, which called it unhelpful. In Tel Aviv, a few hundred left-wing Israelis hit the streets to call on the government to respect the resolution. Yet at the end of the day, nothing fundamentally changed on the ground. Dani Dayan, a prominent settler leader, observed that the view from his living room in the West Bank settlement of Ma'ale Shomron was exactly the same before and after the UN vote.[11]

A few weeks before the passage of the resolution, Netanyahu's government collapsed, and elections were called for January of 2013. A brief conflict with Hamas in November of 2012 had almost prompted an Israeli ground invasion, and Netanyahu campaigned on national security. His primary focus was on the dangers posed by Iran's nuclear program, while the opposition focused on the economy. The one issue largely ignored during the campaign was the peace process with the Palestinians. This was significant. In the previous three Israeli elections—2009, 2006, and 2003—a fierce discussion about the future of the settlements and the conflict had featured prominently. The fact that the Palestinian issue didn't enter the public discourse in 2012 underscored how distant the peace process seemed to everyday Israelis, and how little influence the UN resolution actually had.

Polls showed that Netanyahu and Likud were going to coast to a comfortable win on election day. Yet when Israeli voters went to the polls on January 22, everything changed. Likud received fewer votes than the polls had projected, and Netanyahu was now forced to forge a more centrist coalition with parties that were calling to renew negotiations with Abbas. One of those parties was led by Tzipi Livni, the former foreign minister under Olmert, who was now going to be Netanyahu's top peace negotiator. Suddenly, the peace process was back on the table.

Two months later, in March 2013, Barack Obama arrived in the region for his first presidential visit to Israel and the West Bank. At his side was his new secretary of state, John Kerry, who had long held a special interest in Israel. He saw Netanyahu as a personal friend (their relationship stretched back decades), and he had also met Abbas during his many years as a US senator. Kerry was also friendly with Saeb Erekat, the PA's top negotiator. To this day, Erekat likes to brag to Western officials about how Kerry (and Senator John McCain) "campaigned" for him in the 2006 Palestinian parliamentary elections, when he was running to represent his hometown of Jericho.[12]

As the newly appointed secretary of state, Kerry made it clear early on that unlike Hillary Clinton—who had stepped away from the Israeli-Palestinian conflict during her last two years in office—he planned to invest a lot of time and energy in it. "I believe the window for a two-state solution is shutting," he said. "I think we have some period of time—a year to year-and-a-half to two years, or it's over."[13] That's why, he explained, it was urgent for the United States to make another serious attempt at brokering peace, before it became too late.

All of that was lingering in the air when Obama came to Jerusalem and Ramallah in March 2013. "The decision to have Kerry come along was a big decision," says one senior administration official who was involved in organizing the trip. "For the president, Iran and Syria were the most important priorities [during the visit], but for Kerry, Israel-Palestine was. The president told both Peres and Netanyahu that 'John is going to spend a lot of time here.'"[14]

Abbas seemed to recognize this. In the press conference after his meeting with Obama and Kerry, Abbas praised Kerry's role: "I have renewed confidence that the United States, represented by his excellency President Obama and Mr. John Kerry, shall intensify its efforts to remove the obstacles ahead of the efforts to achieve a just peace."[15] He then thanked Obama for the United States' continued support of the PA, and asserted that "Palestine has taken long and additional steps for making peace," a clear reference to the 194 campaign.[16]

When Obama and Kerry met for dinner with Netanyahu at his official residence, Netanyahu told them he was willing to enter new negotiations with Abbas, as long as the Palestinian president would agree to do so without any preconditions. Abbas, however, was still demanding that Israel cease all settlement building before he entered any new talks. Obama's insistence on the settlement moratorium in 2009 had hamstrung Abbas permanently: he could not demand less of Israel than what the American president had demanded before.

Netanyahu told Obama that if negotiations were to start again he was ready to make the hard compromises necessary for a historic agreement.[17] "Netanyahu explained that he could agree to evacuate large parts of the West Bank so that a Palestinian state could be established, but argued that he could only do it in a slow and gradual process, over a number of years, perhaps even a decade," says a senior official with knowledge of the conversation.[18]

Obama was happy to hear the first part of Netanyahu's perspective, but not the second. "The American president is an impatient negotiator," explains a former senior Obama administration official. "First of all, because he's a president, these guys tend to think in four-year periods. So if Bibi wanted to have this spread across many years, the administration would be doing all the hard work but not getting the credit."[19] Still, despite the obvious gaps in how both sides viewed the timeline, Obama and Netanyahu agreed that Kerry would dive right into the process of restarting the negotiations.

Netanyahu, however, didn't merely agree to restart an official negotiation channel. He also offered to activate a secret negotiation channel between him and Abbas that had existed during the previous talks in 2010–2011. Dubbed "the London channel," it was a series of informal meetings between Netanyahu's lawyer, Yitzhak Molcho, and Abbas's longtime negotiating proxy, Hussein Agha. Netanyahu believed this channel could prove more successful than any kind of public and formal negotiations. Obama was skeptical, according to one of his former aides, but decided to give it a shot.[20]

As Kerry began his push for restarting negotiations, Abbas was in a bind. On the one hand, the longtime negotiator was naturally inclined to embrace new peace talks. On the other hand, he was still just as constrained domestically as before. So long as Hamas ruled in Gaza he could not legitimately say he spoke for all Palestinians. He also had a long history with Netanyahu, and he felt the Israeli leader did not embrace the existence of a sovereign Palestinian state in the West Bank. All of this came after his popular campaign at the United Nations. Thousands of his supporters had cheered Abbas's triumphant return from the UN General Assembly just months before, and now a new secretary of state was attempting to lure him back into unpopular peace talks.

Kerry forged ahead. He believed that Netanyahu's new government, in which Livni and another centrist politician—Yair Lapid—had a major presence, would be easier to negotiate with. In addition, Kerry told Abbas that, in his own conversations with Netanyahu, he had heard "surprising things" that justified new negotiations.[21] Abbas listened but remained skeptical. He had more experience than Kerry in negotiating with Netanyahu and wasn't sold. In addition, some Palestinian officials sensed that while Kerry was truly committed to working hard for an agreement, the White House was keeping its distance. In Ramallah, this was not seen as a promising sign. "I was in the White House when Obama told Kerry: 'John, lower your expectations,'" recalls Palestinian negotiator Mohammad Shtayyeh. "John then said: 'My expectations are in the basement.' [Obama] didn't empower his own secretary for this."[22]

Yet rejecting Kerry's initiative could cost Abbas dearly. His Palestine 194 campaign relied on international support. If Abbas turned away from a good faith, American-led peace effort, he would be sending a signal of intransigence to the international community, thus weakening the argument he was making that internationalization was necessary because he didn't have a partner in Israel. This reality left Abbas with only one choice. He agreed to restart the peace talks but insisted that they be limited to a period of nine months. If Kerry could elicit concessions from Netanyahu within that timeframe, all the better for Abbas. But if he could not, Abbas wanted an exit ramp that would swiftly take him back to the UN and the international arena.

Compounding the dilemma for Abbas was the fact that Hamas was steadily gaining popularity in public opinion polls, largely as a result of the Shalit deal. Polls showed that roughly three in every four Palestinians thought Hamas had triumphed over Israel in the prisoner deal.[23] At a time when Hamas was surging in popularity (that same poll found nearly 40 percent of Palestinians said they supported the group more after the deal), looking too flexible with the peace process could hurt Abbas even further at home. The Palestinian president candidly explained this situation to Kerry and insisted that in order to enter a limited period of nine months of negotiations he would need one major visible concession from Netanyahu, even before the talks got under way, since few on the Palestinian street believed he would get much from Netanyahu within the negotiations.

In his conversations with Kerry during the spring of 2013, Abbas raised three possible concessions. The first option was to have Netanyahu recognize the 1967 borders as the basis for negotiations. Abbas knew Netanyahu would never accept this, but he had raised it in Obama's first term and wanted it raised again. Similarly, he knew his second demand was just as unlikely: another settlement freeze. Netanyahu wouldn't find enough support for such a move, even within his own party.

Abbas's third demand was the most realistic one: a release of approximately one hundred Palestinian prisoners from Israeli jails, most of them veteran terrorists and fighters who had been detained since before the Oslo period. Abbas had one goal in this demand: competing with Hamas. The Islamist terror group had years prior secured the release of over a thousand Palestinian prisoners by kidnapping an Israeli soldier. If Abbas wanted to show Palestinians that peace talks were just as rewarding as terror, he needed to get prisoners released through diplomacy.

In one conversation with a senior American official, Abbas complained that "Hamas kidnapped one Israeli soldier and Netanyahu gave them a thousand prisoners for his release. My security forces have returned to Israel more than a hundred Israelis who wandered into our territories, and we got zero appreciation for it."[24] Indeed, Abbas's security forces had a policy of escorting Israelis who entered Palestinian cities and towns by mistake into the safe arms of the Israeli military. "If I behaved like Hamas, I could have a hundred Shalit deals by now—there would be no more Palestinians in Israeli prisons. But I choose to do the humane thing and get nothing in return," Abbas lamented.

Netanyahu, however, was constrained. "I can't get that through my cabinet," he told Kerry as soon as the secretary of state proposed the prisoner release.[25] For Netanyahu, the biggest problem was that some of the prisoners demanded by Abbas were Arab-Israeli citizens convicted in terror attacks. Netanyahu worried that their release could create a dangerous precedent. Yet four months after Kerry's visit with Obama, the political circumstances changed. Reports emerged that the European Union was about to restrict its government institutions from doing business with Israeli entities that operated beyond the 1967 lines.[26] This was bad news for Netanyahu, as it raised the possibility of international sanctions against Israeli settlements. Suddenly, a new round of US-sponsored peace talks seemed like a convenient way out for the prime minister.

Kerry, sensing Netanyahu's vulnerability, called the Israeli leader on Friday, July 19, and presented him with one last offer: Israel would release 104 prisoners from a specific list prepared by Abbas's office—including the Arab-Israeli ones; in return, Abbas would halt the Palestine 194 campaign while negotiations continued for the next nine months.[27]

Netanyahu told Kerry he could accept this offer, but then added two conditions of his own: first, that the prisoners wouldn't all be released at once, but rather, in four "batches" over the nine-month period; and second, that Israel would be able to continue building in the settlements during the talks.[28] He explained that this was necessary for him in order to maintain his coalition partners on the right. Kerry replied that the United States has always opposed new building in the settlements, but that he understood this was necessary for Netanyahu's internal politics.[29]

In their rush to cut a deal, however, Netanyahu and Kerry glossed over a major misunderstanding on the issue of the prisoners. Netanyahu left the conversation convinced that he and Kerry agreed on releasing only approximately eighty Palestinian prisoners from Abbas's list. Kerry, on the other hand, believed—and reported to Erekat—that Netanyahu accepted the list in full. Only a few days later—and after Kerry had declared the resumption of peace talks—did both sides realize the misunderstanding.[30]

A crisis ensued, with Kerry's staff frantically trying to figure out a formula that would allow both Netanyahu and Abbas to save face. Eventually, it was agreed that the Arab-Israeli prisoners would only be released in the fourth and final batch, and that their release would require a separate vote in the Israeli cabinet.

By the time talks were officially launched in the summer of 2013, Abbas had already won a major victory in getting Israel to release prisoners while not entirely abandoning the Palestine 194 campaign. The clock began ticking in August, when Saeb Erekat, Mohammad Shtayyeh, Tzipi Livni, and Yitzhak Molcho arrived in Washington for a series of meetings with administration officials. In his public appearances at the time, Abbas seemed pleased with his decision.

There was something strange about the John Kerry–led talks from the start. On the one hand, the American secretary of state set out with a highly ambitious goal: reaching a final-status peace agreement within nine months. On the other hand, in the meetings between Livni, Molcho, Erekat, and Shtayyeh, there was no sense of urgency over the looming deadline. The two sides' negotiators could go a week or even two without holding a single meeting. When they did finally sit together, Molcho and Erekat would spend hours discussing procedural matters instead of substance. Molcho, who was also talking to Agha secretly in the London channel, behaved as if the formal talks were unnecessary.[31]

The talks almost fell apart in November 2013 when Netanyahu released the second batch of Palestinian prisoners and partnered the occasion with an announcement of more West Bank settlement units. When the Palestinians publicly attacked the Israeli government for "poisoning the peace talks," Israeli officials claimed that Abbas knew in advance about the settlement announcements.[32] This claim was very dangerous for Abbas, and his associates forcefully denied it. Shtayyeh resigned from the Palestinian negotiating team, and Erekat threatened to do the same.[33]

The Kerry team's response to this crisis was to shift tactics in the talks. Rather than holding lengthy meetings between Abbas and Netanyahu's negotiators, Kerry decided to begin holding separate discussions with each side and later, if and when he had materials to work with, attempt to "bridge" the positions of the two leaders. The idea was that once some common ground emerged, the Americans could produce a framework document that would lay the foundations for a final-status peace agreement—based on the positions expressed by both sides in the separate conversations.[34]

Abbas and his advisers felt Kerry was prioritizing Israel's needs over theirs in a way that would leave them shortchanged once Kerry presented his "bridging document." Their doubts were primarily based on the fact that Kerry devoted much more time to speaking with Netanyahu than Abbas. At one meeting in December, Kerry was supposed to arrive in Ramallah accompanied by General John Allen, the senior US military officer responsible for creating a security plan for the day after the signing of the agreement. When Kerry showed up without Allen, Abbas asked about his whereabouts, to which Kerry replied that Allen had to stay behind in Jerusalem and work more with the Israelis.[35]

American officials who were involved in the talks don't deny the fact that Kerry indeed devoted more time to Netanyahu, but they reject Abbas's conclusions. According to their reasoning, it was important for Kerry to press harder on Netanyahu because if he could get Netanyahu to accept the idea of a contiguous Palestinian state in the West Bank, the negotiations would then enter what American negotiators would later describe as a "zone of a possible agreement."[36]

This didn't stop Abbas from believing he was being cut out. The Americans only realized just how angry and bitter Abbas was in February, when Kerry and Abbas met at a hotel in central Paris and the Palestinian leader "exploded" in a rant about how he felt Netanyahu was misleading Kerry into writing a document that would be heavily tilted in Israel's favor. The next morning, Kerry tried to convince Erekat that Abbas was too suspicious and that in his talks with Netanyahu he had been able to "move" the Israeli Prime Minister on a number of issues.[37] The Palestinians weren't convinced. Abbas wanted to see something concrete, and Kerry wasn't yet ready.

In his conversations with Netanyahu, Kerry was indeed seeing movement from the Israeli prime minister. Their top aides exchanged several drafts for Kerry's "framework document" and, by February, Netanyahu was willing to accept a document that stated that "[t]he new secure and recognized border between Israel and Palestine will be negotiated based on the 1967 lines with mutual agreed swaps."[38] In Kerry's eyes, this was one of his greatest achievements during the negotiations.

On other issues, however, Netanyahu wasn't willing to compromise. When discussing future security arrangements, Netanyahu insisted on a long-term Israeli presence along the Jordan Valley, which meant that Israeli soldiers would continue to be stationed within the borders of a newly established Palestinian state and would have authority to conduct raids and operations against terrorism there. Abbas was willing to accept this condition for a period of three to five years, but Netanyahu demanded more than double that period. An incensed Abbas replied, "Whoever proposes 10 or 15 years for a transition period does not want to withdraw."[39]

Netanyahu also told Kerry that he wouldn't accept a document that directly referred to a Palestinian capital in East Jerusalem. All the American attempts to find workaround language on this issue failed to convince the Israeli leader. The furthest he was willing to go was vague wording about "Palestinian aspirations" regarding Jerusalem.[40] Abbas, for his part, was having none of it. An American framework document that failed to even mention a Palestinian capital in East Jerusalem would be the end of him at home. As he ripped into Kerry in Paris in February, he made this fact abundantly clear.[41]

The next time Abbas and Kerry met was in mid-March of 2014, when the Palestinian leader arrived for a crucial two-day visit in Washington. Kerry's nine-month deadline was only a month and a half away, and this would be the last opportunity for Abbas to discuss the "framework document" together with the secretary of state and, more importantly, with President Obama. But the visit couldn't have gotten off to a worse start. At a lunch at Kerry's residence in Georgetown, the secretary of state asked Abbas if he would be willing to accept a scenario where Netanyahu delayed the release of the fourth batch of prisoners by a few days. Abbas replied that this was impossible, since it would hurt his credibility with the Palestinian public. This was the turning point for Abbas. In his mind, according to a close associate, he thought, If the Americans can't convince Israel to give me these prisoners, how will they ever get *them* to give me East Jerusalem?[42]

The next day, March 17, 2014, Obama met Abbas at the White House and made a last-ditch attempt to convince him to go along with Kerry's proposals.[43] Obama, unlike Kerry, hadn't spent the last several months negotiating with Netanyahu. This was evident when he presented to Abbas language on Jerusalem that was more forth-coming toward the Palestinians.[44] In Obama's version of the "frame-work," there was a clear reference to a Palestinian capital in East Jerusalem.[45] Including this with Kerry's framework document made it arguably the best offer the Palestinians had received from the United States since the Clinton parameters were presented in 2000.

"Don't quibble with this detail or that detail," Obama told Abbas. "The occupation will end. You will get a Palestinian state. You will never have an administration as committed to that as this one."[46] Abbas nodded but didn't give Obama a yes-or-no answer. Instead, he asked for more time to think. It was last time Obama and Abbas would hold a private meeting.

Abbas's reaction to Obama was one of the most telling moments of his presidency. In the face of the best peace offer the Palestinians had received in more than a decade, Abbas simply didn't reply. Just like Ehud Olmert, who in 2008 waited for a phone call from Abbas that never came, Obama waited for a few days to hear back from Abbas before coming to the conclusion that Kerry's attempt at reaching a peace agreement had ended in failure.

In Olmert's case, Abbas seemed to have a reasonable alibi: the Israeli premier was a lame duck without any public legitimacy. There was also a real chance that Tzipi Livni could replace him and then sign a deal with Abbas on the same or even better terms. This time, however, Obama made it clear to Abbas that the chances he would ever receive a better offer from the United States were slim. Pres-idents never have more flexibility to promote peace than in their second term of office—Clinton at Camp David, Bush at Annapolis—when they are free from electoral constraints. Abbas was saying no to an opportunity that would not repeat itself for years.

After the March 17 meeting, Abbas dragged his feet for another few weeks, during which it became clear that Kerry's nine-month deadline—set for April 29—was going to pass without a final-status agreement. Kerry shifted his focus from reaching a historic peace deal to merely extending the talks by another few months, but Abbas refused to prolong the talks before he got the fourth batch of prisoners—and Netanyahu refused to release them before Abbas agreed to prolong the talks. Abbas claimed this was a breach of the original understandings; Netanyahu explained it would be foolish of him to release the prisoners only to see Abbas return to unilateral steps at the UN a few weeks later.

Eventually, on April 23, Abbas signed an agreement—not with Kerry and Netanyahu, but rather with his rivals in Hamas.[47] It was a shocking development. Fatah and Hamas had conducted reconciliation talks off and on for years since 2006, but few observers expected anything more than talk. This new agreement called for an end to the bitter rivalry and the formation of a unity government. The Israeli government, in response, voted to withdraw from the peace talks—and with that, Kerry's peace process was officially over.

To some in the administration, Abbas's conduct in the last month of the talks was somewhat of a mystery. Why, they wondered, didn't he accept Obama's tweaks to the Kerry proposal? Had he said "yes" to Obama, Abbas would have put Netanyahu in an extremely tough spot. Ever since Yasser Arafat rejected Clinton's parameters in 2000 (which Israel accepted), the Palestinians had been viewed as rejectionists.[48] When Abbas ignored Olmert's offer in 2008, he reinforced that image. So, with Obama's offer, Abbas had a rare opportunity to say yes to a document that Netanyahu would have most likely rejected. Even if the talks then collapsed, such a scenario would have given Abbas a chance to change the international perception that the Palestinians were not ready for peace.

Even worse for Abbas was the fact that over the next months, leaked details from within the negotiation rooms seemed to suggest that Netanyahu had taken a surprisingly moderate position on some of the core issues.[49] Whether it was his verbal acceptance of the 1967 borders with land swaps, or his flexible position on the refugee issue (Netanyahu agreed that a limited amount, determined by Israel, would be allowed to enter Israel), Netanyahu gave Kerry more concessions than he'd given any other mediator before.[50] This doesn't mean he was ready for a final peace agreement—his position on Jerusalem, for example, was still a non-starter for the Palestinians—but by the end of 2014 Netanyahu was openly blaming Abbas for turning his back on the peace process after Israel had shown real flexibility, and some in the international community believed he had a point.

Abbas's confidantes responded to that accusation with two qualms. The first was that the Palestinian president didn't have a clear understanding of Netanyahu's concessions due to the lack of transparency on the American side. This was, in part, due to a dispute over just what Obama had presented. "Abu Mazen was never presented with a full offer in writing," says one of his associates. "If the Americans came to Netanyahu and talked to him in general terms about an agreement, without presenting the full document, would he say yes on the spot? Of course not. The Americans should have put down their document, but they kept negotiating over it with the Israeli side. Abu Mazen lost faith in them when he understood this was what was happening."[51]

The second is that they viewed Netanyahu's concessions as meaningless, since he insisted on adding Israeli reservations to any final document. These were problematic, because in the last months of 2013, when the Kerry process was stuck, the "London Channel," involving Yitzhak Molcho and Hussein Agha, was gaining steam—and Netanyahu's concessions in it were similar to the ones he later shared with Kerry.

Agha and Molcho began meeting in the British capital a few months after Netanyahu first proposed the idea in his March 2013 meeting with Obama. By December of that year, they were working together on a document that summarized the progress they had achieved in their conversations. Most of the concessions Kerry eventually managed to get out of Netanyahu (at least verbally) were rooted in Agha and Molcho's work: they agreed that the future border would be based on the 1967 lines (with mutually agreed land swaps) and that the refugee problem would be solved mostly within the future state of Palestine, with some symbolic gesture from Israel. The one issue they failed to agree on, however, was Jerusalem.[52]

Abbas's suspicion and mistrust at the American framework in February and March 2014 raised serious questions—both in Israel and the United States—about the true nature of the London Channel. It was strange that Abbas reacted so angrily toward an American document that had so much in common with the understandings his own negotiator had reached with Molcho in the back channel. Some Israeli officials began fearing that perhaps Agha wasn't truly representing Abbas in the talks.[53]

When the existence of the secret back channel between Abbas and Netanyahu was leaked to Israeli journalist Nahum Barnea in December 2013—at the height of Agha and Molcho's discussions—Abbas declared in a televised interview that "there is no secret channel with Netanyahu, and never was one." He added that the official negotiations led by Kerry's special envoy, Martin Indyk, were "the only channel of communication I have with Netanyahu."[54] Whether he meant these words or was simply using them to protect himself from internal criticism, one thing is clear: when Agha and Molcho's understandings were merged into the Kerry document, Abbas turned his back on them.

Mahmoud Abbas was clearly in a tailspin after his rejection of Obama's offer. In April, he threatened to dismantle the PA and simply quit. "I don't need Netanyahu. I don't need a chief of staff. Give me a junior officer or even a lieutenant and I will deliver the PA keys to him," a despondent Abbas reportedly told a group of Israeli parliamentarians. "Here you are, take charge and I will leave in an hour."[55]

After the 2007 civil war, Abbas had four policy options at any given point in time: negotiations with Israel, launching armed terror against Israel, reconciliation with Hamas, or internationalization at the UN. He had spent his time in office focused on the peace process and negotiations while ignoring the other three. When he walked away from Obama's offer in early 2014, he had only two options left. He could never bring himself to openly support armed terror, but he could try reconciliation and internationalization.

The weight of public pressure was starting to impact Abbas's decision making. The John Kerry–led peace talks had been the target of scorn and derision in Palestinian politics. Several political parties—including the Popular Front for the Liberation of Palestine and the Palestinian People's Party—held demonstrations in Ramallah demanding Abbas end the talks.[56] When he finally did, he found himself in uncharted territory: having public support. Indeed, the Palestinian street was genuinely supportive of Abbas's decision to abandon talks: in a poll taken that March, nearly 86 percent of Palestinians supported joining international organizations.[57] Bolstered by this, Abbas's Fatah party announced a unity agreement with Hamas in April.

Up to that point, Palestinian reconciliation between Fatah and Hamas had been a farce. A number of successive unity "agreements" had been signed in Mecca, Cairo, and Doha before the Shati agreement of 2014, named for the Gaza neighborhood in which it was signed.[58] Like every previous unity pact, this one called for ending the state of low-intensity conflict that dominated the relationship between Fatah and Hamas after the 2007 civil war. It also would result in the formation of a national coalition government.

The agreement meant that most of the PA's cabinet would resign in favor of a new, mutually agreed upon seventeen-member cabinet. The self-proclaimed "government of technocrats" would be unbiased (despite the obvious connections to political parties for several candidates) and charged with preparing for new elections.[59] It was an unprecedented step. Previous unity agreements had fizzled when words became actions, yet here was an ostensible coalition government. That Netanyahu's government openly criticized the move only made it more popular in Palestinian circles. "Mr. Netanyahu and his government were using Palestinian division as an excuse not to make peace," Saeb Erekat complained. "Now they want to use Palestinian reconciliation for the same purpose. This is utterly absurd."[60]

The irony for Abbas was that when he did what he had spent his entire life advocating (peace negotiations) he was punished in the public sphere, but when he changed to a new course (reconciliation and internationalization) he was cheered. In addition, Abbas perhaps missed the fact that one pillar of his new policy—reconciliation with Hamas—would soon come to damage the second pillar, internationalization. Gaining international legitimacy would be more difficult with a government that included a terror group. Hamas's inclusion in any Palestinian Authority government was a nonstarter for the United States and many international donors. By reconciling with Hamas, Abbas had given Netanyahu some powerful ammunition against him.

✦✦✦

In the months leading to the collapse of the 2013–2014 peace talks, John Kerry repeatedly warned the situation in the West Bank and Gaza was "unsustainable," and that in the lack of real progress toward peace, another round of violence would break out, sooner or later.[61] In the summer of 2014, just three months after the talks ended, Kerry's words seemed prophetic.

It started on June 12, 2014, when a Hamas cell in the West Bank kidnapped and murdered three Israeli teenagers. In the initial manhunt, the Israeli army arrested hundreds of Hamas members in the West Bank. Hamas's forces in Gaza responded with blind rocket fire into Israel. A few weeks later, Israeli extremists kidnapped and murdered a sixteen-year old Palestinian boy in Jerusalem. Meanwhile, rocket fire out of Gaza intensified. On July 8, Israel launched Operation Pillar of Defense in Gaza.[62] A fifty-day war of rocket and tunnel attacks, Israeli incursions, and thousands of airstrikes left over two thousand Palestinians and over seventy Israelis dead.[63]

Abbas was distraught. He had signed a unity agreement with Hamas only weeks before; now, the terror group had sparked a new war with Israel. The unity agreement had killed what remained of the John Kerry peace talks, and now he was technically party to Hamas's actions in the war. In short, he had misplayed his hand terribly. Polls during the war showed over 60 percent of Palestinians supported Hamas's position regarding a possible ceasefire, while only 15 percent supported Abbas.[64]

A week after the war started, Abbas appealed to the United Nations to place the Palestinians under "international protection."[65] A week after that, the Palestinian ambassador to the UN made a similar petition. "We call on the Security Council to adopt a resolution that condemns the Israeli military aggression against the Palestinian civilian population in the Gaza Strip . . . and calls for protection of the Palestinian people," pleaded Riyad Mansour.[66] For years, the Palestine Liberation Organization had billed itself as the "sole, legitimate representative" of the Palestinian people. Now, the PLO ambassador was asking for the international community to place them under protection.

When the war ended in late August of 2014, Abbas was politically wounded. Hamas had emerged from the war bloodied, but it was intact and surging in the polls. Thousands of Palestinians had marched from Ramallah to the Israeli checkpoint of Qalandiya in solidarity with Gazans in the middle of the war.[67] With no peace negotiations and a unity government on life support, Abbas now had to deal with a public sentiment that was very clearly swinging in favor of his rivals. In the face of such opposition, he doubled down on his strongman tendencies.

The peace process never recovered from the death blow it received in March 2014, when Abbas walked away from the White House without giving Obama an answer. It was the end of the road for Kerry's effort, but some veterans of Israeli-Palestinian negotiations saw it as even more consequential: the end of the road for any realistic chance to reach a final-status peace agreement, at least in the near future.

To those that hoped Kerry would succeed, one question kept lingering: Why did Abbas act this way? Why didn't he at least go back to Obama with a list of requests or reservations? The answer, quite simply, is that Abbas's hands were tied (in large part by himself) before he even entered the negotiations. His response to losing the election in 2006 was to sequester parts of the Palestinian Authority away from Hamas's control. His response to the 2007 civil war was to consolidate his grip on the West Bank and leave Gaza to Hamas. His response to everything since then was an extension of his desire to survive and stay in power. As his grip on power has tightened, his appeal to everyday Palestinians has waned. He is the master of his court in Ramallah, but of little else. This is not a position from which he could make the painful compromises necessary for a historic peace deal.

The Kerry talks were emblematic of Abbas's troubled domestic position. He could not deliver Gaza nor did he have the political skill set to publicly sell an agreement in the West Bank. His autocracy has therefore risen, which has simultaneously fueled his intransigence. Obama, it seems, was already aware of these problems following the disappointments of his first term. For Kerry, the revelation arrived only after his own attempt ended in failure in 2014.

CHAPTER 11
CLINGING TO POWER
2014–2016

On a cold night in December of 2014, a shocking rumor gripped the Palestinian public: Mahmoud Abbas had suffered a stroke and was incapacitated. No news agency could verify the details, but social networks were abuzz, and Abbas himself was nowhere to be seen. For a few hours, Palestinians speculated about what might lie ahead. Who was in control now? Who would succeed Abbas? What did this mean for the Palestinian national project?

The rumor was false, and in order to disprove it Abbas was forced to do something he very rarely did: walk the streets of Ramallah. With a full television crew in tow, Abbas marched through the city's commercial center, greeting shop owners and citizens alike. Many were surprised to see their president mingling on the streets. His health wasn't mentioned in most of the reports on his unusual fieldtrip, but everyone understood exactly what message he was trying to convey. One American journalist joked on Twitter that Abbas "went out to look at bread tonight to dispel rumors he had a stroke."[1] Within an hour, he was back inside the muqata'a.[2]

The uncertainty of that moment encapsulates the waning years of the Abbas era. With no anointed successor and little in the way of a second-tier leadership, no one knows for certain what the future holds for the Palestinian people after Abbas. The same is also true when discussing Abbas's legacy. What is his greatest achievement? How will history judge his failures? And what is the message he will leave behind to his people as they look toward a future without him?

When the reign of Abbas's predecessor, Yasser Arafat, was

entering its final months, the Palestinian public had a general idea of who would replace the Old Man. Arafat may have feuded with his deputies, even playing them off each other at times, but at least he *had* deputies throughout his career, and everyone knew who they were and that they could lead the movement one day. In the 1980s, the leading names were Khalil al-Wazir and Salah Khalaf, two founding leaders of Fatah. After both al-Wazir and Khalaf were assassinated, Abbas and Ahmed Qurie emerged as the leaders-in-waiting, both boosted by their roles in the Oslo process. Indeed, by the time of Arafat's demise there was a clear second-level of leadership within the Palestinian movement. None of that has existed under the rule of Mahmoud Abbas.

Rather than a handful of second-tier leaders waiting in the wings, there has been a plethora of third-tier politicians vying to position themselves for the post-Abbas vacuum. As David Makovsky, an American negotiator in the 2013–2014 talks, puts it, "I don't see any towering figure. I feel these guys are just strong enough to block the next guy, but not strong enough to take over."[3]

When everyone acts in their own self-interest, factions emerge, and when that happens, chaos typically ensues. Whether it's the streets of Nablus, where angry gunmen loosely affiliated with Fatah battle with the PA security forces, or the Israeli prison in which Marwan Barghouthi issues political edicts, or Abu Dhabi, where Mohammad Dahlan courts regional leaders and plans his rise to power—the longer Abbas avoids preparing for his exit, the more his rivals fuel the chaos.

All of this is wrapped under the uncertainty about what the actual succession process will be when Abbas vacates the scene. There are a number of scenarios if he does so willingly, but it's less clear what would happen if Abbas vacates his seat unwillingly, or, in other words, through a sudden death or illness. It is a source of anxiety in the minds of many Palestinians, who have watched their octogenarian leader endure multiple heart operations—including a heart catheterization procedure in October of 2016.[4]

In such a scenario, Palestinian Basic Law dictates that "the Speaker of the Palestinian Legislative Council shall temporarily assume the powers and duties of the Presidency of the National

Authority for a period not to exceed sixty (60) days, during which free and direct elections to elect a new President shall take place in accordance with the Palestinian Election Law."[5] This was what happened in 2004 when Arafat passed away.

The trouble with repeating that process today is that the speaker of the Palestinian parliament is a member of Hamas. Because of its electoral victory in 2006, Hamas has a majority stake in the parliament and, as such, control of the speakership. Were Abbas to die suddenly, the governing legal structure of the Palestinian Authority would give control over the presidency to Hamas. Palestinian law may mandate that the power is temporary while elections are prepared, but there are few within Fatah who think that Hamas would ever willingly give up control of the PA after gaining it in the first place. Furthermore, Israel and the United States would cut off funding and coordination with any Hamas-led Palestinian Authority.

Abbas's refusal to name a successor raises the possibility of the rise of the very rivals he wishes to sideline. Whether it's Marwan Barghouthi, Fatah's terror leader of the Second Intifada, who garners public acclaim from an Israeli prison, or Jibril Rajoub, the former head of West Bank security forces who commands respect from the security forces, or Mohammad Dahlan, the de facto leader of the opposition abroad who pumps money and guns into the West Bank and Gaza, Palestinians may not see a viable second-tier leadership, but they do see several cadres emerging who are jostling for position in the post-Abbas era.

This is, then, Mahmoud Abbas's legacy in Palestinian politics. Apart from the peace process or Palestine's standing in the world, what matters most is the state in which the Palestinian leader leaves local politics. Arafat bequeathed a united West Bank and Gaza to a leader of his own party in a timely and fair presidential election. Abbas will leave his heir with a divided Palestinian territory, a myopic Fatah party, and an emboldened Hamas. There is no guarantee the next leader will even be from Abbas's own party. Abbas began his rule of the Palestinian Authority with a sense of promise. He will end it as an autocrat.

◆◆◆

Since the collapse of the John Kerry–led peace talks in 2014, the evolution of Mahmoud Abbas from bureaucrat to despot has accelerated. The leader who has surpassed a decade in office is virtually unrecognizable to some who have known him for years. He falls asleep in meetings, regularly lashes out at his deputies, and even refuses to light his own cigarettes. Visitors to Abbas's office have been stunned to see the aging leader press a button on his desk to have an aide march in and light a cigarette for him. "It reminds me of Mubarak," commented one former senior Israeli official.[6]

In 2007, after losing Gaza, Abbas grew increasingly intransigent and paranoid. This transformation solidified seven years later during the Kerry talks. Abbas seemingly cares about nothing beyond staying in power in Ramallah now. His efforts are almost entirely focused on attacking his rivals and cracking down on domestic dissent.

In Palestinian circles, it's impossible to discuss Abbas's rivals without mentioning Mohammad Dahlan. The former protégé of Arafat, darling of the Clinton and Bush administrations, and head of the PA security forces in Gaza, has fashioned himself into the leader of the anti-Abbas opposition after falling out with the aging leader. "Abu Mazen lays siege to anyone who deals with Dahlan," says Ala'a Yaghi, a Fatah parliamentarian associated with Dahlan. "He won't give them money, the muqata'a won't facilitate their work, the security services won't deal with them. Basically, they treat us worse than Hamas."[7]

Losing Gaza was the turning point. Dahlan was long seen by Abbas and the old guard Palestinian leadership as a threatening upstart. Cozy with the United States and Israel and popular among the security services, Dahlan was almost instantly a threat to Abbas. When Gaza fell to Hamas under his watch in 2007, Abbas hung the defeat around his neck. Dahlan retreated to the West Bank, successfully forced himself onto the Fatah Central Committee at the 2009 conference, then suddenly found himself exiled by Abbas in 2011.[8] Abbas unleashed every tool at his disposal that year to marginalize him. He booted Dahlan from Fatah, issued a warrant for his arrest, and essentially chased him out of the West Bank.

Since then, Dahlan has made his home in the United Arab Emirates as the in-house advisor to the crown prince of Abu Dhabi, Sheikh Mohammed bin Zayan al-Nahyan.[9] From his perch in the wealthy emirate, Dahlan has raised money and positioned himself as the region's ambassador-for-hire. In 2015, he negotiated an agreement between Egypt, Sudan, and Ethiopia over construction of a dam on the Nile River.[10] That year, he was also reportedly involved in the negotiations with Libya's rebels.[11] Through his contacts, he even reportedly bought citizenship for his family and friends in Serbia.[12]

But, most importantly for Dahlan, he has slowly built himself into a leading opposition figure in Palestinian politics. He's poured money into the West Bank and Gaza, funding scholarships and mass weddings to increase his popularity on the street.[13] He's blasted Abbas regularly and courted his rivals, including Hamas and Islamic Jihad. In August of 2015, he called upon Abbas to include Hamas and Islamic Jihad in the broader PLO umbrella.[14] His wife regularly goes to Gaza and speaks on his behalf. Anti-Abbas rallies—sponsored by Dahlan—sprout up often in the Gaza Strip. One even featured pictures of Abbas in a noose.[15]

The aging leader is obsessed with Dahlan. During the 2014 peace talks, Abbas heard a rumor that Martin Indyk, the head of the American peace team, was seen sitting next to Dahlan at an international conference in Abu Dhabi. What had happened, in fact, was that Dahlan tried to approach Indyk and strike up a conversation with him, but Indyk—aware of how this could affect his dealings with Abbas— avoided Dahlan and told him to stay away. Yet for Abbas, the very fact that the two were seen together in the same room was reason for suspicion, causing a change in his attitude toward Kerry's chief negotiator.[16] Eventually, things were straightened out, but for the American negotiating team this was a painful example of Abbas's paranoia.

Dahlan, however, is not Abbas's only rival at home. He's just the only one out of the president's immediate reach. To oppose Abbas in the West Bank means subjecting oneself to his myriad networks of influence.

Take, for example, Salam Fayyad. Beloved by Washington and highly appreciated in Israel, the renowned economist was Abbas's longtime reformer. He was finance minister when Abbas was prime minister, and then became prime minister in Abbas's presidency from 2007 to 2013. Fayyad's two-year plan to build the transparent institutions necessary for a functioning Palestinian state was much-heralded in the West when it was launched in 2009. Yet Fayyadism, as foreign journalists liked to call his project of state-building, could never survive Abbas's political ambitions and paranoia.

When Abbas launched the Palestine 194 campaign in 2011, Fayyad refused to get on board. His job as prime minister was to raise donor funds to keep the Palestinian Authority afloat, a job made significantly harder if the PA was joining international organizations and thus complicating aid programs from the United States, which cannot give to international organizations that grant Palestine the same status as member countries. But Fayyad's opposition was rooted in principle. Fayyad believed that actually building state institutions was more important than celebrating diplomatic "achievements." Fayyad's objection was so strong that he broke his hand pounding on a table in one 2012 meeting.[17] By April of 2013, he had to go. He resigned as prime minister amid intense pressure from Abbas and his loyalists.

Abbas was not content with merely forcing Fayyad out of office. When the former prime minister set up a new nonprofit organization called Future for Palestine, Abbas immediately turned it into a target. The organization, which focuses on renewable energy and other developmental projects in the West Bank, had its funds seized in June 2015 by Abbas.[18] Abbas's justification: the funds had come from the UAE—reportedly under the supervision of Dahlan—and thus proved there was a connection between Abbas's two great rivals.[19] Abbas froze the funds until the courts stepped in and ruled the funds released. But the message was received loud and clear. Fayyad, once a close ally, was now being treated as a threat.

Yasser Abed Rabbo, a longtime member of the PLO's highest decision-making body, the Executive Committee, has also found himself under attack from Abbas. In the past, Abbas trusted Abed Rabbo enough to send him to secretly negotiate directly with Netanyahu. Yet in 2015, following reports of increased communication between Abed Rabbo and Dahlan, Abbas removed Abed Rabbo from his post as secretary general of the PLO's Executive Committee, technically the number-two spot in the organization.[20] Since then, Abed Rabbo, once one of Arafat's most trusted advisors, has been persona non grata in the court of Mahmoud Abbas. At one point, PA security forces even threatened to shut down the offices of a Western-funded pro-peace group in Ramallah that was affiliated with Abed Rabbo.[21] Only after foreign diplomats angrily called Abbas's office did he back down.[22]

Dahlan, Fayyad, and Abed Rabbo are but the most recognizable names. There are plenty more who have suffered Abbas's wrath. Whether it's Bassam Zakarneh, the labor union leader and former associate of Abbas who was fired from his post after leading protests in 2016, or Najat Abu Bakr, a member of Abbas's own party who revealed corruption among the upper echelons and was subsequently chased by armed thugs around Ramallah before seeking refuge in the parliamentary building.[23] In the words of Zakarneh, "This government has a dictatorial spirit."[24]

In January of 2016, the former independent presidential candidate Abdul Sattar Qassem insinuated on Palestine TV that Abbas should be executed for violating the "constitution of the Palestinian Authority."[25] Within days, he was arrested by Palestinian Authority security forces and thrown in prison. He spent several days in prison before the PA security forces insisted his arrest was not political but the result of complaints against him.[26] He was released a couple of days later, but the experience left a jarring impression on the public. "We don't have democracy here at all," complains Qassem; "our newspapers and media are one sided, they just talk about the great achievements of Abu Mazen and Fatah. The situation here is very similar to Arab regimes, the same dictatorship of the Arab regimes is applied here."[27]

Qassem is just one example. Whether it is Salim Sweidan, the owner of Nablus TV, who was arrested for four days for having run a story on the arrest of a Hamas cell in the West Bank, or Mohammad Abdullah Khibaysa, who was arrested for writing on the PA's reported financial corruption, Abbas's PA has increasingly cracked down on the press.[28] The Palestinian Center for Development and Media Freedoms, a watchdog group, reported in 2015 that PA violations against journalists went from a low of 28 in 2013 to 116 in 2015.[29] Indeed, in 2015, that same report found 60 percent of assaults on journalists took place in the West Bank—or, in other words, Abbas's government was more antipress than the government of Hamas in the Gaza Strip. Freedom House's 2015 report gave the Palestinian territories the rating of "not free," in part due to Israel's military presence in the West Bank but also to what the group called "arbitrary arrests, detentions, and assaults by PA security forces" of journalists who "covered politically sensitive issues or criticized the government."[30]

While the Palestinian press has found itself under assault, civil society has also withered under Abbas's watch. On February 23, 2016, thousands of Palestinians converged on Ramallah to protest poor conditions for teachers in the West Bank. According to the teachers' unions, the PA had failed to live up to an agreement signed three years earlier that would raise wages for teachers.[31] In response, the unions announced a strike and marched on Ramallah. According to one estimate, roughly 50,000 Palestinians attended.[32] Abbas's government was merciless in its response. The PA threatened legal actions against the teachers, arrested dozens of union leaders, and set up checkpoints across the West Bank to deter protestors from reaching Ramallah. In Hebron, masked assailants shot up a leading teacher's home, while others attacked a teacher with acid.[33] Palestinians pointed their fingers at Abbas. "The PA has gone crazy," one teacher told an Israeli journalist; "it and its security services are acting as if the people were the enemy."[34]

The teacher protests kicked off a wave of tit-for-tat reprisals. "The first step in implementing their dictatorship was to arrest me and my deputy in November of 2014," says Bassam Zakarneh, the former head of the union of public employees in the West Bank and Gaza.[35] "After that, they arrested 365 union members in two days. And then the PA outlawed the entire union." As the leading civil society figure in the West Bank, Zakarneh has since become a lightning rod of civil dissent against the PA. "During the teacher protests, they bribed the teacher union head with a position of ambassador to try to stop the protests," says Zakarneh. Indeed, Zakarneh says the PA fired that union leader and replaced him with a more cooperative proxy. "The teachers rejected this new leadership, and instead formed their own local unions in each school. The people want real representatives."

No sooner had the teachers' unions ended their strike than new protests rocked the West Bank, this time when Abbas unilaterally changed the PA's social security law. That March, he issued an executive decree changing the existing social security law to include both public and private sector.[36] Critics accused him of forcing companies and NGOs, many of whom had their own social security package, to instead pay into the PA's fund. Within weeks, an estimated ten thousand Palestinians took to the streets of Ramallah.[37] "When the government says they've reached an agreement, they lie," says Zakarneh. "The workers reject these agreements and take to the streets."[38]

In 2016, anti–Palestinian Authority protests sprouted in several Palestinian towns. In Tulkaram, protestors clashed with PA forces in August over access to electricity.[39] In Ama'ari camp, near the capital of Ramallah, clashes with PA forces have become regular.[40] And in Nablus's Balata camp, anti-Abbas sentiment has found a home.

Indeed, Nablus has become the epicenter of the movement against Mahmoud Abbas. In August of 2016, PA forces beat to death Ahmad Halawa, a popular local leader of Fatah's armed wing, the Aqsa Martyrs' Brigade. Accused of masterminding the killing of two PA security force members, Halawa was no man of peace.[41] But the intrafactional killing shocked Nablus residents, and his funeral quickly turned into a massive protest against Abbas and the PA. Roughly twelve thousand Palestinians took to the streets, chanting slogans against Abbas and the *sulta*.[42] A month later, another Palestinian was killed by PA forces.[43] At the funeral of Diyaa Araysha, anti-Abbas protestors took to the streets in Balata camp, chanting slogans reminiscent of the Tahrir Square chants that overthrew Hosni Mubarak in Egypt: "Balata wants the fall of the president."[44]

In Balata camp, the feeling of disillusionment with Abbas was quickly evolving into unrest. "When Abbas was elected, the most important theme at that point was the peace process. So we supported him in the political track, but we needed results and he didn't deliver," says one former member of the Aqsa Martyrs' Brigade in Balata, who asked to remain anonymous.[45] "We don't believe in anything anymore. We don't believe in Abbas. And even us, the sons of Fatah, are unable to believe in Fatah."

By any measure, Abbas has slowly lost touch with his people in the waning years of his presidency. Civil unions are the beating heart of Palestinian political society. For decades, unions have played a critical role in rallying Palestinian politics. Unions under the British Mandate organized riots against the British and Zionist forces, student unions formed the backbone for Arafat and his colleagues to organize Fatah, and unions were heavily utilized during the First Intifada's civil disobedience campaign. But under Abbas, civil society has withered. Rather than opening a dialogue with civil society leaders, Abbas treats them with an iron fist. "I don't think Abu Mazen is capable of dealing with internal issues. I told him I gave him a 0 out of 10 in dealing with internal issues," says Zakarneh. "And maybe this is part of his character. For example, he hasn't visited any of the governorates in years. He hasn't met with mayors or local leaders for years. Abu Mazen just does not have the skill to deal with the people."[46]

One thing seems certain, Abbas's governing style is a poor match to address the Palestinian public's demands. "I am certain that protests like the ones that took place in Nablus will happen elsewhere in the West Bank," insists Tawfiq Tirawi, a member of Fatah's highest body, the Central Committee, and Abbas's former head of intelligence. "The PA is conducting itself in a wrongful fashion."[47]

In Nablus's Balata camp, the former members of Fatah's armed wing sum up their views toward Abbas and the Palestinian Authority: "He disappointed me more than betrayed me," says one former fighter. "But the situation will explode. And once it does no one will be able to contain us."[48]

◆◆◆

Fueling Abbas's war on dissent in the West Bank is his constant battle with his rivals in Gaza, Hamas. The battle has sometimes turned political, as both sides have claimed national unity as a reason for patching up their old grievances. Since Hamas's violent takeover of the Gaza Strip in 2007, Abbas and his rivals in the Islamist group have danced the reconciliation dance ad nauseam. The 2007 Mecca talks led to a reconciliation agreement that was never implemented. In 2008, the two parties signed an agreement in Yemen that was never implemented. In 2011, the two sides reached another agreement in

Cairo, that also was never implemented. The following year, Abbas and Hamas leader Khaled Meshaal signed a reconciliation agreement in Doha that, once again, was never implemented. In 2014, the two sides formed an ostensible national coalition government, yet three months later, Hamas was at war with Israel and the unity government was an afterthought. In June of 2016, Abbas's PA announced it would hold municipal elections in the West Bank and Gaza. A month later, Hamas said they would participate. By September of that year, the PA's Supreme Court had ruled the elections would take place in the Fatah-dominated West Bank only. In October, the elections were postponed indefinitely.[49]

If there was ever a thought that Abbas's Fatah could coexist politically with Hamas, the fact that they could not even agree to hold city council elections together should have effectively ended that dream. Palestinians, though demanding unity between the two largest political parties, have rarely thought it possible. "If they could cohabitate, the several attempts at cohabitation would have worked by now," says Hussein Ibish, a former senior fellow at the Washington, DC–based American Task Force on Palestine. "If you disagree about every aspect of society, I don't see where there's room [to live] together."[50] Blame can be laid on both parties, who view the other's gain at their expense, but for Abbas, especially, there is little room for coexistence with Hamas.

"Hamas is an opponent who will not allow someone from Fatah to be president [after Abbas]," says Tirawi. "There are some Fatah leaders who believe reconciling with Hamas will bring them to the president's seat [when Abbas is gone]. I tell you they are wrong. Reconciliation with them is impossible."[51] Tirawi's viewpoint is rooted in a belief within the upper echelons of the movement that the two sides' fundamentally divergent ideologies prevent them from ever cooperating. "There are people that want a homeland, Fatah, and there is another group that wants a universal program, Hamas," continues Tirawi; "they want to exploit religion for the sake of spreading their overwhelming authority over the world."

If Hamas cannot be reconciled with, then opposing them is Abbas's only option. In close coordination with the Israeli army, Abbas's PA forces have broken up Hamas cells in the West Bank and dismantled the Islamist group's political activities.[52] PA forces have routinely arrested Hamas-affiliated students running in student elections in Palestinian universities.[53] Abbas has coupled his active battle with Hamas with a political one. He has to present his platform as a viable alternative to Hamas's violent "resistance." What Abbas has learned over the last decade was that negotiations—especially when they're not on the horizon or appear fruitless in the eyes of the Palestinian street—rarely are enough to defeat Hamas in the court of public opinion. In the years after the collapse of the 2013-2014 peace talks, Abbas has relied more and more on his internationalization campaign at the UN, Palestine 194, to be the counterpoint to Hamas's terrorism.

When Palestine 194 kicked off in 2011, it was largely a response to the Arab Spring. "When he saw what happened to Mubarak, it was traumatic for him," says Gadi Baltiansky, a former spokesman for Ehud Barak's government and longtime back channel negotiator with the Palestinians. "Mubarak was so strong, to Abbas he was the ultimate leader, and then that happened to him, and it immediately dawned on Abu Mazen [that it could happen to him too]."[54] That May, Abbas announced in the *New York Times* that the Palestinians would be launching a new international campaign.[55]

Initially, the 194 campaign was designed as a way to gain leverage in talks with Israel and show the Palestinian street the old-guard leadership was thinking creatively. Yet the plan had a fatal flaw: it had a short shelf-life. Palestine 194 cannot create a Palestinian state alone. No amount of UN support—or even Security Council resolutions—will turn the PA into a legitimate functioning government with viable institutions or pull the Israeli army out of the West Bank and create an independent Palestinian state.

The problem for Abbas was that once he started this campaign, there was no going back. After a temporary pause, which Abbas accepted in order to accommodate John Kerry during the 2013–2014 peace talks, Abbas resumed the campaign in April 2014 by joining fifteen different international organizations.[56] It made for a good headline in the newspapers, but when the Palestinian public realized one of those fifteen agencies was the UN Convention on Biological Diversity, his strategy suddenly seemed more symbolic than practical.

Things took a more serious turn in December 2014, when Abbas forced a vote at the UN Security Council on a resolution that would set the parameters for a Palestinian state, as well as give Israel two years to withdraw from the West Bank. The resolution was hyped for days in the Palestinian (and Israeli) media, with most of the attention focused on how the Obama administration would react.

Yet in what was perhaps the most important moment to date for the 194 campaign, the Palestinians failed to execute. On the last day of 2014, the resolution received eight votes—just one short of the needed majority.[57] No American veto was necessary; Israel was saved by the abstentions of the United Kingdom, Rwanda, Republic of Korea, Lithuania, and Nigeria—all countries that in the past supported pro-Palestinian resolutions in different international bodies.[58] Abbas's embarrassing defeat was compounded by the fact that had he waited just a few days, the makeup of the Security Council would have changed more favorably with the addition of Egypt and Japan.[59] The entire ordeal ended as yet another missed opportunity for Abbas that left many observers baffled. In Gaza, Hamas's newspaper offered a succinct conclusion: "Fatah did not consult anyone."[60]

The next day, Abbas signed the Statute of Rome, paving the way for the Palestinians to join the International Criminal Court (ICC). On paper, this was unprecedented: the PA could now potentially prosecute Israeli officers at the ICC for their actions in the West Bank and Gaza. When the ICC admitted the Palestinians in April 2014, Ramallah praised the court.[61] Yet a year later, a UN commission found evidence of war crimes on both the Israeli and Palestinian sides in the 2014 Gaza war.[62] And as of 2016, the ICC has yet to bring the type of cases Abbas would hope to see.

All of this underscores the futility of Abbas's international campaign. It is not a strategy for national liberation, as Abbas's aides would describe it, but rather a strategy for political survival. In his eyes, raising the Palestinian flag in international organizations is the best shot at countering the claims that he is irrelevant. And it is seemingly the only policy option he has left. Abbas knows he cannot deliver Gaza, which means he knows cannot sign any agreement on behalf of all Palestinians. All that's left, then, is theatrics.

CHAPTER 12

THE REIGN OF
MAHMOUD ABBAS

Mahmoud Abbas entered the room to a standing ovation.

Inside the Ahmed Shuqayri hall in the muqata'a—named after the first chairman of the PLO—more than a thousand members of his Fatah party were on their feet, singing and dancing to traditional Palestinian songs. Posters of Arafat and the founders of Fatah adorned the walls, as did those depicting Abbas at the United Nations. "We must control our feelings and emotions tonight," the overwhelmed moderator told the raucous crowd, "so we can support our brother Abu Mazen."[1] The date was November 30, 2016, and Abbas had just kicked off the long-awaited Fatah conference the night before.

It was the first time since 2009 that Fatah held a party-wide conference. Conferences are ostensibly held to conduct internal elections and issue new policy platforms. Yet for Abbas, that was not the goal. When he decided earlier in the year to hold the event, his aim was clear: to consolidate his ever-increasing grip on his party. The implementation of this plan started long before the conference itself actually began, when Abbas culled the amount of eligible voters by nearly a thousand, purged his rivals from the party, and insisted that—instead of at a hotel ballroom, like the previous conference—the 2016 conference would be held inside his presidential compound. As Jihad Tummaleh, a Fatah official Abbas had fired just weeks before, put it, "He's having the conference in the muqata'a under his guns. There is no doubt who is in charge."[2]

The conference came on the heels of a difficult year for Abbas. Since the end of 2015, a wave of terror had roiled across Israel and the West Bank. Dozens of Palestinians conducted stabbings and car ramming attacks against Israelis. Over forty died and hundreds were wounded.[3] The attackers were typically young and politically unaffiliated, prompting many Israelis to refer to the wave as a "lone-wolf intifada." Abbas had straddled a fine line throughout this period. His ministers and party officials openly incited against Israel and praised the attacks, while his security forces stepped up security coordination with Israel in an attempt to bring them to a halt. At one point Abbas's chief of intelligence bragged about preventing over two hundred attacks against Israelis. Abbas's political rivals used that interview to once again condemn him and portray the aging president as a "collaborator" with Israel.[4]

So Abbas needed a show of force to overcome the political damage at home. A massive conference, with his rivals forced out and his allies in check, was ideal. And indeed, when Abbas entered the conference hall on the second day of the gathering, a feverish crowd greeted him. During his speech, they frequently interrupted him with pledges of support, crying, "With our blood, with our spirit, we'll sacrifice for Abu Mazen."[5] Abbas rewarded the enthusiastic crowd by speaking for no less than three hours, a tough test of the patience and loyalty of the senior members of his party. At one point around the two-hour mark, a member of the audience grumbled and Abbas interrupted his speech to declare, "Don't worry brother, I know where I am going." The crowd jolted back to life. Abbas defended his decisions to talk with Israelis ("You either talk or you fight, but you have to talk at least") and to attend Shimon Peres's funeral earlier that year, while simultaneously challenging the historic Jewish connection to the land ("Some people talk about 4,000 years and it's not true").[6] Yet despite the time he devoted to those issues in his speech, Israel and the peace process were very low on his list of priorities for the conference. And in the wake of his speech, Abbas ruthlessly and effectively purged his rivals from elected positions within Fatah, while placing his own loyalists in every vacant corner. His once and future foe, Mohammad Dahlan, could only sit in exile and watch as Abbas dismantled his political operation in the West Bank.

Abbas emerged from the conference stronger politically than he'd been at any other point since the losses of 2006 and 2007—but still, it was not enough to deliver statehood to his people. In the weeks afterward, as the Israeli government passed a controversial settlement legalization bill and promised to build thousands of new housing units in Jerusalem, Abbas's image as a helpless leader on the Palestinian street was once again reinforced. He has arguably more control over the Palestinian Authority than Arafat ever did. He is strong enough to fight off rivals like Dahlan and other critics within Fatah. But he does not have the strength to challenge Hamas's control in Gaza or contest Israel's policies. That was true before his triumph at the Fatah conference, and it remained just as true after.

Mahmoud Abbas was a peripheral player in the early stages of the Palestinian national project. He cut out a role for himself in the margins as a negotiator-in-waiting, leveraged that position to elevate the Oslo process, and climbed the ranks to become the natural successor to Yasser Arafat. He started his reform-minded presidency with a democratic mandate and a goal of negotiating an agreement with Israel, yet after losing the elections in 2006 and then Gaza in 2007 his goals shifted seemingly to one singular focus: survival.

Many of his peers and constituents do not share a high opinion of his time in office. "All of our expectations we had for this man of institutions, for this pragmatic man like Abbas, were met with disappointment," says Nasser Juma'a, a Fatah parliamentarian. "None of what he promised was achieved. On the contrary, our situation deteriorated with him."[7] Abbas's rivals in Hamas, for their part, question the very legitimacy of his rule. "Abbas politically, nationally, and historically no longer represents the Palestinian people. He lost his legitimacy as president in 2009, he operates now as president from a very narrow, factional perspective," says Mushir al-Masri, a Hamas parliamentarian. "Most importantly," adds Masri, "his political project [peace negotiations] has failed completely."[8]

Others, like former Palestinian Authority minister Ghassan Khatib, come to Abbas's defense: "I think that President Abbas is a victim of the reality and I think he inherited an impossible situation. I think he's doomed, no matter what he does or says. . . . Certain changes happened in Israel that made Israel less and less compatible to the basic notion of the [peace] process."[9] Khatib insists that Israel, and its governing makeup, dictates Abbas's position: "[He] inherited a reality which was in my view created because of the changes inside Israel. Sometimes I ask myself if another person was in his position, what [they] could do." Ashraf al-Ajrami, another former minister in Abbas's cabinet, adds that "He took a lot of risks for peace, more than most Israelis give him credit for."[10]

A similar split regarding Abbas's legacy exists in the Israeli discourse. During one heated cabinet discussion in Jerusalem, at the height of the 2015 wave of terror attacks in Israel, one senior Israeli general lashed out at a group of right-wing government ministers who talked about Abbas as an enemy. "All of you in this room are going to miss Abu Mazen one day," the general warned,[11] echoing the famous statement by the deceased president Peres, who called Abbas "the best partner Israel has ever had."[12]

This view of Abbas has been rejected by Netanyahu, who routinely accuses Abbas of inciting to violence and running away from the difficult decisions necessary for reaching peace. "Abbas is the number one inciter in the world against Israel and the Jewish people," said Yuval Steinitz, a Likud minister considered close to Netanyahu. "The blood spilled during the latest outbreak of violence is on Abbas's hands."[13] And even within the Israeli left-wing opposition, which is generally more generous in its judgment of the Palestinian president, some now describe him as a disappointment. "Abu Mazen is a pleasant person to talk to, he is polite and doesn't like confrontations. Maybe that's part of the problem with him," says Tzipi Livni, the former foreign minister and peace negotiator. "In my opinion, he has much in common with Netanyahu. They both focus all the time on the small politics and ignore the iceberg appearing in the distance."[14] The sense among Israeli politicians, both on the right and left, is that while they may not have a better partner than Abbas in the future that still doesn't change the way he led his people in the past.

"He was always a man who carried himself with this kind of dignity and sense of pride," recalls Dennis Ross, the longtime American negotiator. In the same breath, however, Ross remembers Abbas as a leader with a long memory: "He is also someone who holds grudges. I've often said about him that he doesn't forgive and he doesn't forget."[15] Veterans of the Bush administration marvel at the change in the Mahmoud Abbas they knew in those years. "He's a better politician in personal terms than we thought, he's tougher than we thought," says Elliott Abrams, Bush's top Middle East advisor. "I think there was a view of him in the Bush years that was much more positive [than today]. The question for all of us then was 'could he deliver'? I think it's a different Mahmoud Abbas. I don't even know if he wants to deliver [an agreement] now. What he wants is to be president forever, to get rich, and to marginalize rivals. That's a different Mahmoud Abbas now."[16]

In the final analysis, Abbas remains an enigma to the Americans who worked with him. "We know that he opposes violence. . . . But as with all Palestinian leaders, you don't know how far they're willing to go in support of an outcome which is very far away from their preferred outcome," says Daniel Kurtzer, a former ambassador to Israel and Egypt. "You always hear: 'We already made our concession in accepting 22 percent of [historic] Palestine, don't ask us for more.' But have they really accepted that concession? At the end of the day, if an Israeli prime minister woke up and said, 'Okay, you can have [the West Bank and Gaza] back, we'll keep a couple of settlements here and there but you can have it,' would they really accept it? Who knows? There's not a strong argument to say that they would."[17]

Beyond the autocracy and paranoia that have come to characterize Abbas's era, some aspects of the man he was before he became president remain. Chief among them is his care for his loved ones. Abbas is an infamous family man, who time and again during his career stepped away from politics to spend more time at home. His inclination has been to protect his family and children at all times, and one of the reasons he is so worried about the identity of his successor is the possible impact that person could have on the Abbas family once he's gone.

But his children may have moved on from their father, at least when it comes to politics. In a 2014 interview with the *New York Times*, Tareq Abbas advocated for a "one-state solution," in which Palestinians would become a part of Israel instead of establishing their own state. "If you don't want to give me independence," said Tareq, "at least give me civil rights."[18] Tareq's break with his father, the man who led the Palestinian push for a two-state solution, is a microcosm of where the Palestinian national movement stands today. Younger Palestinians are increasingly frustrated with the old guard Oslo crowd and in their frustration have begun pushing for a binational state. In that same interview, Palestinian pollster Khalil Shikaki emphasized the growing divide: "Just ask my son, he will tell you that my generation failed and should exit the stage and take its mainstream paradigm, the two-state solution, along with it." This divide could become an unexpected legacy of the Abbas presidency.

Even after over a decade as the leader of his people, Mahmoud Abbas still lives in Yasser Arafat's shadow. He is not the charismatic leader of Palestinians. He cannot convince both West Bankers and Gazans of the merit of his cause. He does not press the flesh in Palestine. He does not appeal to the Palestinian street. He can rally allies behind him in the muqata'a and consolidate his grip on an ever-shrinking political entity, but he has little appeal to those Palestinians in the refugee camps.

The United States and Israel would have to minimize, to as much an extent as possible, the political backlash Abbas would face in publicly compromising on the Palestinian national narrative for an agreement to actually be reached. Without that, a comprehensive peace agreement remains nothing more than an academic pursuit. When there are no political considerations to the peace process—such as when he worked on the Beilin-Abu Mazen agreement—Abbas has more flexibility. Whenever the peace process became real, however, Abbas was too weak to make the necessary compromises.

A Palestinian leader needs both the willingness to sign an agreement and the capacity to deliver on that agreement in the West Bank and Gaza to make peace with Israel. Arafat, who had the capacity but likely not the will, called it the peace of the brave. For a brief moment, in 2005, Abbas seemed to have both. After 2006 and 2007, however, he lost the capacity to lead a Palestine united in the West Bank and Gaza. Since then, he has clung to power but wasn't able to achieve anything palpable for his people. He has morphed into another garden-variety regional autocrat. He spends most days of the year abroad.[19] He is almost never seen on the streets of the West Bank. He may have enough clout to enter another round of negotiations, but he lacks the power to deliver to his people.

Mahmoud Abbas is one of the few remaining founding members of the Palestinian national project. He was born in the British Mandate of Palestine, was raised as a refugee following the war of 1948, and has devoted his entire adult life to the Palestinian cause. Yet, while no one knows for sure what the future holds for his people, they know what he will leave them: a fragmented political culture, a divided territorial body, and a sense of desperation. In the end, the truest test of Abbas's legacy may simply be whether Palestinian nationalism can flourish again after he's gone, or whether he will be remembered as the last Palestinian leader.

NOTES

CHAPTER 1. THE RISE OF MAHMOUD ABBAS

1. Yardena Schwartz, "Exclusive: Shimon Peres on Peace, War and Israel's Future," *Time*, February 15, 2016, http://time.com/4224947/exclusive-shimon-peres-on-peace-war-and-israels-future/ (accessed December 8, 2016).

2. Senior Israeli official, interview with the authors, December 17, 2016.

3. Adam Rasgon, "Abbas: I Came to Peres's Funeral of My Own Volition," *Jerusalem Post*, November 23, 2016, http://www.jpost.com/Arab-Israeli-Conflict/Abbas-I-came-to-Peress-funeral-of-my-own-volition-473438 (accessed December 8, 2016).

4. "Abbas Attends Shimon Peres Funeral Despite Critiques," Ma'an News Agency, September 30, 2016, https://www.maannews.com/Content.aspx?id=773358 (accessed December 8, 2016).

5. Dennis Ross, interview with the authors, July 25, 2016.

6. Institute for Palestine Studies, "Mahmoud Abbas's Call for a Halt to the Militarization of the Intifada," *Journal of Palestine Studies* 32, no. 2 (Winter 2003): 74–78.

CHAPTER 2. THE NEGOTIATOR

1. Ahmad Tibi, interview with the authors, July 27, 2016.

2. Ibid.

3. Ibid.; Yossi Klein, "The Wandering Palestinian" [in Hebrew], *Ha'aretz*, April 16, 2003, http://www.haaretz.co.il/misc/article-print-page/1.876356 (accessed May 26, 2016).

4. Tibi and Klein.

5. Ibid.

6. David Shalit, "The Sky's the Limit" [in Hebrew], *Globes*, February

2, 2004, http://www.globes.co.il/news/article.aspx?did=772764 (accessed November 17, 2016).

7. Tibi, interview with the authors; Klein, "Wandering Palestinian."

8. "Stages in the Life of the President," Mahmoud Abbas: President of the State of Palestine, January 1, 1994, http://president.ps/eng/general.aspx?id=99 (accessed May 26, 2016).

9. Tibi, interview with the authors.

10. Mustafa Abbasi, *Safed During the Mandate Period 1918–1948* (Jerusalem: Yad Yitzhak Ben Zvi Press, 2015), p. 67.

11. Klein, "Wandering Palestinian."

12. Mustafa Abbasi, interview with the authors, July 10, 2016.

13. "Pre-State Israel: The 1936 Arab Riots," Jewish Virtual Library, http://www.jewishvirtuallibrary.org/the-1936-arab-riots (accessed March 2, 2017).

14. Abbasi, interview with the authors.

15. "Stages in the Life of the President," Mahmoud Abbas.

16. Klein, "Wandering Palestinian."

17. Ibid.

18. "Stages in the Life of the President," Mahmoud Abbas.

19. "Primer on Palestine, Israel and the Arab-Israeli Conflict," Middle East Research and Information Project, http://www.merip.org/primer-palestine-israel-arab-israeli-conflict-new#The United Nations Partition Plan (accessed August 31, 2016).

20. Abbasi, *Safed During the Mandate Period*, p. 67.

21. "Stages in the Life of the President," Mahmoud Abbas.

22. Abbasi, interview with the authors.

23. Klein, "Wandering Palestinian."

24. "Stages in the Life of the President," Mahmoud Abbas.

25. Benny Morris, *The Birth of the Palestinian Refugee Problem Revisited* (Cambridge: Cambridge University Press, 2004), p. 604.

26. "Stages in the Life of the President," Mahmoud Abbas.

27. Ibid.

28. Ibid.

29. Ibid.

30. Mustafa Kabha, *The Palestinian People: Seeking Sovereignty and State* (Boulder, CO: Lynne Rienner, 2014), p. 217.

31. Tibi, interview with the authors.

32. Dani Rubinstein, interview with the authors, July 27, 2016.

33. Abbasi, interview with the authors.

34. "Stages in the Life of the President," Mahmoud Abbas.

35. Ibid.

36. Rubinstein, interview with the authors.

37. Hussein Abu Shanb, "Abu Jihad, First in Lead, First in Stones, First in Media" [in Arabic], *Amad News*, April 16, 2016, https://www.amad.ps/ar/Details/118769 (accessed December 19, 2016).

38. Philip Mattar, *Encyclopedia of the Palestinians* (New York: Infobase Publishing, 2005), pp. 276–77.

39. Nazir Magally, interview with the authors, July 11, 2016.

40. Ibid.

41. Yezid Sayigh, *Armed Struggle and the Search for State: The Palestinian National Movement: 1949–1993* (New York: Oxford University Press, 1997), pp. 97–99.

42. Ibid., p. 101.

43. Ibid.

44. Rubinstein, interview with the authors.

45. Efraim Karsh, *Arafat's War: The Man and His Battle for Israeli Conquest* (New York: Grove Press, 2004), p. 37.

46. Tibi, interview with the authors.

47. Rubinstein, interview with the authors; Tibi, interview with the authors.

48. Editors of Encyclopedia Britannica, "Six-Day War," Encyclopedia Britannica, April 30, 2015, https://www.britannica.com/event/Six-Day-War (accessed August 8, 2016).

49. Michael Broning, *Political Parties in Palestine: Leadership and Thought* (New York: Palgrave Macmillan, 2013), p. 58.

50. "1968: Karameh and the Palestinian Revolt," *Telegraph*, May 1, 2002, http://www.telegraph.co.uk/news/1400177/1968-Karameh-and-the-Palestinian-revolt.html (accessed August 8, 2016).

51. Kabha, *Palestinian People*, p. 239.

52. Karsh, *Arafat's War*, p. 40.

53. Barry Rubin, *Revolution until Victory? The Politics and History of the PLO* (Cambridge: Harvard University Press, 1994), p. 23.

54. "1970: Civil War Breaks Out in Jordan," BBC News, http://news.bbc.co.uk/onthisday/hi/dates/stories/september/17/newsid_4575000/4575159.stm (accessed August 31, 2016).

55. William Quandt, Fuad Jabber, and Ann Mosely Lesch, *The Politics of Palestinian Nationalism* (Berkeley: University of California Press, 1973), p. 128.

56. "Profile: Mahmoud Abbas," BBC News, November 29, 2012, http://www.bbc.com/news/world-middle-east-20033995 (accessed August 31, 2016).

57. Mattar, *Encyclopedia of the Palestinians*, p. 352.

58. Tibi, interview with the authors; Magally, interview with the authors.

59. Yossi Beilin, interview with the authors, July 12, 2016; Tibi, interview with the authors; Magally, interview with the authors; Uri Avnery, interview with the authors, July 10, 2016.

60. Tibi, interview with the authors; Magally, interview with the authors.

61. "Stages in the Life of the President," Mahmoud Abbas.

62. Alexander Wolff, "The Mastermind Thirty Years after He Helped Plan the Terror Strike, Abu Daoud Remains in Hiding—And Unrepentant," *Sports Illustrated*, August 26, 2002, http://www.si.com/vault/2002/08/26/8113133/the-mastermind-thirty-years-after-he-helped-plan-the-terror-strike-abu-daoud-remains-in-hidingand-unrepentant (accessed December 29, 2016).

63. Rubinstein, interview with the authors; Tibi, interview with the authors; Magally, interview with the authors.

64. Elhanan Miller, "Mahmoud Abbas and Zionism: From Struggle to Acceptance," Forum for Regional Thinking, September 23, 2016, http://www.regthink.org/en/articles/mahmoud-abbas-and-zionism-from-struggle-to-acceptance (accessed November 17, 2016).

65. "Demographics of Israel: Jewish and Non-Jewish Population of Israel/Palestine," Jewish Virtual Library, http://www.jewishvirtuallibrary.org/jsource/Society_&_Culture/israel_palestine_pop.html (accessed August 31, 2016).

66. Tibi, interview with the authors.

67. Magally, interview with the authors.

68. Kabha, *Palestinian People*, p. 285.

69. "Key Player: Palestinian Authority President Mahmoud Abbas," PBS Newshour, May 9, 2006, http://www.pbs.org/newshour/updates/middle_east-jan-june06-mahmoud-abbas/ (accessed December 29, 2016).

70. Jillian Becker, *The PLO: The Rise and Fall of the Palestine Liberation Organization* (New York: St. Martin's Press, 1984), p. 219.

71. Mahmoud Abbas, *Through Secret Channels: The Road to Oslo: Senior PLO Leader Abu Mazen's Revealing Story of the Negotiations with Israel* (Reading, UK: Garnet, 1995), pp. 13–14.

72. Edward Said, *Peace and Its Discontents: Essays on Palestine in the Middle East Peace Process* (New York: Vintage, 1996), p. 33.

73. Tibi, interview with the authors.

74. Ibid.

75. Benny Morris, "Exposing Abbas," *National Interest*, May 19, 2011, http://nationalinterest.org/commentary/exposing-abbas-5335 (accessed May 27, 2016).

76. Jodi Rudoren, "Mahmoud Abbas Shifts on Holocaust," *New York Times*, April 26, 2014, http://www.nytimes.com/2014/04/27/world/middleeast/palestinian-leader-shifts-on-holocaust.html?_r=0 (accessed May 27, 2016).

77. Yasser Abed Rabbo, interview with the authors, June 29, 2016.

78. "Stages in the Life of the President," Mahmoud Abbas.

79. Jonathan Schanzer, *State of Failure* (New York: Palgrave Macmillan, 2013), p. 96.

80. Barry Rubin and Judith Colp Rubin, *Yasir Arafat: A Political Biography* (London: Continuum, 2003), p. 91.

81. Ibid.

82. Senior PLO official, interview with the authors, June 29, 2016.

83. Ibid.

84. Abed Rabbo, interview with the authors.

85. Magally, interview with the authors.

86. Michal Shmulovich, "24 Years Later, Israel Acknowledges Top-Secret Operation that Killed Fatah Terror Chief," *Times of Israel*, November 1, 2012, http://www.timesofisrael.com/israel-admits-to-top-secret-operation-that-killed-top-fatah-commander-abu-jihad-in-1988/ (accessed March 2, 2017); Sayigh, *Armed Struggle and the Search for State*, p. 654.

87. Abbas, *Through Secret Channels*, p. 21.

88. Kabha, *Palestinian People*, p. 319.

89. F. Robert Hunter, *The Palestinian Uprising: A War By Other Means* (Los Angeles: University of California Press, 1991), p. 152.

90. John Kifner, "Hussein Surrenders Claim on West Bank to the PLO; US Peace Plan in Jeopardy; Internal Tensions," *New York Times*, August 1, 1988, http://www.nytimes.com/1988/08/01/world/hussein-surrenders-claims-west-bank-plo-us-peace-plan-jeopardy-internal-tensions.html (accessed June 4, 2016).

91. Abbas, *Through Secret Channels*, p. 23.

92. Ibid. pp. 33–34.

93. James Gerstenzang, "Bush Suspends Talks with PLO: Terrorism:

President Assails the Organization's Failure to Denounce a Splinter Group's Raid on an Israeli Beach," *Los Angeles Times,* June 21, 1990, http://articles.latimes.com/1990-06-21/news/mn-118_1_splinter-group (accessed December 24, 2016).

94. Magally, interview with the authors.

95. Toufic Haddad, "Palestinian Forced Displacement from Kuwait: The Overdue Accounting," Badil, http://www.badil.org/en/component/k2/item/1514-art07 (accessed December 24, 2016).

96. Hanan Ashrawi, *This Side of Peace: A Personal Account* (New York: Simon & Schuster, 1995), p. 144.

97. Bassam Abu Sharif, *Arafat and the Dream of Palestine* (New York: Palgrave Macmillan, 2009), p. 225.

98. Abbas, *Through Secret Channels,* p. 51.

99. Omar Massalha, *Towards the Long-Promised Peace* (London: Saqi Books, 1994), p. 169.

CHAPTER 3. FROM OSLO TO CAMP DAVID

1. Ahmed Qurie, *From Oslo to Jerusalem: The Palestinian Story of the Secret Negotiations* (New York: I.B. Tauris, 2008), pp. 278–79.

2. "Oslo Accords 1993," YouTube video, 1:25:25, ABC and NBC News footage, posted by "alhofdTV," February 3, 2014, https://www.youtube.com/watch?v=93EFpsZs3d4 (accessed July 31, 2016).

3. Ibid.

4. Ibid.

5. Ibid.

6. Dennis Ross, interview with the authors, July 25, 2016.

7. Shimon Peres, "Declaration of Principles on Interim Self-Government Arrangements: Texts and Speeches," speech, Israel Ministry of Foreign Affairs, 1993, http://ecf.org.il/media_items/1224 (accessed August 31, 2016).

8. Mahmoud Abbas, "Declaration of Principles on Interim Self-Government Arrangements: Texts and Speeches'," (speech, Israel Ministry of Foreign Affairs, 1993), http://ecf.org.il/media_items/1231 (accessed August 31, 2016).

9. "The Oslo Accords and the Arab-Israeli Peace Process," Department of State Office of the Historian, https://history.state.gov/milestones/1993-2000/oslo (accessed August 31, 2016).

10. Qurie, *From Oslo to Jerusalem*, p. 281.

11. Abbas, "Declaration of Principles."

12. Ahmad Tibi, interview with the authors, July 27, 2016.

13. "Demographic Overview: Gaza Strip & West Bank 1992," United States Census Bureau, http://www.census.gov/population/international/data/idb/region.php?N=%20Results%20&T=13&A=both&RT=0&Y=1992&R=-1&C=GZ,WE (accessed August 31, 2016).

14. Mahmoud Abbas, *Through Secret Channels: The Road to Oslo: Senior PLO Leader Abu Mazen's Revealing Story of the Negotiations with Israel* (Reading, UK: Garnet, 1995), pp. 90–92.

15. Dennis Ross, *The Missing Peace: The Inside Story of the Fight for Middle East Peace* (New York: Farrar, Straus, and Giroux, 2004), p. 100.

16. Yair Hirschfeld, interview with the authors, June 21, 2016.

17. Qurie, *From Oslo to Jerusalem*, p. 40.

18. Abbas, *Through Secret Channels*, p. 113.

19. Hirschfeld, interview with the authors.

20. "Oslo Accords," Department of State Office of the Historian.

21. Ross, *The Missing Peace*, p. 119.

22. Yossi Klein, "The Wandering Palestinian" [in Hebrew], *Ha'aretz*, April 16, 2003, http://www.haaretz.co.il/misc/article-print-page/1.876356 (accessed May 26, 2016).

23. Yoel Marcus, "Presidents and Spirit," *Ha'aretz*, August 27, 2010, http://www.haaretz.com/presidents-and-spirit-1.310468 (accessed March 8, 2017).

24. Avi Issacharoff and Chaim Levinson, "Settlers Remember Gunman Goldstein; Hebron Riots Continue," *Ha'aretz*, February 28, 2010, http://www.haaretz.com/settlers-remember-gunman-goldstein-hebron-riots-continue-1.263834 (accessed August 31, 2016).

25. Michael Parks, "Israel Quietly OKs West Bank Expansion, Angering PLO," *Los Angeles Times*, September 27, 1994, http://articles.latimes.com/1994-09-27/news/mn-43677_1_west-bank (accessed March 8, 2017).

26. "Deri Leaves Rabin Government, But Party May Back Peace Plan," Jewish Telegraphic Agency, September 13, 1993, http://www.jta.org/1993/09/13/archive/deri-leaves-rabin-government-but-party-may-back-peace-plan (accessed August 31, 2016).

27. Moshe Negby, *Coming Apart: The Unraveling of Democracy in Israel* (Jerusalem: Keter Books, 2004), pp. 211–14.

28. Dan Ephron, *Killing a King: The Assassination of Yitzhak Rabin and the Remaking of Israel* (New York: W.W. Norton & Company, 2015), p. 46.

29. "Hamas Covenant 1988," Yale Law School, August 18, 1988, http://avalon.law.yale.edu/20th_century/hamas.asp (accessed December 20, 2016).

30. Israel Ministry of Foreign Affairs, *The Israeli-Palestinian Interim Agreement* (Washington, DC: September 28, 1995), http://www.mfa.gov .il/mfa/foreignpolicy/peace/guide/pages/the%20israeli-palestinian%20 interim%20agreement.aspx (accessed August 31, 2016).

31. Yasser Abed Rabbo, interview with the authors, June 29, 2016.

32. Jim Zanotti, "The Palestinians: Background and US Relations," Congressional Research Service, January 31, 2014, https://fas.org/sgp/ crs/mideast/RL34074.pdf (accessed August 31, 2016).

33. Nimrod Novik, interview with authors, June 22, 2016; Yossi Beilin, interview with the authors, July 12, 2016.

34. Novik, interview with authors.

35. Beilin, interview with the authors.

36. Walid Khalidi, "Thinking the Unthinkable: A Sovereign Palestinian State," *Foreign Affairs*, July 1978, https://www.foreignaffairs. com/articles/palestinian-authority/1978-07-01/thinking-unthinkable -sovereign-palestinian-state (accessed August 31, 2016).

37. Israeli associate of Ahmad Khalidi, interview with the authors, July 2016.

38. Yair Hirschfield, *Track-Two Diplomacy Toward an Israeli-Palestinian Solution, 1978–2014* (Baltimore: Johns Hopkins University Press), p. 369.

39. Novik, interview with authors.

40. Yossi Beilin and Mahmoud Abbas, "Israel-Palestinian Peace Process: The Beilin-Abu Mazen Document," Jewish Virtual Library, 1995, http://ecf.org.il/media_items/566 (accessed August 31, 2016).

41. Ibid.

42. Michael Herzog, "Minding the Gaps: Territorial Issues in Israeli-Palestinian Peacemaking," *The Washington Institute for Near East Policy*, December 2011, https://www.washingtoninstitute.org/uploads/ Documents/pubs/PolicyFocus116.pdf (accessed March 8, 2017).

43. Beilin and Abbas, "Israel-Palestinian Peace Process: The Beilin-Abu Mazen Document."

44. Ibid.

45. Ibid.

46. Novik, interview with authors; Beilin, interview with the authors.

47. Novik, interview with authors.

48. Former Abbas aide, interview with the authors, June 13, 2016.

49. Ibid.

50. Abed Rabbo, interview with the authors.

51. Novik, interview with authors.

52. Abed Rabbo, interview with the authors.

53. Novik, interview with authors.

54. Ibid.

55. Scott Macleod, "We Became More Than Friends," *Time*, November 20, 2016, http://content.time.com/time/magazine/article/0,9171 ,983726,00.html (accessed August 31, 2016).

56. Joel Greenberg, "Assassination in Israel: Arafat; Arafat Visits Israel to Give Condolences to Leah Rabin," *New York Times*, November 10, 1995, http://www.nytimes.com/1995/11/10/world/assassination-israel-arafat-arafat -visits-israel-give-condolences-leah-rabin.html (accessed August 31, 2016).

57. Ross, interview with the authors.

58. "The Commissioners," Central Elections Commission: Palestine, 2017, http://www.elections.ps/tabid/710/language/en-US/Default.aspx (accessed August 31, 2016).

59. Walter Rodgers, "Palestinians Turn Out for Historic Vote," CNN, January 20, 1996, http://edition.cnn.com/WORLD/9601/palestine_elex/ (accessed August 31, 2016).

60. "The 1996 Presidential and Legislative Elections," Central Elections Commission: Palestine, http://www.elections.ps/Portals/0/pdf/ Resultselection1996.pdf (accessed August 31, 2016).

61. Mary Curtius, "Arafat's Fatah Wins Big in Historic Vote," *Los Angeles Times*, January 22, 1996, http://articles.latimes.com/1996-01-22/ news/mn-27439_1_palestinian-leader-arafat (accessed August 31, 2016).

62. Patrick Cockburn, "How the Phone Bomb Was Set Up," *Independent*, January 8, 1996, http://www.independent.co.uk/news/world/ how-the-phone-bomb-was-set-up-1323096.html (accessed August 31, 2016).

63. "Fatal Terrorist Attacks in Israel (Sept 1993–1999)," Israel Ministry of Foreign Affairs, September 24, 2000, http://www.mfa.gov.il/ mfa/foreignpolicy/terrorism/palestinian/pages/fatal%20terrorist%20 attacks%20in%20israel%20since%20the%20dop%20-s.aspx (accessed August 31, 2016).

64. Novik, interview with authors; Beilin, interview with the authors; Hirschfeld, interview with the authors.

65. Beilin, interview with the authors.

66. Beilin, interview with the authors; Hirschfeld, interview with the authors.

67. Abed Rabbo, interview with the authors.

68. "Israeli Election Results: May 1996," Israel Ministry of Foreign Affairs, 2013, http://www.mfa.gov.il/MFA/AboutIsrael/History/Pages/Israeli%20Election%20Results-%20May%201996.aspx (accessed August 31, 2016).

69. Yair Hirschfeld, *Track-Two Diplomacy toward an Israeli-Palestinian Solution 1978–2014* (Washington, DC: Woodrow Wilson Press, 2014), p. 188.

70. Ross, *Missing Peace*, p. 263.

71. Abed Rabbo, interview with the authors.

72. Ross, *Missing Peace*, p. 263.

73. Novik, interview with authors.

74. Ibid.

75. Ross, interview with the authors.

76. David Landau, *Arik: The Life of Ariel Sharon* (New York: Alfred A. Knopf, 2013), p. 304.

77. Ross, *Missing Peace*, p. 393.

78. Ibid., p. 492.

79. Martin Indyk, *Innocent Abroad: An Intimate Account of American Peace Diplomacy in the Middle East* (New York: Simon & Schuster, 2009), pp. 70–71.

80. Ibid.

81. Ross, interview with the authors.

82. Martin Indyk, interview with the authors, September 6, 2016.

83. Abed Rabbo, interview with the authors.

84. Ross, interview with the authors.

85. Senior PLO official, interview with the authors, June 29, 2016.

86. Ahmed Qurie, *Beyond Oslo, the Struggle for Palestine: Inside the Middle East Peace Process from Rabin's Death to Camp David* (New York: I.B. Tauris, 2008), p. 75.

87. Ibid., p. 80.

88. Dani Rubinstein, "Abu Mazen's Troubles Will Continue" [in Hebrew], *Ha'aretz*, April 29, 2003, http://www.haaretz.co.il/misc/1.878565 (accessed August 31, 2016).

89. Munib al-Masri, interview with the authors, August 28, 2016.

90. Novik, interview with authors.

91. Dan Ephron, "Exiled in Abu Dhabi, Mohammed Dahlan Dreams of Gaza," *Newsweek*, March 2, 2015, http://www.newsweek.com/2015/03/20/exiled-abu-dhabi-mohammed-dahlan-dreams-gaza-310349.html (accessed December 19, 2016).

92. "Palestinian National Council Address," C-SPAN video, 1:20:00,

December 14, 1998, https://www.c-span.org/video/?116641-1/palestinian
-national-council-address (accessed August 31, 2016).

93. Ross, *Missing Peace*, p. 486.

94. Deborah Sontag, "Clinton in the Mideast: The Overview; Clinton
Watches as Palestinians Drop Call for Israel's Destruction," *New York
Times*, December 15, 1998, http://www.nytimes.com/1998/12/15/world/
clinton-mideast-overview-clinton-watches-palestinians-drop-call-for-israel-s
.html (accessed August 31, 2016).

95. Indyk, *Innocent Abroad*, p. 199.

96. Ross, *Missing Peace*, p. 486.

97. Qurie, *Beyond Oslo, the Struggle for Palestine*, p. 73.

98. Ross, *Missing Peace*, p. 492.

99. Will Lester, "US Aides Hired for Israel Vote," *Washington Post*,
January 20, 2001, http://www.washingtonpost.com/wp-srv/aponline/
20010130/aponline150101_001.htm (accessed December 10, 2016).

100. Ross, *Missing Peace*, p. 492.

101. Gilad Sher, interview with the authors, June 14, 2016.

102. Former Abbas aide, interview with the authors, June 14, 2016.

103. Nizar Farsakh, interview with the authors, June 15, 2016.

104. Dani Rubinstein, interview with the authors, July 27, 2016.

105. Jonathan Schanzer, "The Brothers Abbas: Are the Sons of the
Palestinian President Growing Rich off Their Father's System?" *Foreign
Policy*, June 5, 2012, http://foreignpolicy.com/2012/06/05/the-brothers
-abbas/ (accessed August 31, 2016).

106. Tricia McDermott, "Arafat's Billions: One Man's Quest to Track Down
Unaccounted-For Public Funds," CBS News, November 7, 2003, http://www
.cbsnews.com/news/arafats-billions/ (accessed August 31, 2016).

107. Former Senior Israeli official, interview with the authors,
December 26, 2016.

108. Sher, interview with the authors.

109. Beilin, interview with the authors.

110. Sher, interview with the authors.

111. Ibid.

112. Ibid.

113. Tibi, interview with the authors.

114. Ibid.

115. Novik, interview with authors.

116. Ross, *Missing Peace*, p. 611.

117. Qurie, *Beyond Oslo, the Struggle for Palestine*, pp. 111–13.

118. Sher, interview with the authors.

119. Ibid.

120. Ibid.

121. Qurie, *Beyond Oslo, the Struggle for Palestine*, p. 115.

122. Novik, interview with authors.

123. Ross, *Missing Peace*, p. 624.

124. Novik, interview with authors.

125. Qurie, *Beyond Oslo, the Struggle for Palestine*, p. 160.

126. Michael Hirsh, "Clinton to Arafat: It's All Your Fault," *Newsweek*, June 26, 2001, http://www.newsweek.com/clinton-arafat-its-all-your -fault-153779 (accessed August 31, 2016).

127. Indyk, *Innocent Abroad*, p. 339.

128. Benny Morris, "Camp David and After: An Exchange (1. An Interview with Ehud Barak)," *New York Review of Books*, June 13, 2002, http://www.nybooks.com/articles/2002/06/13/camp-david-and-after-an -exchange-1-an-interview-wi/ (accessed August 31, 2016).

129. Akram Hanieh, "The Camp David Papers," *Journal of Palestine Studies* 30, no. 2 (Winter 2001): 75–97.

130. Robert Malley and Hussein Agha, "Camp David: The Tragedy of Errors," *New York Review of Books*, August 9, 2001, http://www.nybooks .com/articles/2001/08/09/camp-david-the-tragedy-of-errors/ (accessed August 31, 2016).

131. "Mahmoud Abbas (Abu Mazin), Report on the Camp David Summit, Gaza, 9 September 2000 (Excerpts)," *Journal of Palestine Studies* 30, no. 2 (Winter 2001): 157–90.

132. Ibid.

133. Former Abbas aide, interview with the authors.

134. Ross, interview with the authors.

135. Sher, interview with the authors.

136. Gadi Baltiansky, interview with the authors, July 12, 2016.

137. Ibid.

138. Indyk, *Innocent Abroad*, p. 311.

139. Sher, interview with the authors.

140. Former Abbas aide, interview with the authors.

141. "Abu Mazen: Had Camp David Convened Again, We Would Take the Same Positions Part I," Middle East Media Research Institute, August 6, 2001, http://www.memri.org/report/en/print489.htm (accessed August 31, 2016).

142. Ross, interview with the authors.

143. Ross, *Missing Peace*, p. 668.

144. Ross, interview with the authors.

145. Former Abbas aide, interview with the authors.

146. Ibid.

147. Landau, *Arik: The Life of Ariel Sharon*, p. 335.

148. "Abu Mazen: Had Camp David Convened Again, Part I," Middle East Media Research Institute; Abu Mazen: Had Camp David Convened Again, We Would Take the Same Positions Part II," Middle East Media Research Institute, August 6, 2001, https://www.memri.org/reports/abu-mazen-had-camp-david-convened-again-we-would-take-same-positions-part-ii (accessed March 8, 2017).

149. Morris, "Camp David and After."

150. Landau, *Arik: The Life of Ariel Sharon*, pp. 334–36.

151. Dennis Ross, "Iran Cannot Be a Partner in the Struggle against ISIS," Washington Institute for Near East Policy, September 11, 2016, http://www.washingtoninstitute.org/policy-analysis/view/iran-cannot-be-a-partner-in-the-struggle-against-isis (accessed November 10, 2016).

152. David Matz, "Trying to Understand the Taba Talks: An In-Depth Analysis of What Happened at the Taba Peace Talks, and Why They Failed," *Palestine-Israel Journal* 10, no. 3 (2003), http://www.pij.org/details.php?id=32 (accessed August 31, 2016).

153. Ben Caspit, "Two Years to the Intifada" [in Hebrew], *Ma'ariv*, September 5, 2002, http://www.nrg.co.il/online/archive/ART/344/233.html (accessed August 31, 2016).

CHAPTER 4. YEARS OF TERROR

1. Former Senior Israeli intelligence official, interview with the authors, August 18, 2016.

2. David Landau, *Arik: The Life of Ariel Sharon* (New York: Alfred A. Knopf, 2013), p. 369.

3. Qaddura Fares, interview with the authors, September 18, 2016.

4. Former Senior Israeli intelligence official, interview with the authors.

5. Raymond Whitaker, "A Strange Voice Said: I Just Killed Your Husband," *Independent*, October 13, 2000, http://www.independent.co.uk/news/world/middle-east/a-strange-voice-said-i-just-killed-your-husband-635341.html (accessed October 13, 2016).

6. Former Abbas aide, interview with the authors, June 14, 2016.

7. Avi Dichter, interview with the authors, August 18, 2016.

8. Ahmad Tibi, interview with the authors, July 27, 2016.

9. Ahmed Qurie, *Peace Negotiations in Palestine: From the Second Intifada to the Roadmap* (London: I.B. Tauris, 2015), pp. 34–35.

10. Bill Clinton, *My Life* (New York: Knopf, 2004), pp. 936–37.

11. Ibid.

12. Ibid., pp. 944–45.

13. Itamar Marcus and Nan Jacques Zilberdik, "Arafat Planned and Led the Intifada: Testimonies from PA Leaders and Others," Palestinian Media Watch, November 28, 2011, http://palwatch.org/main .aspx?fi=157&doc_id=5875 (accessed October 13, 2016).

14. Nasser Juma'a, interview with the authors, September 14, 2016.

15. Martin Indyk, interview with the authors, September 6, 2016.

16. Munib al-Masri, interview with the authors, August 28, 2016.

17. Nimrod Novik, interview with authors, June 22, 2016.

18. Juma'a, interview with the authors.

19. Fares, interview with the authors.

20. Michael Broning, *Political Parties in Palestine: Leadership and Thought* (New York: Palgrave Macmillan, 2013), p. 73.

21. Eli Avidar, *The Abyss: Bridging the Divide Between Israel and the Arab World* (Maryland: Rowman & Littlefield, 2015), p. 3.

22. Indyk, interview with the authors.

23. Yasser Abed Rabbo, interview with the authors, June 29, 2016.

24. "Mahmoud Abbas's Call for a Halt to the Militarization of the Intifada," *Journal of Palestine Studies* 32, no. 2 (Winter 2003): 74–78.

25. Jonathan Schanzer, *Hamas vs. Fatah: The Struggle for Palestine* (New York: Palgrave Macmillan, 2008), pp. 58–60.

26. Tracy Wilkinson, "Arafat Lives with Enemy Breathing Down His Neck," *Los Angeles Times*, April 4, 2002, http://articles.latimes.com/2002/ apr/04/news/mn-36194 (accessed October 13, 2016).

27. Martin Indyk, *Innocent Abroad: An Intimate Account of American Peace Diplomacy in the Middle East* (New York: Simon & Schuster, 2009), p. 14.

28. Elliott Abrams, interview with the authors, June 13, 2016.

29. Ibid.

30. "Statement by IDF Chief-of-Staff Lt.-Gen. Shaul Mofaz Regarding Interception of Ship Karine A," Israel Ministry of Foreign Affairs, January 4, 2002, http://mfa.gov.il/MFA/PressRoom/2002/Pages/Statement%20 by%20IDF%20Chief-of-Staff%20Lt-Gen%20Shaul%20Mofaz.aspx (accessed October 13, 2016).

31. Abrams, interview with the authors.

32. Juma'a, interview with the authors.

33. "Eldest Son of PLO No. 2 Dies," Al Bawaba, June 16, 2002, http://www.albawaba.com/news/eldest-son-plo-no-2-dies (accessed October 13, 2016).

34. Tibi, interview with the authors.

35. Fares, interview with the authors; Danny Rubinstein, "He Will Bury All His Successors" [in Hebrew], *Ha'aretz*, June 23, 2002, http://www.haaretz.co.il/misc/1.804233 (accessed November 15, 2016).

36. Dichter, interview with the authors.

37. Aaron David Miller, interview with the authors, November 2, 2016.

38. Robert Malley and Hussein Agha, "Three Men in a Boat," *New York Review of Books*, August 14, 2003, http://www.nybooks.com/articles/2003/08/14/three-men-in-a-boat/ (accessed October 13, 2016).

39. Ibid.

CHAPTER 5. OUR MAN IN RAMALLAH

1. Dov Weisglass, interview with the authors, July 23, 2016.

2. Ibid.

3. David Landau, *Arik: The Life of Ariel Sharon* (New York: Alfred A. Knopf, 2013), p. 444.

4. Weisglass, interview with the authors.

5. Ibid.

6. Merav Levi, "Sharon-Abu Mazen Meeting Was Very Successful, Israel Promises to Ease Restrictions" [in Hebrew], *News 1*, http://www.news1.co.il/Archive/001-D-24572-00.html (accessed November 18, 2016).

7. Weisglass, interview with the authors.

8. Robin Wright and Mary Curtius, "Sharon's Washington Trip Will Test US and Israel as Partners," *Los Angeles Times*, May 5, 2002, http://articles.latimes.com/2002/may/05/world/fg-usiz5 (accessed September 1, 2016).

9. Elliott Abrams, *Tested by Zion: The Bush Administration and the Israeli-Palestinian Conflict* (Cambridge: Cambridge University Press, 2013), p. 36.

10. Ibid., p. 39.

11. Elliott Abrams, interview with the authors, June 13, 2016.

12. "Statements by President George Bush and Prime Minister Ariel Sharon Following Their Meeting at the White House," Israel Ministry

of Foreign Affairs, May 7, 2002, http://mfa.gov.il/MFA/ForeignPolicy/
MFADocuments/Yearbook2002/Pages/Statements%20by%20
President%20George%20Bush%20and%20Prime%20Mini.aspx (accessed
September 1, 2016).

13. "Full Text of George Bush's Speech," *Guardian*, June 25, 2002,
https://www.theguardian.com/world/2002/jun/25/israel.usa (accessed
September 1, 2016).

14. Abrams, *Tested by Zion*, p. 42.

15. "Roadmap for Peace in the Middle East: Israeli/Palestinian
Reciprocal Action, Quartet Support," US Department of State, Bureau
of Public Affairs, July 16, 2003, http://2001-2009.state.gov/r/pa/ei/
rls/22520.htm (accessed September 1, 2016).

16. Aaron David Miller, interview with the authors, November 2, 2016.

17. Weisglass, interview with the authors.

18. Weisglass, interview with the authors; Abrams, interview with the
authors.

19. Radi Jarai, interview with the authors, July 3, 2016.

20. Yasser Abed Rabbo, interview with the authors, June 29, 2016.

21. Former Abbas aide, interview with the authors, June 14, 2016.

22. Greg Myre, "Palestinian Becomes Premier, Diminishing Arafat's
Power," *New York Times*, March 20, 2003, http://www.nytimes.com/
2003/03/20/world/palestinian-becomes-premier-diminishing
-arafat-s-power.html (accessed September 1, 2016).

23. Ashraf al-Ajrami, interview with the authors, July 25, 2016.

24. "Palestinians Fail to Settle Deadlock," BBC News, April 23,
2003, http://news.bbc.co.uk/2/hi/middle_east/2967031.stm (accessed
September 1, 2016).

25. Former Abbas aide, interview with the authors.

26. James Bennet, "Palestinian Chief Denounces Terror," *New
York Times*, April 30, 2003, http://www.nytimes.com/2003/04/30/
international/middleeast/30MIDE.html?pagewanted=all (accessed
September 1, 2016).

27. Weisglass, interview with the authors.

28. Mahmoud Abbas, "PM Abbas' Aqaba Summit Speech," *Ha'aretz*,
June 4, 2003, http://www.haaretz.com/news/pm-abbas-aqaba-summit
-speech-1.90374 (accessed September 1, 2016).

29. Abed Rabbo, interview with the authors.

30. "PM Abbas' Aqaba Summit Speech," *Ha'aretz*.

31. Abed Rabbo, interview with the authors.

32. Yael Yehoshua, "Palestinian Reactions to Abu Mazen's Speech at the Aqaba Summit," Middle East Media Research Institute, June 25, 2003, http://www.memri.org/report/en/0/0/0/0/0/0/895.htm (accessed September 1, 2016).

33. Ibid.

34. Hussein Ibish, interview with the authors, July 18, 2016.

35. Former Abbas aide, interview with the authors.

36. Ibid.

37. Amos Harel, Aluf Benn, and Arnon Regular, "Arafat Tells Envoy: Abbas Is a Traitor," *Ha'aretz*, July 11, 2003, http://www.haaretz.com/arafat-tells-envoy-abbas-is-a-traitor-1.93832 (accessed September 1, 2016).

38. Nathan J. Brown, "Evaluating Palestinian Reform," *Carnegie Papers*, no. 59, *Carnegie Endowment for International Peace*, June 2005, http://carnegieendowment.org/files/CP59.brown.FINAL.pdf (accessed September 1, 2016).

39. James Bennet, "Palestinian Focus: The Internal Fight," *New York Times*, July 1, 2003, http://www.nytimes.com/2003/07/01/international/middleeast/01ASSE.html?pagewanted=all (accessed September 1, 2016).

40. Landau, *Arik: The Life of Ariel Sharon*, p. 452.

41. Ibid., pp. 453–54.

42. Ibid., p. 453.

43. Ibid.

44. Weisglass, interview with the authors.

45. "Bus Bomb Carnage in Jerusalem," BBC News, August 20, 2003, http://news.bbc.co.uk/2/hi/middle_east/3165279.stm (accessed November 17, 2016).

46. Avi Dichter, interview with the authors, August 18, 2016.

47. "Palestinian Prime Minister Abbas Resigns," CNN, September 6, 2003, http://edition.cnn.com/2003/WORLD/meast/09/06/mideast/ (accessed September 1, 2016).

48. Chris McGreal, "Ridiculed and Betrayed: Why Abbas Blames Arafat," *Guardian*, September 7, 2003, https://www.theguardian.com/world/2003/sep/08/israel (accessed September 1, 2016).

49. Nizar Farsakh, interview with the authors, June 15, 2016.

50. Former Abbas aide, interview with the authors.

51. Ghaith al-Omari, interview with the authors, June 18, 2016.

52. Ibid.

53. James Bennet, "Arafat Wants No. 2 Man in the PLO as the Premier," *New York Times*, March 7, 2003, http://www.nytimes.com/

2003/03/07/world/arafat-wants-no-2-man-in-the-plo-as-the-premier.html (accessed September 1, 2016).

54. Ghaith al-Omari, interview with the authors.

55. Abrams, interview with the authors.

56. Weisglass, interview with the authors.

57. "Prime Minister's Speech at the Herzliya Conference," *Ha'aretz*, December 18, 2003, http://www.haaretz.com/news/prime-minister-s -speech-at-the-herzliya-conference-1.109089 (accessed September 1, 2016).

58. Mahmoud Abbas, *Through Secret Channels: The Road to Oslo: Senior PLO Leader Abu Mazen's Revealing Story of the Negotiations with Israel* (Reading, UK: Garnet, 1995), p. 37.

CHAPTER 6. PRESIDENT ABBAS

1. Judith Miller, "Yasir Arafat, Father and Leader of Palestinian Nationalism, Dies at 75," *New York Times*, November 11, 2004, http://www .nytimes.com/2004/11/11/world/middleeast/yasir-arafat-father-and -leader-of-palestinian-nationalism.html?_r=0 (accessed July 11, 2016).

2. "Leaders Gather in Egypt for Arafat's Funeral," CNN, November 11, 2004, http://www.cnn.com/2004/WORLD/meast/11/11/arafat .main/ (accessed July 18, 2016).

3. Yasser Abed Rabbo, interview with the authors, June 29, 2016.

4. Ibid.

5. Ibid.

6. "Arab and Muslim Dignitaries Attend Military Funeral in Cairo," *Irish Times*, November 13, 2004, http://www.irishtimes.com/news/ arab-and-muslim-dignitaries-attend-military-funeral-in-cairo-1.1166249 (accessed July 18, 2016).

7. "Official Funeral Service for Yasser Arafat," C-SPAN, 29:20, November 12, 2004, http://www.c-span.org/video/?184424-1/official -funeral-service-yasser-arafat (accessed July 18, 2016).

8. "Chaotic Crowds Crash Arafat Burial: Thousands Swarm Helicopter," CNN, November 12, 2004, http://www.cnn.com/2004/ WORLD/meast/11/12/arafat.main/ (accessed July 18, 2016).

9. Sari Nusseibeh with Anthony David, *Once Upon a Country: A Palestinian Life* (New York: Picador, 2007), p. 10.

10. "Ramadan—1425 Hijri," Habibur, https://habibur.com/hijri/ 1425/9/ (accessed November 10, 2016).

11. Nusseibeh with David, *Once Upon a Country*, p. 10.

12. Robert Malley and Hussein Agha, "The Last Palestinian," *New York Review of Books*, February 10, 2005, http://www.nybooks.com/articles/2005/02/10/the-last-palestinian/ (accessed November 10, 2016).

13. Abed Rabbo, interview with the authors.

14. Ghaith al-Omari, interview with the authors, June 14, 2016.

15. Elliott Abrams, interview with the authors, June 13, 2016.

16. "Full Text of George Bush's Speech," *Guardian*, June 25, 2002, https://www.theguardian.com/world/2002/jun/25/israel.usa (accessed November 10, 2016).

17. Robert Danin, interview with the authors, November 8, 2016.

18. Dov Weisglass, interview with the authors, July 23, 2016.

19. Nader Said, interview with the authors, May 17, 2016.

20. Ibid.

21. Ibid.

22. Mohammad Shtayyeh, interview with the authors, July 4, 2016.

23. Ibid.

24. Conal Urquhart, "Israel Jails Jewish Woman for Meeting Palestinian Militant," *Guardian*, December 22, 2005, https://www.theguardian.com/world/2005/dec/23/israel (accessed July 9, 2016).

25. Shtayyeh, interview with the authors.

26. Ashraf al-Ajrami, interview with the authors, July 26, 2016.

27. Ibid.

28. Mustafa Barghouthi, interview with the authors, July 4, 2016.

29. Arnon Regular, "Mustafa Barghouti Briefly Arrested for Campaigning Illegally in Jerusalem," *Ha'aretz*, December 28, 2004, http://www.haaretz.com/mustafa-barghouti-briefly-arrested-for-campaigning-illegally-in-jerusalem-1.145365 (accessed July 16, 2016).

30. Barghouthi, interview with the authors.

31. "Abu Mazen's Rivals in Election: The Palestinian Media Discriminates against Us," Middle East Media Research Institute Reports, December 29, 2004, http://www.memri.org/report/en/0/0/0/0/0/0/1285.htm (accessed July 11, 2016).

32. Barghouthi, interview with the authors; Shtayyeh, interview with the authors.

33. Shtayyeh, interview with the authors.

34. "National Democratic Institute, *Final Report on the Palestinian Presidential Election*" (Washington, DC: January 9, 2005), https://www.cartercenter.org/documents/2123.pdf (accessed July 10, 2016).

35. Ibid.

36. Shtayyeh, interview with the authors.

37. "2005: Abbas Triumphs in Palestinian Elections," BBC, January 9, 2005, http://news.bbc.co.uk/onthisday/hi/dates/stories/january/9/newsid_4514000/4514342.stm (accessed July 10, 2016).

38. "Abbas Wins His Mandate in Presidential Poll," *Telegraph*, January 10, 2005, http://www.telegraph.co.uk/news/1480835/Abbas-wins-his-mandate-in-presidential-poll.html (accessed July 10, 2016).

39. "Abbas Declared Victor in Palestinian Election: New President Ready for 'Difficult Mission' en Route to Statehood," CNN, January 11, 2005, http://edition.cnn.com/2005/WORLD/meast/01/10/palestinian.elections/ (accessed July 10, 2016).

40. "Presidential Election Final Results," Central Elections Commission (Palestinian Authority), http://www.elections.ps/Portals/0/pdf/SummaryPresidentialElectionsFinalResults2005.pdf (accessed July 10, 2016).

41. Barghouthi, interview with the authors.

42. "The 1996 Presidential and Legislative Elections," Central Elections Commission (Palestinian Authority), http://www.elections.ps/Portals/0/pdf/Resultselection1996.pdf (accessed July 10, 2016).

43. "PA President Mahmud Abbas, Inaugural Address to the Palestinian Council, Ramallah, 15 January 2005 (Excerpts)," *Journal of Palestine Studies* 34, no. 3 (Spring 2005): 159–86.

44. Ibid.

45. Ibid.

46. Ibid.

47. Condoleezza Rice, *No Higher Honor: A Memoir of My Years in Washington* (New York: Broadway Books, 2011), p. 332.

48. "Israel Holds off Military Offensive," Associated Press, January 18, 2005, http://www.taipeitimes.com/News/world/archives/2005/01/18/2003219917 (accessed September 1, 2016).

49. "Transcript of Mahmoud Abbas' Speech at Egypt Summit," CNN, February 8, 2005, http://www.cnn.com/2005/WORLD/meast/02/08/transcript.abbas/ (accessed September 1, 2016).

50. Arnon Regular, "New Palestinian Cabinet Takes Office," *Ha'aretz*, February 24, 2005, http://www.haaretz.com/news/new-palestinian-cabinet-takes-office-1.151191 (accessed September 1, 2016).

51. "Abbas Decides to Challenge Powerful Militant Groups," Associated Press, April 4, 2005, http://www.tulsaworld.com/archives/

abbas-decides-to-challenge-powerful-militant-groups/article_98ffd291
-ec37-5696-be69-89a422b81e98.html (accessed September 1, 2016).

52. "Gunmen Break up Fatah Party Meeting in Challenge to Abbas," Associated Press, March 10, 2005, http://usatoday30.usatoday.com/news/world/2005-03-10-mideast_x.htm (accessed September 1, 2016).

53. "Abbas Decides to Challenge Powerful Militant Groups," Associated Press.

54. Ibid.

55. "Israel Formally Gives up Jericho," BBC News, March 16, 2005, http://news.bbc.co.uk/2/hi/middle_east/4353109.stm (accessed September 1, 2016).

56. "Israel Completes Handover of West Bank Town: Gate Blocking Traffic into Tulkarem Blocked," Associated Press, March 22, 2005, http://www.nbcnews.com/id/7183904/ns/world_news/t/israel-completes-handover-west-bank-town/#.V5Ajz5MrLsl (accessed September 1, 2016).

57. Peter Baker and Glenn Kessler, "Bush Offers Palestinians Aid," *Washington Post*, May 27, 2005, http://www.washingtonpost.com/wp-dyn/content/article/2005/05/26/AR2005052600292.html (accessed November 17, 2016).

58. "Bush Pledges $50 Million to Palestinian Authority," CNN, May 26, 2005, http://www.cnn.com/2005/WORLD/meast/05/26/abbas.bush/ (accessed March 13, 2017).

59. Greg Myre, "The Mideast Turmoil: Reaction; Palestinians and Other Arabs Assail Bush for Stand on Israel," *New York Times*, April 15, 2004, http://www.nytimes.com/2004/04/15/world/mideast-turmoil-reaction-palestinians-other-arabs-assail-bush-for-stand-israel.html?_r=0 (accessed September 1, 2016).

60. Al-Ajrami, interview with the authors.

61. David Landau, *Arik: The Life of Ariel Sharon* (New York: Alfred A. Knopf, 2013), p. 453.

62. Weisglass, interview with the authors.

63. Al-Ajrami, interview with the authors.

64. Daniel Kurtzer, interview with the authors, November 9, 2016.

65. Al-Ajrami, interview with the authors.

66. Weisglass, interview with the authors.

CHAPTER 7. LOSING PALESTINE

1. Ali Waked, "Bargouthi Gives Interviews: We Will Build a Unity Government" [in Hebrew], Ynet News, January 22, 2006, http://www.ynet.co.il/articles/0,7340,L-3204617,00.html (accessed November 17, 2016).

2. Ibid.

3. "PA President Mahmud Abbas, Inaugural Address to the Palestinian Council, Ramallah, 15 January 2005 (Excerpts)," *Journal of Palestine Studies* 34, no. 3 (Spring 2005): 159–86.

4. Daniel Kurtzer, Scott Lasensky, William Quandt, Steven Spiegel, and Shibley Telhami, *The Peace Puzzle: America's Quest for Arab-Israeli Peace, 1989–2011* (Cornell: Cornell University Press, 2012), p. 199.

5. Condoleezza Rice, *No Higher Honor: A Memoir of My Years in Washington* (New York: Broadway Books, 2011), p. 415.

6. Kurtzer et al., *Peace Puzzle*, p. 200.

7. "Hamas Leader in Gaza Dr. Mahmoud Al-Zahar: We'll Join the Legislative Council—and Keep our Guns," Middle East Media Research Institute Reports, November 18, 2005, http://www.memri.org/report/en/0/0/0/0/0/0/1531.htm (accessed October 18, 2016).

8. Elliott Abrams, interview with the authors, June 13, 2016.

9. Elliott Abrams, *Tested by Zion: The Bush Administration and the Israeli-Palestinian Conflict* (Cambridge: Cambridge University Press, 2013), p. 146.

10. Robert Danin, interview with the authors, November 2, 2016.

11. Abrams, interview with the authors.

12. Senior Hamas official, interview with the authors, June 29, 2016.

13. Avi Issacharoff, "How the US Failed to Thwart Hamas' Rise to Power" [in Hebrew], Walla! News, May 17, 2003, http://news.walla.co.il/item/2642814 (accessed December 21, 2016).

14. Roei Nahmias, "2006: A Year of Escalation and Downslide" [in Hebrew], Ynet News, January 2, 2006, http://www.ynet.co.il/articles/0,7340,L-3193441,00.html (accessed November 18, 2016).

15. Qaddura Fares, interview with the authors, September 18, 2016.

16. Ibid.

17. Ibid.

18. Aaron Pina, *Palestinian Elections* (Washington, DC: Congressional Research Service, February 9, 2006), https://www.fas.org/sgp/crs/mideast/RL33269.pdf (accessed October 18, 2016).

19. Dov Weisglass, interview with the authors, July 23, 2016.

20. Ibid.

21. Abrams, *Tested by Zion*, p. 151.

22. Emilio Dabed, "Toward a Constitutional Dictatorship in the West Bank?" Nakba Files, http://nakbafiles.org/2016/06/09/toward-a -constitutional-dictatorship-in-the-west-bank (accessed October 18, 2016).

23. Pina, *Palestinian Elections*.

24. National Democratic Institute for International Affairs, *Final Report on the Palestinian Legislative Council Elections* (Washington, DC: January 25, 2006), https://www.ndi.org/files/2068_ps_elect_012506.pdf (accessed October 18, 2016).

25. "The Second 2006 PLC Elections: The Final Distribution of PLC Seats," Central Elections Commission: Palestine, http://www.elections.ps/ Portals/0/pdf/The%20final%20distribution%20of%20PLC%20seats.pdf (accessed October 18, 2016).

26. Pina, *Palestinian Elections*.

27. Fares, interview with the authors.

28. "The Second 2006 PLC Elections: The Final Results for the Electoral Districts," Central Elections Commission: Palestine, http:// www.elections.ps/Portals/0/pdf/FinalresultsElectoralDistricts2006.pdf (accessed October 18, 2016).

29. Steven Erlanger, "Victory Ends 40 Years of Political Domination by Arafat's Party," *New York Times,* January 26, 2006, http://www.nytimes .com/2006/01/26/international/middleeast/victory-ends-40-years-of -political-domination-by.html (accessed October 18, 2016).

30. Mohammad Shtayyeh, interview with the authors, July 4, 2016.

31. Scott Wilson, "Hamas Sweeps Palestinian Elections, Complicating Peace Efforts in Mideast," *Washington Post,* January 27, 2006, http:// www.washingtonpost.com/wp-dyn/content/article/2006/01/26/ AR2006012600372.html (accessed October 18, 2016).

32. Ala'a Yaghi, interview with the authors, July 4, 2016.

33. Mustafa Barghouthi, interview with the authors, July 2016.

34. Mahmoud Muslih, interview with the authors, July 4, 2016.

35. "Spiegel Interview with Hamas Leader Khaled Mashaal: 'Our People Will Never Rest,'" *Der Spiegel,* February 6, 2006, http://www.spiegel .de/international/spiegel/spiegel-interview-with-hamas-leader-khaled -mashaal-our-people-will-never-rest-a-399153.html (accessed October 18, 2016).

36. Yaghi, interview with the authors.

37. Muslih, interview with the authors.

38. Hussein Ibish, interview with the authors, July 18, 2016.

39. Danin, interview with the authors.

40. "George W. Bush: The President's News Conference," The American Presidency Project, January 26, 2006, http://www.presidency.ucsb.edu/ws/index.php?pid=65146 (accessed October 18, 2016).

41. Glenn Kessler, "Bush Is Conciliatory in Accepting Victory of Hamas," *Washington Post*, January 27, 2006, http://www.washingtonpost.com/wp-dyn/content/article/2006/01/26/AR2006012601009.html (accessed October 18, 2016).

42. "Bush: President's News Conference," The American Presidency Project.

43. Abrams, interview with the authors.

44. Ari Shavit, "Watching Hamas," *New Yorker*, February 6, 2006, http://www.newyorker.com/magazine/2006/02/06/watching-hamas (accessed October 18, 2016).

45. "Transcript: Khaled Meshaal Interview," BBC News, February 8, 2006, http://news.bbc.co.uk/2/hi/middle_east/4693382.stm (accessed October 18, 2016).

46. Greg Myre, "Hamas Warns Abbas Not to Make Changes to Palestinian Authority," *New York Times*, February 8, 2006, http://www.nytimes.com/2006/02/08/world/africa/hamas-warns-abbas-not-to-make-changes-to-palestinian-authority.html (accessed October 18, 2016).

47. Former Abbas aide, interview with the authors, June 18, 2016.

48. John Kifner and Greg Myre, "Palestinians' Hamas Leader Faces Many Problems," *New York Times*, April 6, 2006, http://www.nytimes.com/2006/04/06/world/middleeast/06cnd-hamas.html (accessed December 12, 2016).

49. Robert Tait, "Hamas Leader's Daughter Treated in Israeli Hospital," *Telegraph*, October 20, 2014, http://www.telegraph.co.uk/news/worldnews/middleeast/israel/11174416/Hamas-leaders-daughter-treated-in-Israeli-hospital.html (accessed December 21, 2016); Mohammed Omer, "Hamas Forms a Government: Ismail Haniyeh—From Refugee Camp to Prime Minister's Office," *Washington Report on Middle East Affairs*, May/June 2006, http://www.wrmea.org/2006-may-june/hamas-forms-a-government.html (accessed October 18, 2016).

50. "Hamas Leader Forms New Cabinet, Minus Moderates," *Sydney Morning Herald*, March 20, 2006, http://www.smh.com.au/news/world/hamas-leader-forms-new-cabinet-minus-moderates/2006/03/19/1142703216788.html (accessed October 18, 2016).

51. Senior Hamas official, interview with the authors.

52. Former Abbas aide, interview with the authors.

53. Senior Hamas official, interview with the authors.

54. Associated Press, "Palestinian Security Deploys, Abbas Demands Hamas Militia Be Removed," *USA Today*, May 18, 2006, http://usatoday30 .usatoday.com/news/world/2006-05-18-palestine_x.htm (accessed October 18, 2016).

55. "Abbas Orders Alert after Rampage," BBC News, June 13, 2006, http://news.bbc.co.uk/2/hi/middle_east/5074108.stm (accessed October 18, 2016).

56. Associated Press, "Shooting Resumes, Gaza Cease-Fire Ends," *USA Today*, December 18, 2006, http://usatoday30.usatoday.com/news/ world/2006-12-17-palestinians_x.htm (accessed October 18, 2016).

57. Ronny Shaked, "Abbas Escapes Assassination Attempt," YNet News, January 28, 2007, http://www.ynetnews.com/articles/ 0,7340,L-3357655,00.html (accessed October 18, 2016).

58. Former PLO official, interview with the authors, June 15, 2016.

59. Ibid.

60. Senior Hamas official, interview with the authors.

61. Rory McCarthy, "Rival Palestinian Factions Agree to Form Coalition Government," *Guardian*, February 9, 2007, https://www.the guardian.com/world/2007/feb/09/israel (accessed October 18, 2016).

62. Senior Hamas official, interview with the authors.

63. David Rose, "The Gaza Bombshell," *Vanity Fair*, April 2008, http:// www.vanityfair.com/news/2008/04/gaza200804 (accessed October 18, 2016).

64. Muslih, interview with the authors.

65. "Black Pages in the Absence of Justice: Report on Bloody Fighting in the Gaza Strip from 7 to 14 June 2007," Palestine Center for Human Rights, October 1, 2007, http://www.pchrgaza.org/files/Reports/English/ pdf_spec/Gaza%20Conflict%20-%20Eng%209%20october.pdf (accessed October 16, 2016).

66. "Palestinian Horror: 2 Thrown to Death," *New York Daily News*, June 11, 2007, http://www.nydailynews.com/news/world/palestinian -horror-2-thrown-death-article-1.222464 (accessed October 18, 2016).

67. Associated Press, "Palestinian Gunmen Target Haniyeh's Home in Gaza," *Ha'aretz*, June 10, 2007, http://www.haaretz.com/news/palestinian -gunmen-target-haniyeh-s-home-in-gaza-1.222703 (accessed October 18, 2016).

68. "Black Pages in the Absence of Justice," Palestine Center for Human Rights.

69. "Hamas Battles for Control of Gaza," BBC News, June 13, 2007, http://news.bbc.co.uk/2/hi/middle_east/6748811.stm (accessed October 18, 2016).

70. Jonathan Schanzer, *Hamas vs. Fatah: The Struggle for Palestine* (New York: Palgrave Macmillan, 2008), pp. 107–108.

71. "Black Pages in the Absence of Justice," Palestine Center for Human Rights.

72. Rose, "Gaza Bombshell."

73. Efraim Sneh, interview with the authors, July 13, 2016.

74. Ibid.

75. Amos Yadlin, "Military Intelligence Director Yadlin Comments on Gaza, Syria and Lebanon," WikiLeaks, June 13, 2007, https://wikileaks .org/plusd/cables/07TELAVIV1733_a.html (accessed October 18, 2016).

76. Ibid.

77. Avi Dichter, interview with the authors, August 18, 2016.

78. "Mahmoud Abbas: No to Dialogue with the Murderers; This Is Not a Struggle between Fatah and Hamas, But Between the National Project and the Emirate of Darkness and Backwardness," Middle East Media Research Institute Reports, June 26, 2007, http://www.memri.org/report/ en/0/0/0/0/0/0/2266.htm (accessed October 18, 2016).

79. Senior Hamas official, interview with the authors.

80. "Black Pages in the Absence of Justice," Palestine Center for Human Rights.

81. Dichter, interview with the authors.

82. "GI Chief al-Tirawi Offers Ideas on PASF Control, Predicts Conflict with Hamas," WikiLeaks, February 24, 2006, https://wikileaks.org/ plusd/cables/06JERUSALEM799_a.html (accessed October 18, 2016).

83. Tawfiq Tirawi, interview with the authors, September 19, 2016.

84. Ghassan Khatib, interview with the authors, September 19, 2016.

85. Yaghi, interview with the authors.

86. Haytham al-Halabi, interview with the authors, September 14, 2016.

87. Gideon Levy, "Zakariya Zubeidi Presents," *Ha'aretz*, June 28, 2007, http://www.haaretz.com/israel-news/zakariya-zubeidi-presents-1.224244 (accessed October 18, 2016).

CHAPTER 8. AN OFFER HE COULDN'T REFUSE?

1. Tzipi Livni, interview with the authors, July 14, 2016.

2. Stuart Winer, "Hand-Drawn Map Shows What Olmert Offered for Peace," *Times of Israel*, May 23, 2013, http://www.timesofisrael.com/hand-drawn-map-shows-what-olmert-offered-for-peace/ (accessed October 18, 2016).

3. Raviv Drucker, "Olmert, Abu Mazen, and Barak Discuss the Peace Process" [in Hebrew], Israeli Channel 10, November 17, 2015, http://news.nana10.co.il/Article/?ArticleID=1158791 (accessed November 14, 2016).

4. Avi Issacharoff, "The Hope, the Fear, and the Accusations: The Peace Agreement That Stayed on a Napkin" [in Hebrew], Walla! News, May 24, 2013, http://news.walla.co.il/item/2644736 (accessed November 14, 2016).

5. Drucker, "Olmert, Abu Mazen, and Barak.""

6. Ibid.

7. Ibid.

8. Issacharoff, "The Hope, the Fear, and the Accusations."

9. Ibid.

10. Drucker, "Olmert, Abu Mazen, and Barak."

11. ."The Most Detailed Offer to End the Conflict" [in Hebrew], Ynet News, January 28, 2011, http://www.ynet.co.il/articles/0,7340,L-4020380,00.html (accessed November 15, 2016).

12. Drucker, "Olmert, Abu Mazen, and Barak."

13. Ibid.

14. Ibid.

15. Drucker, "Olmert, Abu Mazen, and Barak."

16. Ibid.

17. Ibid.

18. Livni, interview with the authors.

19. Steven Erlanger, "Quest for Mideast Peace: Can Leaders Deliver?" *New York Times*, November 25, 2007, http://www.nytimes.com/2007/11/25/world/africa/25iht-assess.1.8467861.html (accessed October 18, 2016).

20. James A. Baker, III, Lee H. Hamilton, et al., *The Iraq Study Group Report* (Houston, TX: Baker Institute, December 6, 2006), http://www.bakerinstitute.org/research/the-iraq-study-group-report/ (accessed December 14, 2016).

21. Condoleezza Rice, *No Higher Honor: A Memoir of My Years in Washington* (New York: Broadway Books, 2011), p. 600.

22. Elliott Abrams, *Tested by Zion: The Bush Administration and the Israeli-Palestinian Conflict* (Cambridge: Cambridge University Press, 2013), p. 248.

23. "Annapolis Agreement: Full Text," *Guardian*, November 27, 2007, https://www.theguardian.com/world/2007/nov/27/israel.usa1 (accessed October 18, 2016).

24. "George W. Bush: Interview with Nahum Barnea and Shimon Shiffer of Yedioth Ahronoth," The American Presidency Project, January 2, 2008, http://www.presidency.ucsb.edu/ws/?pid=76254 (accessed November 15, 2016).

25. Yoram Raved, interview with Mr. Tibon, April 1, 2014.

26. Ibid.

27. Ibid.

28. The Israeli minutes of these meetings were provided to the authors of this book. The minutes cited in this chapter summarize at least five meetings that took place in Spain between July 2006 and February 2008. The minutes are in Hebrew and were produced by the Israeli participants following each meeting. Mr. Agha and Mr. Khalidi did not confirm the veracity of these documents.

29. Document obtained by the authors.

30. Ibid.

31. Ibid.

32. Ibid.

33. Raved, interview with the authors.

34. Document obtained by the authors.

35. Ibid.

36. Ibid.

37. Former PLO official, interview with the authors, June 15, 2016.

38. "30 Years, 4 Prisoner Exchange Deals: Will There Be Another to Return Israelis in Gaza?" YNet News, July 11, 2015, http://www.ynetnews .com/articles/0,7340,L-4678530,00.html (accessed October 18, 2016).

39. Former PLO official, interview with the authors.

40. Rice, *No Higher Honor*, p. 651.

41. Ibid., pp. 651–53.

42. Alison Leigh Cowan, "Olmert Tied to New York Developer in Scandal," *New York Times*, May 7, 2008, http://www.nytimes.com/2008/05/07/world/africa/07iht-07olmert.12632880.html?_r=0 (accessed October 18, 2016).

43. Drucker, "Olmert, Abu Mazen, and Barak."

44. Elior Levy, "Abu Mazen and the Conspiracy: Who Brought Down Olmert?" [in Hebrew], Ynet News, October 9, 2011, http://www.ynet .co.il/articles/0,7340,L-4132794,00.html (accessed November 14, 2016).

45. Avi Issacharoff, "Abu Mazen: The Draft of Olmert's Offer Is Not Serious" [in Hebrew], *Ha'aretz*, August 12, 2008, http://www.haaretz.co.il/ misc/1.1554369 (accessed November 14, 2016).

46. Drucker, "Olmert, Abu Mazen, and Barak."

47. Rice, *No Higher Honor*, p. 724.

48. Elliott Abrams, interview with the authors, June 13, 2016.

49. Abrams, *Tested by Zion*, p. 285.

50. Ben Birnbaum, "The End of the Two-State Solution: Why the Window Is Closing on Middle-East Peace," *New Republic*, March 11, 2013, https://newrepublic.com/article/112617/israel-palestine-and-end-two -state-solution (accessed October 18, 2016).

51. Livni, interview with the authors.

52. Drucker, "Olmert, Abu Mazen, and Barak."

53. Former PLO official, interview with the authors.

54. Daniel Kurtzer, interview with the authors, November 9, 2016.

55. Aaron David Miller, interview with the authors, November 2, 2016.

56. Yair Hirschfeld, interview with the authors, June 21, 2016.

57. Amit Segal, "Abu Mazen Was Right," Amit Segal [in Hebrew], November 21, 2015, http://www.amitsegal.co.il/%D7%9B%D7%9C%D7 %9C%D7%99/%D7%90%D7%91%D7%95-%D7%9E%D7%90%D7%96 %D7%9F-%D7%A6%D7%93%D7%A7-%D7%95%D7%A2%D7%95%D7 %93-%D7%A9%D7%AA%D7%99-%D7%94%D7%A2%D7%A8%D7%95 %D7%AA-%D7%A2%D7%9C-%D7%94%D7%9B%D7%A0%D7%A1 %D7%AA-%D7%95%D7%A2/ (accessed November 18, 2016).

CHAPTER 9. BETWEEN BARACK AND BIBI

1. Aryeh Shalev, *Israel's Intelligence Assessment before the Yom Kippur War: Disentangling Deception and Distraction* (East Sussex: Sussex Academic Press, 2010), p. 15.

2. Tim Butcher, "Israel Attack on Gaza: Fragile Peace Shattered Again," *Telegraph*, December 27, 2008, http://www.telegraph.co.uk/news/ worldnews/middleeast/palestinianauthority/3981502/Israel-attack-on -Gaza-Fragile-peace-shattered-again.html (accessed November 15, 2016).

3. Yaakov Lappin, "IDF Releases Cast Lead Casualty Numbers," *Jerusalem Post*, March 26, 2009, http://www.webcitation.org/5niwZTV9K (accessed November 15, 2016); Canadians for Justice and Peace in the Middle East, "Israel's 'Operation Cast Lead' 1,400 Palestinian Deaths, 5000 Wounded: Palestinian Doctor Offers Message of Reconciliation after Loss of Three Daughters," Centre for Research on Globalization, June 2, 2010, http://www.globalresearch.ca/israel-s-operation-cast-lead-1-400 -palestinians-deaths-5000-wounded/19524 (accessed November 15, 2016).

4. "UN Divided on Gaza Resolution: Security Council Meeting Ends without Vote as Aid Groups Warn of Humanitarian Catastrophe," Al Jazeera, January 1, 2009, http://www.aljazeera.com/news/middle east/2009/01/20091114211413246.html (accessed November 15, 2016).

5. Mohammad Yaghi, "The Impact of the Gaza Conflict on Palestinian Politics," Washington Institute for Near East Policy, December 31, 2008, http://www.washingtoninstitute.org/policy-analysis/view/the -impact-of-the-gaza-conflict-on-palestinian-politics (accessed November 15, 2016).

6. Tzipi Livni, interview with the authors, July 14, 2016.

7. "Responses to the War in Gaza," *London Review of Books*, January 29, 2009, http://www.lrb.co.uk/v31/n02/gaza-writers/responses-to-the -war-in-gaza (accessed November 15, 2016).

8. Peter Wallsten, "Allies of Palestinians See a Friend in Obama," *Los Angeles Times*, April 10, 2008, http://articles.latimes.com/2008/apr/10/ nation/na-obamamideast10 (accessed March 14, 2017).

9. Oliver Burkeman and Ed Pilkington, "Obama: The First 100 Hours," *Guardian*, January 23, 2009, https://www.theguardian.com/ world/2009/jan/24/barack-obama-inauguration (accessed November 15, 2016).

10. Daniel Shapiro, "1. Today seems like a good day to debunk this oft-repeated but erroneous claim: That Obama's first call as POTUS was to Abbas. It wasn't," Twitter post, March 10, 2017, 4:29 a.m., https://twitter .com/DanielBShapiro/status/840177671585878016 (accessed March 14, 2017).

11. Roni Sofer, "Obama Calls Abbas, Olmert on First Day," YNet News, January 21, 2009, http://www.ynetnews.com/articles/0,7340,L-3659961,00 .html (accessed November 15, 2016).

12. "Nabil Shaath on Int'l Peace Conference: Anything Is Better Than US-Led Negotiations; Do We Need to Hijack Planes Again to Stir Interest in Our Cause?" Middle East Media Research Institute video, 2:24, February

1, 2016, http://www.memri.org/clip_transcript/en/5301.htm (accessed November 15, 2016).

13. Patrick Martin, "Palestinians Stunned by First Presidential Phone Call," *Globe and Mail,* January 21, 2009, http://www.theglobeandmail .com/news/world/palestinians-stunned-by-first-presidential-phone-call/ article1147500/ (accessed November 15, 2016).

14. Jeff Zeleny, "Obama Meets with Israeli and Palestinian Leaders," *New York Times,* July 24, 2008, http://www.nytimes.com/2008/07/24/us/ politics/24obama.html (accessed November 15, 2016).

15. "Barack Obama Administration: Remarks by President Obama and President Abbas," Jewish Virtual Library, May 28, 2009, http://www .jewishvirtuallibrary.org/remarks-by-president-obama-and-president -abbas-may-2009 (accessed March 12, 2017).

16. Barak Ravid, "Palestinians Reject Netanyahu's 'Economic Peace' Plan: Top PA Officials Refuse to Meet Israelis over Issue, Worry Israel Will Use Plan to Avoid Political Process," *Ha'aretz,* July 9, 2009, http://www .haaretz.com/palestinians-reject-netanyahu-s-economic-peace-plan -1.279616 (accessed November 15, 2016).

17. "Remarks by President Obama and President Abbas," Jewish Virtual Library.

18. Ibid.

19. Ibid.

20. "Text: Obama's Speech in Cairo," *New York Times,* June 4, 2009, http://www.nytimes.com/2009/06/04/us/politics/04obama.text.html (accessed March 13, 2017).

21. Kevin Flower, Paula Hancocks, Mike Schwartz and Kareem Khadder, "Obama's Speech Draws Mixed Reviews in Middle East," CNN, June 4, 2009, http://www.cnn.com/2009/POLITICS/06/04/obama .mideast.reactions/index.html?iref=nextin (accessed November 15, 2016).

22. Benjamin Netanyahu, "Full Text of Netanyahu's Foreign Policy Speech at Bar Ilan," *Ha'aretz,* June 14, 2009, http://www.haaretz.com/ news/full-text-of-netanyahu-s-foreign-policy-speech-at-bar-ilan-1.277922 (accessed November 15, 2016).

23. Yair Rosenberg, "Did Netanyahu Invent the Demand That Israel Be Recognized as a Jewish State? The Short Answer Is 'No.' The Long Answer Is Also 'No,'" *Tablet,* January 21, 2014, http://www.tabletmag.com/ scroll/160131/did-netanyahu-invent-the-demand-that-israel-be-recognized -as-a-jewish-state (accessed November 15, 2016).

24. "The Palestine Papers: Talking Points for Erekat Re: Israeli

Preconditions," Al Jazeera, November 15, 2007, http://www.aj transparency.com/en/projects/thepalestinepapers/20121823746218853 .html (accessed November 15, 2016).

25. "Transcript: Saeb Erekat," Al Jazeera, April 2, 2014, http://www .aljazeera.com/programmes/headtohead/2014/03/transcript-dr-saeb -erekat-201432611433441126.html (accessed November 15, 2016).

26. Amit Segal, "Netanyahu's Father Exposes the Trick" [in Hebrew], Channel 2 News, July 8, 2009, http://www.mako.co.il/news-channel2/ Channel-2-Newscast/Article-a7831a348cf7321004.htm (accessed November 15, 2016)

27. Isabel Kershner, "Netanyahu Backs Palestinian State, with Caveats," *New York Times*, June 14, 2009, http://www.nytimes.com/2009/ 06/15/world/middleeast/15mideast.html (accessed November 15, 2016).

28. International Crisis Group, "Palestine: Salvaging Fatah," *Middle East Report* 91, November 12, 2009, https://d2071andvip0wj.cloudfront .net/91-palestine-salvaging-fatah.pdf (accessed November 15, 2016).

29. *The Fatah Constitution*, Israel Palestine Creative Regional Initiatives, July 25, 1964, http://www.ipcri.org/index.php/publications/historical -documents/168-fatah-constitution (accessed November 15, 2016).

30. Mohamed El-Sharkawy, "Fatah's Seventh General Congress: Revival or Division?" *Al Ahram*, November 10, 2016, http://weekly.ahram .org.eg/News/17811/19/Fatah%E2%80%99s-Seventh-General-Congress –Revival–or–division-.aspx (accessed November 15, 2016).

31. International Crisis Group, "Palestine: Salvaging Fatah."

32. Ibid.

33. Ibid.

34. Isabel Kershner, "Abbas Urges 'New Start' at Fatah Conference," *New York Times*, August 4, 2009, http://www.nytimes.com/2009/08/05/ world/middleeast/05fatah.html (accessed November 15, 2016).

35. International Crisis Group, "Palestine: Salvaging Fatah."

36. Haytham al-Halabi, interview with the authors, September 14, 2016.

37. Rory McCarthy, "Fatah Holds First Party Conference for 20 Years," *Guardian*, August 4, 2009, https://www.theguardian.com/world/2009/ aug/04/fatah-conference-abbas-west-bank (accessed November 15, 2016).

38. Al-Halabi, interview with the authors.

39. International Crisis Group, "Palestine: Salvaging Fatah."

40. Al-Halabi, interview with the authors.

41. Ibid.

42. Mohammed Assadi, "Abbas Says Nothing 'Unsound' about Fatah Election," Reuters, August 13, 2009, http://www.reuters.com/article/us-palestinians-fatah-election-idUSLD42082220090813 (accessed November 15, 2016).

43. "Sixth General Fatah Conference Gets Underway in Bethlehem," YouTube video, 3:20, posted by "AP Archive," July 23, 2015, https://www.youtube.com/watch?v=6HvJVCFfc6A (accessed November 15, 2016).

44. "Palestinian Public Opinion Poll No (33)," Palestinian Center for Policy and Survey Research, August 13–15, 2009, http://www.pcpsr.org/en/node/220 (accessed November 15, 2016); "Palestinian Public Opinion Poll No (34)," Palestinian Center for Policy and Survey Research, December 10-12, 2009, http://www.pcpsr.org/en/node/219 (accessed November 15, 2016).

45. Mohsen Moh'd Saleh, "On the Experience of the Palestinian Liberation Organization," *Palestine Chronicle*, October 23, 2012, http://palestinechronicle.com/old/view_article_details.php?id=19655 (accessed November 15, 2016).

46. Ben Birnbaum, "The Visionary: A Palestinian Reformer's Downfall," *New Republic*, May 4, 2012, https://newrepublic.com/article/103096/fayyad-palestinian-state-reform-israel-abbas-minister (accessed November 15, 2016).

47. Thomas Friedman, "Green Shoots in Palestine," *New York Times*, August 4, 2009, http://www.nytimes.com/2009/08/05/opinion/05friedman.html (accessed November 15, 2016).

48. Attila Somfalvi, "Peres: Fayyad—Palestinians' 1st 'Ben-Gurionist,'" YNet News, February 2, 2010, http://www.ynetnews.com/articles/0,7340,L-3843457,00.html (accessed November 15, 2016).

49. Palestinian National Authority, "Palestine: Ending the Occupation, Establishing the State," Program of the Thirteenth Government, August 2009, https://unispal.un.org/DPA/DPR/unispal.nsf/0/A013B65A5984E671852576B800581931 (accessed November 15, 2016).

50. Isabel Kershner, "Palestinian Leader Maps Out Plan for Workings of Independent State," *New York Times*, August 26, 2009, http://query.nytimes.com/gst/fullpage.html?res=9901E1DF1139F935A1575BC0A96F9C8B63 (accessed November 15, 2016).

51. David Makovsky, "The Fayyad Resignation: Scapegoating a State-Builder," Washington Institute for Near East Policy, April 16, 2013, http://www.washingtoninstitute.org/policy-analysis/view/the-fayad-resignation-scapegoating-a-state-builder (accessed December 22, 2016).

52. Reuters, "Fatah Officials Demand Abbas Fires Western-Backed Fayyad," *Ha'aretz*, March 3, 2011, http://www.haaretz.com/israel-news/fatah-officials-demand-abbas-fires-western-backed-fayyad-1.346968 (accessed December 22, 2016).

53. Grant Rumley, "The Purge of Abbas's Adversaries Looms over Ramallah," *Weekly Standard*, November 29, 2016, http://www.weekly standard.com/the-purge-of-abbass-adversaries-looms-over-ramallah/article/2005588 (accessed December 27, 2016).

54. Human Rights Council, *Human Rights in Palestine and Other Occupied Arab Territories: Report of the United Nations Fact-Finding Mission on the Gaza Conflict* (UN General Assembly, September 25, 2009), http://www2.ohchr.org/english/bodies/hrcouncil/docs/12session/A-HRC-12-48.pdf (accessed November 15, 2016).

55. Ibid.

56. Hanan Greenberg, Amit Cohen, Maya Bengal, and Amir Bohbot, "The Goldstone Report, Abu Mazen's Tapes and the Blackmail" [in Hebrew], NRG, October 5, 2009, http://www.nrg.co.il/online/1/ART1/949/920.html (accessed November 15, 2016).

57. Uri Blau and Daniel Dolev, "Panama Papers: Leaks Reveal Abbas' Son's $1m Holding in Company with Ties to Palestinian Authority," *Ha'aretz*, April 7, 2016, http://www.haaretz.com/middle-east-news/1.713347 (accessed November 15, 2016).

58. Akiva Eldar, "The Head of the Shin Bet Threatened Abbas: Give up on Goldstone or We'll Turn the West Bank into a Second Gaza" [in Hebrew], *Ha'aretz*, January 17, 2010, http://www.haaretz.co.il/news/politics/1.1184872 (accessed November 15, 2016).

59. S. Farhan Mustafa, "PA Stonewalled the Goldstone Vote: PA, with US Encouragement, Delayed a UN Vote on the Goldstone Report into War Crimes Committed during Israel's Gaza War," Al Jazeera, January 26, 2011, http://www.aljazeera.com/palestinepapers/2011/01/2011126123125167974.html (accessed November 15, 2016).

60. Nasser Najjar, "Hamas Piles Up Pressure on Abbas," *Gulf News Palestine*, October 11, 2009, http://gulfnews.com/news/mena/palestine/hamas-piles-up-pressure-on-abbas-1.512888 (accessed November 15, 2016); Avi Issacharoff, "Hamas Accuses Abbas of Treason for 'Justifying' Gaza War: Syria Postpones Abbas' Scheduled Visit in Damascus over PA Decision to Delay Vote on Goldstone Report," *Ha'aretz*, October 5, 2009, http://www.haaretz.com/news/hamas-accuses-abbas-of-treason-for-justifying-gaza-war-1.6656 (accessed November 15, 2016).

61. Mohammed Assadi, "Palestinians Slam Abbas over UN Gaza Report Delay," Reuters, October 4, 2009, http://www.reuters.com/article/idUSL4539077 (accessed November 15, 2016).

62. Avi Issacharoff and Jackie Hugie, "Balad Party Will Call on Abu Mazen to Resign over Goldstone Affair" [in Hebrew], *Ha'aretz*, October 6, 2009, http://www.haaretz.co.il/news/politics/1.1283831 (accessed November 15, 2016).

63. Assadi, "Palestinians Slam Abbas."

64. Khaled Abu Toameh, "Abbas Blames Aides for Motion's Removal," *Jerusalem Post*, October 5, 2009, http://www.americantaskforce.org/daily_news_article/2009/10/06/1254801600_14 (accessed November 15, 2016).

65. Isabel Kershner and Neil MacFarquhar, "Furor Sends Palestinians into Shift on UN Report," *New York Times*, October 7, 2009, http://www.nytimes.com/2009/10/08/world/middleeast/08mideast.html?_r=1&ref=middleeast (accessed November 15, 2016).

66. Tzvi Yehezkeli and Reshef Saar, "Masha'al Attacks Abu Mazen: Saved Israel from the Goldstone Report" [in Hebrew], Channel 10 News, October 11, 2009, http://10tv.nana10.co.il/Article/?ArticleID=670605 (accessed November 15, 2016).

67. Curtis Doebbler, "UN Rights Body Endorses Goldstone Report," Ma'an News Agency, October 16, 2009, http://www.maannews.com/Content.aspx?id=232673 (accessed November 15, 2016).

68. Yair Altman, "Yesha Chair: US' Offer Is Poisonous Pill," YNet News, October 2, 2010, http://www.ynetnews.com/articles/0,7340,L-3962806,00.html (accessed November 15, 2016).

69. "How a Slap Sparked Tunisia's Revolution," CBS News, February 22, 2011, http://www.cbsnews.com/news/how-a-slap-sparked-tunisias-revolution-22-02-2011/ (accessed November 15, 2016).

70. "Palestinian Public Opinion Poll No (39)," Palestinian Center for Policy and Survey Research, March 17–19, 2011, http://www.pcpsr.org/en/node/214 (accessed November 15, 2016).

71. Seumas Milne and Ian Black, "The Story Behind the Palestine Papers," *Guardian*, January 23, 2011, https://www.theguardian.com/world/2011/jan/23/story-behind-leaked-palestine-papers (accessed November 15, 2016).

72. "Palestine Papers: Meeting Minutes Dr. Saeb Erekat—Sen. George Mitchell," Al Jazeera, October 21, 2009, http://ajtransparency.com/files/4899.pdf (accessed November 15, 2016).

73. "Palestine Papers: Minutes of the General Plenary Meeting,"

Al Jazeera, June 30, 2008, http://ajtransparency.com/files/2826.pdf (accessed November 15, 2016).

74. "Palestine Papers: Trilateral Meeting Minutes," Al Jazeera, June 15, 2008, http://ajtransparency.com/files/2825.pdf (accessed November 15, 2016).

75. Joshua Mitnick, "How Leaked Palestinian Documents Will Affect Abbas, Peace Process," *Christian Science Monitor,* January 24, 2011, http://www.csmonitor.com/World/Middle-East/2011/0124/How-leaked-Palestinian-documents-will-affect-Abbas-peace-process (accessed November 15, 2016).

76. "Abbas: Concessions in Palestine Papers Came from Israel, Not Us," *Ha'aretz,* January 24, 2011, http://www.haaretz.com/israel-news/abbas-concessions-in-palestine-papers-came-from-israel-not-us-1.338882 (accessed November 15, 2016).

77. "Palestine Papers: Al Jazeera, Guardian Release Documents on Israeli-Palestinian Conflict," *Huffington Post,* May 25, 2011, http://www.huffingtonpost.com/2011/01/23/palestine-papers-israel-conflict-wikileaks-documents-released_n_812776.html (accessed November 15, 2016).

78. "Palestinian Public Opinion Poll No (39)."

79. Nizar Farsakh, interview with the authors, June 15, 2016.

80. *Towards New Strategies for Palestinian National Liberation,* Palestine Strategy Group, August 2011, http://www.palestinestrategygroup.ps/wp-content/uploads/2015/09/Report-2011.pdf (accessed November 15, 2016).

81. "Yasser Arafat's Speech at the UN General Assembly Olive Branch Speech," YouTube video, 1:05, posted by "oterbulbul," November 24, 2012, https://www.youtube.com/watch?v=LVXN6EiqKFY (accessed November 15, 2016).

82. Agence France-Presse, "United Nations Observer Status: Facts," *National,* November 28, 2012, http://www.thenational.ae/news/world/middle-east/united-nations-observer-status-facts (accessed November 15, 2016).

83. Dennis Ross, *The Missing Peace: The Inside Story of the Fight for Middle East Peace* (New York: Farrar, Straus and Giroux, 2004), p. 491.

84. "United States Vetoes Security Council Resolution on Israeli Settlements," UN News Centre, February 18, 2011, http://www.un.org/apps/news/story.asp?NewsID=37572#.WA5IjvkrKCg (accessed November 15, 2016).

85. Newsweek Staff, "Palestinian Leader Mahmoud Abbas's Frustra-

tion with Obama," *Newsweek,* April 24, 2011, http://www.newsweek.com/palestinian-leader-mahmoud-abbass-frustration-obama-66509 (accessed November 15, 2016).

86. Ibid.

87. "United States Vetoes Security Council."

88. "Palestinian Public Opinion Poll No (41)," Palestinian Center for Policy and Survey Research, September 15–17, 2011, http://www.pcpsr.org/en/node/212 (accessed November 15, 2016).

89. Mahmoud Abbas, "The Long Overdue Palestinian State," *New York Times,* May 16, 2011, http://www.nytimes.com/2011/05/17/opinion/17abbas.html (accessed November 15, 2016).

90. Ibid.

91. Steven Erlanger and Scott Sayare, "UNESCO Accepts Palestinians as Full Members," *New York Times,* October 31, 2011, http://www.nytimes.com/2011/11/01/world/middleeast/unesco-approves-full-membership-for-palestinians.html (accessed November 15, 2016).

92. Barak Ravid, "With UNESCO Membership Granted, Palestinians Seek to Join 16 More UN Agencies: World Health Organization, Intellectual Property Organization, and Atomic Agency Are among the Organizations Where the PA Will Request Full Membership," *Ha'aretz,* November 1, 2011, http://www.haaretz.com/israel-news/with-unesco-membership-granted-palestinians-seek-to-join-16-more-un-agencies-1.393134 (accessed November 15, 2016).

93. Ethan Bronner and Isabel Kershner, "Palestinians Set Bid for UN Seat, Clashing with US," *New York Times,* September 16, 2011, http://www.nytimes.com/2011/09/17/world/middleeast/Abbas-Security-Council-United-Nations-Vote.html (accessed November 15, 2016).

94. Chris McGreal, "Palestinians Braced for Fresh Setback in UN Statehood Bid: European Nations Set to Back US Opposition to Move, Meaning Washington Does Not Have to Exercise Its Security Council Veto," *Guardian,* November 9, 2011, https://www.theguardian.com/world/2011/nov/09/palestinians-setback-un-statehood-bid (accessed November 15, 2016).

95. Chris McGreal, "UN Vote on Palestinian State Put Off Amid Lack of Support: Palestinians to Decide Whether to Press Statehood Issue after Mustering Only Eight of Nine Votes Needed to Win Approval," *Guardian,* November 11, 2011, https://www.theguardian.com/world/2011/nov/11/united-nations-delays-palestinian-statehood-vote (accessed November 15, 2016).

96. Tony Karon, "Gilad Shalit and the End of the Israeli-Palestinian Peace Process," *Time*, October 17, 2011, http://world.time.com/2011/10/17/gilad-shalit-and-the-end-of-the-israeli-palestinian-peace-process/ (accessed November 15, 2016).

97. Walter Reich, "Saving Shalit, Encouraging Terror," *New York Times*, October 18, 2011, http://www.nytimes.com/2011/10/18/opinion/saving -a-soldier-encouraging-terror.html (accessed November 15, 2016).

98. "Gilad Shalit Prisoner Swap Was Partly a Response to 2011 Social Protests, Ex-Cabinet Secretary Says," *Ha'aretz*, June 25, 2016, http://www .haaretz.com/israel-news/1.727060 (accessed November 15, 2016).

CHAPTER 10. NEGOTIATOR NO MORE

1. Gadi Baltiansky, interview with the authors, July 12, 2016.

2. Grant Rumley and Amir Tibon, "The Death and Life of the Two-State Solution," *Foreign Affairs*, July/August 2015, https://www.foreign affairs.com/articles/israel/2015-06-16/death-and-life-two-state-solution (accessed December 27, 2016).

3. Isabel Kershner, "Spreading Palestinian Protests Focus on Leaders," *New York Times*, September 10, 2012, http://www.nytimes.com/2012/09/11/world/middleeast/spreading-palestinian-protests-focus-on -leaders.html (accessed November 16, 2016).

4. "Protests across West Bank against High Cost of Living," Ma'an News Agency, September 4, 2012, http://www.maannews.com/Content .aspx?id=517262 (accessed December 15, 2016).

5. Mahmoud Abbas, "Abbas' Remarks to the UN General Assembly, September 2012," Council on Foreign Relations, September 27, 2012, http://www.cfr.org/palestine/abbas-remarks-un-general-assembly -september-2012/p29168 (accessed November 16, 2016).

6. "Full Speech: Mahmoud Abbas Addresses the UN," YouTube video, 21:53, posted by "Al Jazeera English," November 29, 2012, https://www.youtube.com/watch?v=Hsv0GUNcGG8 (accessed November 16, 2016).

7. The Learning Network, "Nov. 29, 1947 | UN Partitions Palestine, Allowing for Creation of Israel," *New York Times*, November 29, 2011, http://learning.blogs.nytimes.com/2011/11/29/nov-29-1947-united -nations-partitions-palestine-allowing-for-creation-of-israel/?_r=0 (accessed November 16, 2016).

8. "General Assembly Votes Overwhelmingly to Accord Palestine 'Non-Member Observer State' Status in United Nations," United Nations, November 29, 2012, http://www.un.org/press/en/2012/ga11317.doc.htm (accessed November 16, 2016).

9. Ewen MacAskill and Chris McGreal, "UN General Assembly Makes Resounding Vote in Favour of Palestinian Statehood," *Guardian*, November 29, 2012, https://www.theguardian.com/world/2012/nov/29/united-nations-vote-palestine-state (accessed November 16, 2016).

10. "Palestinians Celebrate Status Upgrade at UN: Overwhelming Majority of States Vote to Give Palestine Non-Member Observer Status, Despite Israeli and US Opposition," Al Jazeera, November 30, 2012, http://www.aljazeera.com/news/middleeast/2012/11/201211292 23421111270.html (accessed November 16, 2016).

11. Rumley and Tibon, "Death and Life of the Two-State Solution."

12. Saeb Erekat, briefing to Western policymakers, Ramallah, September 17, 2016.

13. Harriet Sherwood, "Kerry: Two Years Left to Reach Two-State Solution in Middle East Peace Process," *Guardian*, April 18, 2013, https://www.theguardian.com/world/2013/apr/18/kerry-two-state-solution-middle-east (accessed November 16, 2016).

14. Senior US official, interview with Mr. Tibon, June 8, 2014.

15. "Full Text: Obama, Abbas Remarks in Ramallah," Ma'an News Agency, March 21, 2013, http://www.maannews.com/Content .aspx?id=577528 (accessed November 16, 2016).

16. Ibid.

17. Senior Israeli official, interview with Mr. Tibon, July 14, 2014.

18. Ibid.

19. Senior US official, interview with Mr. Tibon.

20. Ibid.

21. Ibid.

22. Mohammad Shtayyeh, briefing to national security professionals, Ramallah, September 17, 2016.

23. "Palestinian Public Opinion Poll No (42)," Palestinian Center for Policy and Survey Research, December 15–17, 2011, http://www.pcpsr .org/en/node/211 (accessed November 16, 2016).

24. Former senior US official, interview with Mr. Tibon, July 7, 2013.

25. Ben Birnbaum and Amir Tibon, "The Explosive, Inside Story of How John Kerry Built an Israel-Palestine Peace Plan—and Watched it Crumble," *New Republic*, July 20, 2014, https://newrepublic.com/

article/118751/how-israel-palestine-peace-deal-died (accessed November 16, 2016).

26. Barak Ravid, "EU's New Policy on Israeli Settlements: The Full Guidelines," *Ha'aretz*, July 16, 2013, http://www.haaretz.com/israel-news/ .premium-1.536155 (accessed November 16, 2016).

27. Birnbaum and Tibon, "Explosive, Inside Story."

28. Ibid.

29. Ibid.

30. Ibid.

31. Ibid.

32. Ibid.

33. "Abbas Accepts Resignation of Palestinian Peace Negotiator Shtayyeh," *Jerusalem Post*, November 22, 2013, http://www.jpost.com/ Diplomacy-and-Politics/Abbas-accepts-resignation-of-Palestinian-peace -negotiator-Shtayyeh-332671 (accessed November 16, 2016).

34. Birnbaum and Tibon, "Explosive, Inside Story."

35. Ibid.

36. Martin Indyk, "*The Pursuit of Middle East Peace: A Status Report*" (Washington, DC: Washington Institute for Near East Policy, May 8, 2014), https://www.washingtoninstitute.org/uploads/Documents/other/ IndykKeynote20140508.pdf (accessed December 27, 2016).

37. Birnbaum and Tibon, "Explosive, Inside Story."

38. Ibid.

39. Associated Press, "Palestinians 'Could Accept' Three-Year Israeli West Bank Withdrawal," *Japan Times*, January 29, 2014, http://www .japantimes.co.jp/news/2014/01/29/world/palestinians-could-accept -three-year-israeli-west-bank-withdrawal/#.WF06T1MrKCh (accessed December 23, 2016).

40. Birnbaum and Tibon, "Explosive, Inside Story."

41. Ibid.

42. Ibid.

43. "Remarks by President Obama and President Abbas of the Palestinian Authority," The White House, March 17, 2014, https:// obamawhitehouse.archives.gov/the-press-office/2014/03/17/remarks -president-obama-and-president-abbas-palestinian-authority (accessed March 13, 2017).

44. Birnbaum and Tibon, "Explosive, Inside Story."

45. Ibid.

46. Ibid.

47. Jack Khoury and Barak Ravid, "Hamas, Fatah Sign Reconciliation Agreement," *Ha'aretz*, April 23, 2014, http://www.haaretz.com/middle -east-news/1.586924 (accessed November 16, 2016).

48. "Remarks and Questions from the Palestinian Negotiating Team Regarding the United States Proposal," Negotiations Affairs Department— PLO, January 1, 2001, http://www.nad-plo.org/etemplate.php?id=98 (accessed November 16, 2016).

49. Barak Ravid, "The Secret Fruits of the Peace Talks, a Future Point of Departure?" *Ha'aretz*, July 5, 2014, http://www.haaretz.com/peace/ .premium-1.603028 (accessed November 16, 2016).

50. Birnbaum and Tibon, "Explosive, Inside Story."

51. Ahmad Tibi, interview with the authors, December 27, 2016.

52. Amir Tibon, "The Secret Back Channel that Doomed the Israel -Palestine Negotiations," *New Republic*, November 26, 2014, https:// newrepublic.com/article/120413/secret-negotiations-between-yitzhak -molho-abbas-representative (accessed November 16, 2016).

53. Tibon, "Secret Back Channel."

54. Ibid.

55. "Official: PLO Members Consider Disbanding PA," Ma'an News Agency, April 19, 2014, http://www.maannews.com/Content.aspx?id =691203 (accessed November 16, 2016).

56. Leona Vicario, "Palestinian Politicians Say No to the Negotiations with Israel No Negotiations Protest," *Palestine Monitor*, October 6, 2013, http://palestinemonitor.org/details.php?id=32l69oa5246ychwqic96e (accessed November 16, 2016).

57. "Poll No. 185," Palestinian Center for Public Opinion, March 29, 2014, http://www.pcpo.org/index.php/polls/108-poll-no-185 (accessed November 16, 2016).

58. Ehud Yaari and Neri Zilber, "The Hamas-Fatah Reconciliation Agreement: Too Early to Judge," Washington Institute for Near East Policy, April 24, 2014, http://www.washingtoninstitute.org/policy-analysis/view/ the-hamas-fatah-reconciliation-agreement-too-early-to-judge (accessed November 16, 2016).

59. Jodi Rudoren and Michael Gordon, "Palestinian Rivals Announce Unity Pact, Drawing US and Israeli Rebuke," *New York Times*, April 23, 2014, http://www.nytimes.com/2014/04/24/world/middleeast/ palestinian-factions-announce-deal-on-unity-government.html (accessed November 16, 2016).

60. Ibid.

61. "Kerry: Israeli, Palestinian Status Quo Unsustainable," Voice of America News, December 8, 2014, http://www.voahausa.com/a/kerry -israel-palestinians-islamic-state/2550881.html (accessed November 16, 2016).

62. Jerusalem Associated Press, "Israeli-Palestinian Violence in 2014: Timeline," *Guardian*, November 18, 2014, https://www.theguardian .com/world/2014/nov/18/israel-palestinian-violence-timeline (accessed November 16, 2016).

63. "Key Figures on the 2014 Hostilities," Office for the Coordination of Humanitarian Affairs, June 2015, http://gaza.ochaopt.org/2015/06/ key-figures-on-the-2014-hostilities/ (accessed November 16, 2016).

64. "22 July 2014: Results of a West Bank-Only Public Opinion Poll and a Specialized Poll for Opinion Leaders Focusing on the Current War in Gaza," Arab World for Research and Development, July 23, 2014, http://www.awrad.org/page.php?id=uccNJV1m8pa9859017A7SHvVPyPcs (accessed November 16, 2016).

65. "Abbas to UN: Put Palestine under International Protection," Ma'an News Agency, July 13, 2014, http://www.maannews.com/Content .aspx?id=712733 (accessed November 16, 2016).

66. Riyad Mansour, "18 July 2014: Statement by Ambassador Dr. Riyad Mansour before the United Nations Security Council, Emergency Meeting," Permanent Observer Mission of the State of Palestine to the United Nations New York, July 18, 2014, http://palestineun.org/18-july -2014-statement-by-ambassador-dr-riyad-mansour-before-the-united-nations -security-council-emergency-meeting/ (accessed November 16, 2016).

67. Neri Zilber, "What Will Happen if the Palestinians Really End Security Cooperation?" *The Tower*, April 2015, http://www.thetower.org/ article/what-will-happen-if-the-palestinians-really-end-security -cooperation/ (accessed November 16, 2016).

CHAPTER 11. CLINGING TO POWER

1. Gregg Carlstrom, "Via Ma'an, Mahmoud Abbas went out to look at bread tonight to dispel rumors he had a stroke," Twitter post, December 5, 2014, 12:13 p.m., https://twitter.com/glcarlstrom/ status/540962091994066945 (accessed November 16, 2016).

2. Khaled Abu Toameh, "Palestinian Internal Strife Sparks Rumors about Abbas's Health," *Jerusalem Post*, December 7, 2014, http://www.jpost

.com/Middle-East/Palestinian-internal-strife-sparks-rumors-about-Abbass
-health-383913 (accessed November 16, 2016).

3. David Makovsky, interview with the authors, September 29, 2016.

4. Avi Issacharoff, "After Feeling 'Tired,' Abbas Undergoes Heart Test in Hospital: West Bank Medical Official Says Cardiac Catheterization Performed on 81-Year-Old Palestinian Leader, Who Was Found to Be Fit," *Times of Israel*, October 6, 2016, http://www.timesofisrael.com/after -feeling-tired-abbas-undergoes-heart-test-in-hospital/ (accessed November 16, 2016).

5. "2003 Amended Basic Law," Palestinian Basic Law, March 18, 2003, http://www.palestinianbasiclaw.org/basic-law/2003-amended-basic -law (accessed November 16, 2016).

6. Gadi Baltiansky, interview with the authors, July 12, 2016.

7. Ala'a Yaghi, interview with the authors, July 4, 2016.

8. Grant Rumley, "In Palestine, Mahmoud Abbas vs Mohammad Dahlan," *National Interest*, January 3, 2015, http://nationalinterest.org/ feature/palestine-mahmoud-abbas-vs-mohammad-dahlan-11953 (accessed November 16, 2016).

9. "Dahlan: The Mastermind for Mohammad bin Zayed and Issuer of Security and Foreign Policy for the Emirates" [in Arabic], *El Shaab*, http:// www.elshaab.org/news/154176/%D8%AF%D8%AD%D9%84%D8%A7 %D9%86-%D8%A7%D9%84%D8%B9%D9%82%D9%84-%D8%A7%D9 %84%D9%85%D8%AF%D8%A8%D8%B1-%D9%84%D9%80-%D9 %85%D8%AD%D9%85%D8%AF-%D8%A8%D9%86-%D8%B2%D8 %A7%D9%8A%D8%AF-%D9%88%D8%B1%D8%A7%D8%B3%D9 %85-%D8%A7%D9%84%D8 (accessed November 16, 2016).

10. Jack Moore, "Exiled Palestinian Leader Looks for Regional Allies in Mediation of Nile Dam Deal," *Newsweek*, April 28, 2015, http://www .newsweek.com/exiled-palestinian-leader-looks-regional-allies-mediation -nile-dam-deal-326036 (accessed November 16, 2016).

11. "New Sisi Leak Reveals More on Dahlan's Role in Libya," Middle East Monitor, March 13, 2015, https://www.middleeastmonitor.com/ 20150313-new-sisi-leak-reveals-more-on-dahlans-role-in-libya/ (accessed November 16, 2016).

12. Ivan Angelovski and Lawrence Marzouk, "Mahmoud Abbas Rival Given Serbian Citizenship, Documents Reveal," *Guardian*, January 30, 2015, https://www.theguardian.com/world/2015/jan/30/palestinian -president-rival-given-serbian-citizenship (accessed November 16, 2016).

13. Mohammed Omer, "Is a Mass Wedding in Gaza Part of a UAE-

Dahlan Arranged Marriage?" Middle East Eye, April 13, 2015, http://www.middleeasteye.net/in-depth/features/uae-gets-game-1623032740 (accessed November 16, 2016).

14. "Dahlan Calls to Integrate Hamas and Islamic Jihad into the PLO," Ma'an News Agency, August 28, 2015, https://www.maannews.com/Content.aspx?id=767309 (accessed November 16, 2016).

15. "Supporters of Dismissed Fatah Leader Muhammad Dahlan Burn Pictures of Abbas in Gaza," Ma'an News Agency, October 7, 2016, http://www.maannews.com/Content.aspx?id=773457 (accessed November 16, 2016).

16. Martin Indyk, interview with the authors, September 6, 2016.

17. Thomas Friedman, "Goodbye to All That," New York Times, April 23, 2013, http://www.nytimes.com/2013/04/24/opinion/friedman-goodbye-to-all-that.html (accessed November 16, 2016).

18. "Palestinians Seize Former Premier's Funds," Yahoo! News, June 23, 2015, https://www.yahoo.com/news/palestinians-seize-former-premiers-funds-145612520.html?ref=gs (accessed November 16, 2016).

19. Rori Donaghy, "Revealed: How Palestinian President Made an Enemy of the UAE," Middle East Eye, July 19, 2016, http://www.middleeasteye.net/news/revealed-how-mahmoud-abbas-made-enemy-uae-461002456 (accessed November 16, 2016).

20. "Abbas Fires Deputy Abed Rabbo in PLO Power Struggle: In a Bid to Sideline Potential Rivals, Palestinian Authority Chief Sacks Long-Time Critic; Cabinet Asks PM for Reshuffle," Times of Israel, July 1, 2015, http://www.timesofisrael.com/abbas-fires-deputy-abed-rabbo-in-plo-power-struggle/ (accessed November 16, 2016).

21. Barak Ravid, "Abbas Orders Palestinian Branch of Geneva Initiative Closed over Political Rivalry," Ha'aretz, August 20, 2015, http://www.haaretz.com/israel-news/.premium-1.672006 (accessed December 15, 2016).

22. Ali Sawafta, "Abbas Reopens Palestinian Branch of Geneva Initiative NGO after EU Pressure, Officials Say: Some Claimed the Palestinian Peace Coalition (PPC) Was Shut Down to Minimize Influence of Political Opponent Yasser Abed Rabbo," Ha'aretz, August 27, 2015, http://www.haaretz.com/israel-news/1.673276 (accessed December 16, 2016).

23. Jonathan Schanzer and Grant Rumley, "Palestine's Anti-Corruption Crusader," Daily Beast, March 14, 2016, http://www.thedailybeast.com/articles/2016/03/14/palestine-s-anti-corruption-crusader.html (accessed November 16, 2016).

24. Bassam Zakarneh, interview with the authors, September 16, 2016.

25. Maayan Groisman, "Palestinian Political Analyst Incites to Kill Palestinian Authority President Abbas," *Jerusalem Post*, January 31, 2016, http://www.jpost.com/Arab-Israeli-Conflict/Palestinian-political-analyst -incites-to-kill-Palestinian-Authority-President-Abbas-443373 (accessed November 16, 2016).

26. Khaled Abu Toameh, "Palestinian Forces Arrest Professor Accused of Calling for Abbas Execution," *Jerusalem Post*, February 2, 2016, http:// www.jpost.com/Middle-East/Palestinian-forces-arrest-professor-accused-of -calling-for-Abbas-execution-443634 (accessed November 16, 2016).

27. Abdul Sattar Qassem, interview with the authors, June 30, 2016.

28. Daoud Kuttab, "Arrest of Palestinian Journalist Reflection of 'Political Chaos,'" Al Monitor, January 14, 2016, http://www.al-monitor .com/pulse/originals/2016/01/palestinian-journalist-sweidan-release .html (accessed November 16, 2016); "PA Security Forces Arrest Five Citizens and Detain Three Others" [in Arabic], *Al Resalah*, July 26, 2016, http://alresalah.ps/ar/post/144928/%D8%A3%D9%85%D9%86-%D8 %A7%D9%84%D8%B3%D9%84%D8%B7%D8%A9-%D9%8A%D8%B9 %D8%AA%D9%82%D9%84-5-%D9%85%D9%88%D8%A7%D8%B7 %D9%86%D9%8A%D9%86-%D9%88%D9%8A%D8%B3%D8%AA%D8 %AF%D8%B9%D9%8A-3-%D8%A2%D8%AE%D8%B1%D9%8A%D9%86 (accessed November 16, 2016).

29. "*The Violations of Media Freedoms in Palestine*" Palestinian Center for Development and Media Freedoms, 2015, http://www.madacenter.org/ images/text_editor/annualRepE2015-.pdf (accessed November 16, 2016).

30. "West Bank and Gaza Strip," Freedom House: Freedom of the Press 2015, 2015, https://freedomhouse.org/report/freedom-press/ 2015/west-bank-and-gaza-strip (accessed November 16, 2016).

31. "Thousands of Palestinian Teachers Demonstrate across West Bank," Ma'an News Agency, March 1, 2016, http://www.maannews.com/ Content.aspx?id=770505 (accessed November 16, 2016).

32. Elia Ghorbiah, "'March of 50,000' Palestinian Teachers Defy Roadblocks to Protest Pay: Organisers Say That up to 50,000 Teachers Marched in Ramallah Today as Tensions with the PA Escalate," Middle East Eye, February 23, 2016, http://www.middleeasteye.net/news/palestinian -teachers-defy-roadblocks-protest-about-pay-536302724 (accessed November 16, 2016).

33. "Gunshots Fired at Homes of Two Palestinian Teachers in Hebron," Ma'an News Agency, March 3, 2016, http://www.maannews .com/Content.aspx?id=770546 (accessed November 16, 2016); Maayan

Groisman, "Hamas and Fatah Play the Blame Game Following Acid Attack on Palestinian Teacher," *Jerusalem Post*, March 2, 2016, http://www.jpost .com/Middle-East/Hamas-and-Fatah-play-the-blame-game-following-acid -attack-on-Palestinian-teacher-446662 (accessed November 16, 2016).

34. Amira Hass, "Palestinian Authority Treats Its Own People as the Enemy," *Ha'aretz*, February 24, 2016, http://www.haaretz.com/opinion/ .premium-1.705076 (accessed November 16, 2016).

35. Zakarneh, interview with the authors.

36. "Thousands Rally against PA Approval of Controversial Social Security Law," Ma'an News Agency, April 19, 2016, https://www.maan news.com/Content.aspx?id=771207 (accessed November 16, 2016).

37. Emily Mulder, "PA Executive Governing 'Alone in an Empty Space': Backlash over New Social Security Law Highlights Broader Concerns about Concentration of Palestinian Government Powers," Al Jazeera, July 12, 2016, http://www.aljazeera.com/news/2016/07/pa -executive-governing-empty-space-160707123914572.html (accessed November 16, 2016).

38. Zakarneh, interview with the authors.

39. Adam Rasgon, "Tulkarem Electricity Crisis Leads to Clash between PA and Local Municipality," *Jerusalem Post*, August 3, 2016, http://www .jpost.com/Middle-East/Tulkarem-electricity-crisis-leads-to-clash-between -PA-and-local-municipality-463124 (accessed November 16, 2016).

40. "Clashes between Boys of Amari Camp and PA Security Forces," YouTube video, 1:52, posted by "Wattan News Agency," June 30, 2014, https://www.youtube.com/watch?v=WH4Rf4T0J9k (accessed November 16, 2016).

41. Alexandra Sims, "Violent Protests Break Out in West Bank Over Palestinian Prisoner 'Beaten to Death' in Police Custody: Ahmed Izz Halawa Died on Tuesday after Being Detained at Juneid Prison in Nablus," *Independent*, August 24, 2016, http://www.independent.co.uk/news/ world/middle-east/violent-protests-break-out-in-west-bank-over-palestinian -prisoner-beaten-to-death-in-police-custody-a7208176.html (accessed November 16, 2016).

42. Adam Rasgon and Udi Shaham, "Thousands Turn Nablus Funeral into Protest against PA," *Jerusalem Post*, August 28, 2016, http://www.jpost. com/Arab-Israeli-Conflict/12000-turn-funeral-procession-into -demonstration-against-the-PA-in-Nablus-466264 (accessed November 16, 2016).

43. "Conflicting Reports over Deadly Shooting by Palestinian Police in

Nablus," Ma'an News Agency, September 28, 2016, http://www.maannews
.com/Content.aspx?id=773337 (accessed November 16, 2016).

44. "Funeral of Man Killed in Nablus Turns Into Protest Against President and Abbas and the PA Leaders" [in Arabic], *Ahwal el-Balad*, October 2, 2016, http://ahwalelbelad.com/news/75680.html (accessed March 15, 2017).

45. Former Aqsa Martyrs' Brigades member, interview with the authors, June 30, 2016.

46. Zakarneh, interview with the authors.

47. Tawfiq Tirawi, interview with the authors, September 19, 2016.

48. Former Aqsa Martyrs' Brigades member, interview with the authors.

49. Grant Rumley and Mor Yahalom, "Palestine's Democratic Deficit," *Foreign Affairs*, October 12, 2016, https://www.foreignaffairs.com/articles/ palestinian-authority/2016-10-12/palestines-democratic-deficit (accessed November 16, 2016).

50. Hussein Ibish, interview with the authors, July 18, 2016.

51. Tirawi, interview with the authors.

52. "Palestinian Forces Arrest Dozens of Hamas Members in West Bank," BBC News, July 3, 2015, http://www.bbc.com/news/world-middle -east-33384295 (accessed December 16, 2016).

53. Jihad Abaza, "Palestinian Authority Forces Arrest Students Affiliated with Hamas: Students, Arrested after Winning Student Council Elections and Writing Critical Facebook Posts, Say They Were Mistreated in Security Detentions," *Daily News Egypt*, May 8, 2015, http://www.daily newsegypt.com/2015/05/08/258063/ (accessed December 16, 2016).

54. Baltiansky, interview with the authors.

55. Mahmoud Abbas, "The Long Overdue Palestinian State," *New York Times*, May 16, 2011, http://www.nytimes.com/2011/05/17/ opinion/17abbas.html?_r=0 (accessed November 16, 2016).

56. Grant Rumley, "Suicide by Statehood: Palestine's Push for International Recognition Is Tanking John Kerry's Peace Talks. Was This Abbas's Plan All Along?" *Foreign Policy*, April 2, 2014, http://foreignpolicy .com/2014/04/02/suicide-by-statehood/ (accessed November 16, 2016).

57. Associated Press, "UN Security Council Rejects Palestinian Statehood Bill," *Guardian*, December 30, 2014, https://www.theguardian .com/world/2014/dec/30/un-security-council-rejects-palestinian -statehood-bid (accessed November 16, 2016).

58. "UN Security Council Rejects Palestinian Resolution," BBC News,

December 31, 2014, http://www.bbc.com/news/world-middle
-east-30639764 (accessed November 16, 2016).

59. "Egypt, Japan, Senegal, Ukraine, and Uruguay Elected to Serve on UN Security Council," UN News Centre, October 15, 2015, http://www.un.org/apps/news/story.asp?NewsID=52275#.WCzCfC0rKCg (accessed November 16, 2016).

60. "UN Security Council Rejects," BBC News.

61. Peter Beaumont, "Palestinian Authority Becomes Member of International Criminal Court," *Guardian*, April 1, 2015, https://www.theguardian.com/law/2015/apr/01/palestinian-authority-becomes
-member-of-international-criminal-court (accessed November 16, 2016).

62. Jodi Rudoren and Somini Sengupta, "UN Report on Gaza Finds Evidence of War Crimes by Israel and by Palestinian Militants," *New York Times*, June 22, 2015, http://www.nytimes.com/2015/06/23/world/middleeast/israel-gaza-report.html?_r=0 (accessed November 18, 2016).

CHAPTER 12. THE REIGN OF MAHMOUD ABBAS

1. Seventh Fatah congress, November 29–30, 2016, Mr. Rumley was in attendance.

2. Jihad Tummaleh, interview with the authors, November 28, 2016.

3. "Wave of Terror 2015/16," Israel Ministry of Foreign Affairs, November 1, 2016, http://mfa.gov.il/MFA/ForeignPolicy/Terrorism/Palestinian/Pages/Wave-of-terror-October-2015.aspx (accessed December 26, 2016).

4. "A Joint Press Statement on Majed Faraj's Remarks," press release, Hamas [in Arabic], January 21, 2016, http://hamas.ps/ar/post/4714/ (accessed December 26, 2016).

5. Seventh Fatah congress.

6. Ibid. Mahmoud Abbas went off script in his speech to the Fatah conference in November 2016 to say this line about Jewish connection to the land.

7. Nasser Juma'a, interview with the authors, September 14, 2016.

8. Mushir al-Masri, telephone interview with the authors, September 19, 2016.

9. Ghassan Khatib, interview with the authors, September 19, 2016.

10. Ashraf al-Ajrami, interview with the authors, July 25, 2016.

11. Senior Israeli official, interview with Mr. Tibon, January 3, 2016.

12. "Peres: Abbas 'Risking His Life' in Stance against Terrorism: In Remarks Contrasting with Netanyahu's More Wary Stance, President Hails PA Leader as Best Peace Partner Israel Has Ever Had," *Times of Israel*, June 22, 2014, http://www.timesofisrael.com/peres-abbas-risking-his-life-in -stance-against-terrorism/ (accessed December 9, 2016).

13. Yoni Hersch, "Steinitz: Blood Spilled in Latest Violence is 'On Abbas' Hands,'" *Israel Hayom*, October 19, 2015, http://www.israelhayom .com/site/newsletter_article.php?id=29017 (accessed December 27, 2016).

14. Tzipi Livni, interview with the authors, July 14, 2016.

15. Dennis Ross, interview with the authors, July 25, 2016.

16. Elliott Abrams, interview with the authors, June 13, 2016.

17. Daniel Kurtzer, interview with the authors, November 9, 2016.

18. Jodi Rudoren, "A Divide among Palestinians on a Two-State Solution," *New York Times*, March 18, 2014, https://www.nytimes.com/ 2014/03/19/world/middleeast/a-divide-among-palestinians-on-a-two -state-solution.html?_r=0 (accessed December 23, 2016).

19. "Report: Abbas Spends More Time Abroad than at Home," i24 News, June 28, 2015, http://www.i24news.tv/en/news/international/ middle-east/76464-150628-report-abbas-spends-more-time-abroad-than-at -home (accessed December 16, 2016).

INDEX